FORMULA 1
ALL THE RACES

FORMULA 1
ALL THE RACES

# THE 100 GREATEST RACES

**To Gregor Grant, founder of *Autosport* magazine 75 years ago. In those early decades when F1 news was so scarce, *Autosport* was my weekly therapy for Formula fever. The *Autosport* Podcasts bring me full circle. RS**

First published in 2025 by Veloce, an imprint of David and Charles Limited.
Tel +44 (0)1305 260068 / e-mail info@veloce.co.uk / web www.veloce.co.uk

Published in October 2025

ISBN: 9781836440581



British Library Cataloguing in Publication Data – A catalogue record for this book is available from the British Library.

Design and layout by Richard Parsons.

Printed and bound through Asia Pacific Offset Group Ltd.

**Author's acknowledgments**
Special thanks to Kevin Turner, Karun Chandhok, and designer Richard Parsons for joining me on the 100GR journey. And thanks to *Autosport*, Doug Nye and others for the content they generously made available. RS

**Photograph credits**
All photographs are from Motorsport Images apart from: Alamy, pages 6, 7, 9, 41, 56, 69, 70, 98, 110, 113, 121, 124, 133, 134, 141, 151, 152, 153, 155 and the back cover, and Getty Images, pages 39, 140, and the front cover.

FORMULA 1
ALL THE RACES

# THE 100 GREATEST RACES

**ROGER SMITH** AND **KEVIN TURNER**
FOREWORD BY **KARUN CHANDHOK**

# FORMULA 1 ALL THE RACES

The team that curated 'The 100 Greatest Races' prepare for their first podcast on the book at *Autosport*'s offices. From left to right, Karun Chandhok, former F1 driver and TV commentator; Roger Smith, F1 author and project leader; Kevin Turner, *Autosport*'s Chief Editor and podcast chairman. Look out for them on https://www.autosport.com/podcast/

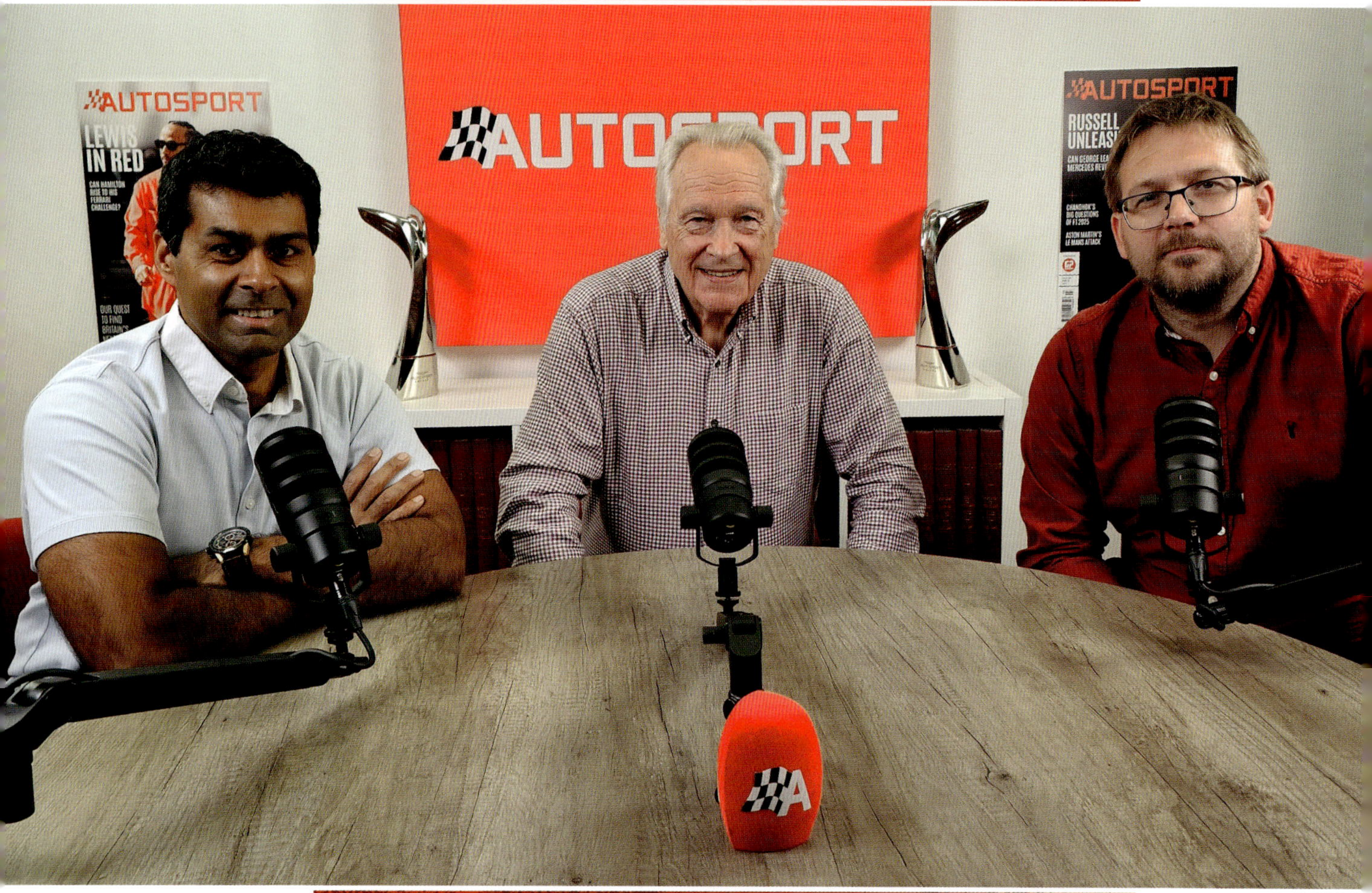

# CONTENTS


| | | |
|---|---|---|
| | **FOREWORD**<br>BY KARUN CHANDHOK | **6** |
| | **INTRODUCTION**<br>THE 100 GREATEST RACES | **8** |
| **CHAPTER 1** | **THRILLERS**<br>LATE DRAMA, TIGHT FINISHES | **10** |
| **CHAPTER 2** | **DUELS**<br>FIRST AMONG EQUALS | **24** |
| **CHAPTER 3** | **COMEBACKS**<br>THROUGH THE FIELD | **38** |
| **CHAPTER 4** | **WHAT THE …?**<br>BIZARRE HAPPENINGS | **52** |
| **CHAPTER 5** | **EPICS**<br>AGAINST THE ODDS | **66** |
| **CHAPTER 6** | **REGENMEISTERS**<br>WINNERS IN THE RAIN | **80** |
| **CHAPTER 7** | **SURPRISES**<br>SHOCK VICTORIES | **94** |
| **CHAPTER 8** | **PASS MASTERS**<br>DRAMATIC OVERTAKES | **108** |
| **CHAPTER 9** | **FOLKLORE**<br>UNFORGETTABLE CONTESTS | **122** |
| **CHAPTER 10** | **DECIDERS**<br>DOWN TO THE WIRE | **136** |
| **CHAPTER 11** | **THE GOAT**<br>THE GREATEST OF ALL TIME | **150** |
| | **EPILOGUE**<br>THE EYE OF THE BEHOLDER | **156** |
| | **ABBREVIATIONS** | **157** |
| | **SOURCES AND BIBLIOGRAPHY** | **157** |
| | **APPENDIX** | **158** |
| | **AUTHOR BIOGRAPHIES** | **160** |

## KARUN CHANDHOK

# FOREWORD

One of the things I love most about Formula 1 is how much richer the experience becomes when you understand its history. The drama we see on track today, whether it's a title decider in Abu Dhabi or a bold move around the outside at Silverstone, gains real depth when viewed through the lens of the sport's past. F1 has given us seven-and-a-half decades of unforgettable stories, characters, and moments that continue to echo through the paddock today.

That's why a book like The 100 Greatest Races is so welcome. What I particularly enjoyed about this one is the imaginative way it's been structured. Rather than simply ranking races from 1 to 100, the authors have taken ten different themes, like overtaking masterclasses, shock wins, or epic drives against the odds, and grouped classic races accordingly. It's a clever approach that not only brings variety, but also shines a light on the different elements that make Formula 1 so compelling.

I've known both authors for years and have always been struck by their encyclopaedic knowledge of the sport, not to mention the passion and attention to detail they bring to everything they do. You can trust that this isn't just a list pulled together from highlight reels or nostalgia; it's the product of deep research, sound judgement, and genuine love for the sport.

Whether you're a long-time fan or a more recent convert to Formula 1, this book will remind you why you fell in love with it in the first place. It's also likely to introduce you to a few races you may not have seen before, giving you the perfect excuse to dive back into the archives.

Enjoy the journey through these 100 classics. I certainly did.

**Karun Chandhok, 2025**

Racing driver Karun Chandhok at the wheel of his Lotus-Renault at the 2011 German Grand Prix

Commentator Karun Chandhok shares his insightful perspectives and deep historical knowledge with his Sky Sports F1 viewers

# INTRODUCTION

On May 13, 2025, Formula 1 celebrated its 75th anniversary, a momentous milestone for a sport steeped in drama, innovation, and the relentless pursuit of excellence. It all began at Silverstone in 1950 with the inaugural 'Grand Prix' for the FIA World Championship of Drivers. Since then, 1,120 Grands Prix races have been run across six continents, producing 34 World Champions from 15 nations, three of whom have claimed the crown five times or more.

What better way to commemorate Formula 1's illustrious past than to pinpoint the races that truly define Grand Prix racing, the best of the very best? *'The 100 Greatest Races'* spotlights the heart-stopping moments, the unforgettable battles, and the iconic performances that have left their indelible mark on the sport. From the closest finishes and wet-weather masterclasses to awe-inspiring comeback drives and shocking upsets, this superb collection of races celebrates the finest displays of skill, bravery, and sheer determination.

This book is more than a tribute, it's an exploration of what makes the FIA Formula 1 World Championship the pinnacle of motorsport. Whether it's the split-second decisions of drivers, the groundbreaking ingenuity of teams, or the sheer unpredictability of racing, *'The 100 Greatest Races'* captures the essence of Formula 1's enduring magic and its unrivalled ability to thrill and inspire fans around the globe.

**The start of the very first FIA World Championship Grand Prix held at Silverstone International Circuit on 13th May, 1950**

The start of the 1,120th FIA World Championship Grand Prix held at Miami International Autodrome on 4th May, 2025, close on 75 years to the day since the first. These 1,120 Grands Prix races embody the scope from which *The 100 Greatest Races* have been selected, the 11 Indy 500 races included in the Championship from 1950 to 1960 having been omitted

Authors Roger Smith and Kevin Turner targeted Formula 1's 75th anniversary as the perfect occasion to unveil *'The 100 Greatest Races'*. It's a project they have been building towards over many years, Roger through his 'Formula 1 All the Races' series of books, and Kevin as Chief Editor of that icon of British motorsport journalism, *Autosport* magazine. Karun Chandhok, former F1 driver, F1 commentator, and renowned Formula 1 historian has kindly written the book's Foreword as well as keeping a watching brief on the project.

Drawing on this wealth of experience and knowledge, the authors have collaborated for a number of years to formulate a race ratings methodology that grades each and every F1 race. Much like a pair of Klondike prospectors, they have applied their system to rigorously sieve through over 1000 races to unearth those nuggets of Grand Prix Gold. From there, identification of the recurring dynamics and themes that define Formula 1's greatest moments became possible. These themes lend the book the titles to each of ten distinct chapters that comprise a carefully curated collection of ten exceptional races. Each chapter's top ten is then ranked to generate a 3, 2, 1 'podium' as the authors push the envelope by controversially concluding the book with their pick of *The GOAT*, the Greatest Race Of All Time.

Through a compelling blend of high-octane text and stunning authentic photography, *'The 100 Greatest Races'* invites fans to relive the magic of the sport's greatest moments and celebrate the defining events that have shaped its legacy. Readers embark on an exhilarating odyssey through the annals of Formula 1 history, where every race is a testament to the passion, skill, and relentless pursuit of excellence that defines Formula 1.

## CHAPTER 1

# THRILLERS

## LATE DRAMA, TIGHT FINISHES

Few moments in Formula 1 rival the sheer thrill of a race decided in its closing stages, whether through a dramatic last-lap overtake or an agonisingly close finish. These unforgettable edge-of-your-seat spectacles are the ultimate crowd pleasers, and no one circuit has staged them more often than Monza: the temple of speed.

In this collection of Formula 1's greatest thrillers, the *Autodromo Nazionale di Monza* features no fewer than four times. For nearly 30 seasons, before chicanes and 'dirty' air diminished the noble art of slipstreaming, Monza's long straights and flowing corners provided the ultimate battleground for such duels. A driver could latch onto the car ahead, let it do all the work of punching a hole in the air, and so get towed along in its wake before darting out to seize the advantage. At Monza, this frequently led to multi-car battles, drivers ducking and diving in close company for lap after lap and victory decided in one final mad dash to the finish line.

A close climax always raises the pulses but, in the split-second world of Formula 1, even one second isn't that close. A Grand Prix finish isn't utterly electrifying until the gap is measured in tenths – about one car-length on a typical circuit. And if it's less than 0.1 seconds, the cars will be side-by-side, wheel-to-wheel as they scream past the chequered flag. Monza holds the record for the closest finish in history: a scarcely believable 0.010 seconds!

Monza may have set the standard for heart-stopping finishes, but it is far from the only stage for late drama and tight finishes. Across the decades, Formula 1 has delivered heart-stopping thrillers at circuits around the world.

Few moments in Formula 1 are as electrifying as a final-lap overtake for the lead, a breathtaking climax for both driver and crowd. Yet, such feats are rare. Across more than 1000 Grands Prix, victory has been snatched on the last lap just 26 times. Many resulted from fuel miscalculations or mechanical failure, but a select few were decided purely in the heat of battle – a relentless chase to the flag. Would the leader keep their nerve and defend to the bitter end, or would the chaser force a mistake in sight of glory? This chapter revisits the races where the tension never let up as the battles raged to the very last lap.

**MONZA MAY HAVE SET THE STANDARD FOR HEART-STOPPING FINISHES, BUT IT IS FAR FROM THE ONLY STAGE FOR LATE DRAMA AND TIGHT FINISHES. ACROSS THE DECADES, FORMULA 1 HAS DELIVERED HEART-STOPPING THRILLERS AT CIRCUITS AROUND THE WORLD**

# 10 THRILLERS

# Hamilton passed Rosberg for a sensational last lap victory

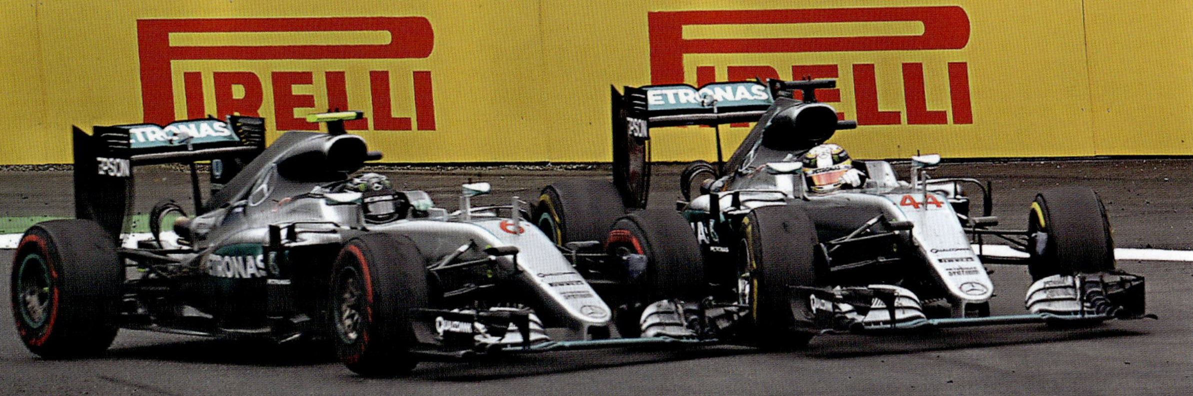


A picture paints a thousand words. By 2016 Rosberg had worked out that he had to get tougher to beat Hamilton. This indiscretion cost him points and a penalty but not the Championship

## Race 944 — 2016 AUSTRIAN GP Red Bull Ring

**Round 9/21** — **3 July 2016**

## LEWIS HAMILTON

**Mercedes F1 W07** 210.203kph, 130.614mph

On the final lap, Hamilton got a run on leader Rosberg to attempt a wide outside pass around turn 2. From the inside line, Rosberg left his turn-in so late that he crashed into his teammate, shunting Lewis off-track. Not only was he penalised for the affray, but Rosberg's car was also badly damaged too, passed by winner Hamilton and by Verstappen and Räikkönen. Until he lost his head, Nico had driven well from a gearbox-penalised P6 grid slot. His two-stop plan had proved superior to Hamilton's one-stop, a strategy forced on Lewis by the one-stopping Ferraris. But after leader Sebastian Vettel's right rear tyre exploded on lap 26, Rosberg led Hamilton. At their second stops, Hamilton failed to undercut Rosberg, leaving him 16 laps to make the pass, doing so at turn 2 on that final, frenetic lap.

| Pos | Driver | Car | Time/gap | Grid (pen) | Stops | Tyres (s/ss/us) |
|---|---|---|---|---|---|---|
| 1 | Lewis Hamilton | Mercedes | 1h 27m 38.107s | 1 | 2 | uss |
| 2 | Max Verstappen | Red Bull-TAG Heuer | –5.719s | 8 | 1 | ss |
| 3 | Kimi Räikkönen | Ferrari | –6.024s | 4 | 1 | ss |
| 4 | Nico Rosberg | Mercedes | –26.710s[1] | 6 (-5) | 2 | uss |
| 5 | Daniel Ricciardo | Red Bull-TAG Heuer | –30.981s | 5 | 2 | ssu |
| 6 | Jenson Button | McLaren-Honda | –37.706s | 3 | 2 | uss |

[1] Including 10s penalty

**POLE POSITION** Hamilton, Mercedes, 1m 7.922s (0.543s), 229.286kph, 142.471mph
**LAPS** 71 x 4.326 km, 2.688 miles
**DISTANCE** 307.020 km, 190.773 miles
**STARTERS/FINISHERS** 22/20
**WEATHER** Overcast, cool, dry
**LAP LEADERS** Hamilton 1-21, 71 (22); Räikkönen 22 (1); Vettel 23-26 (4); Rosberg 27-55, 61-70 (39); Verstappen 56-60 (5); SC 27-31 (5)
**WINNER'S LAPS** 1-21 P1, 22 P4, 23-26 P3, 27-54 P2, 55-62 P3, 63-70 P2, 71 P1
**FASTEST LAP** Hamilton, Mercedes, 1m 8.411s (Lap 67), 227.647kph, 141.453mph
**CHAMPIONSHIP** Rosberg 153, Hamilton 142, Vettel 96, Räikkönen 96, Ricciardo 88

RACE POD

9 THRILLERS

# One lap from a famous victory, Hill's hobbled Arrows was overtaken

Former Williams teammates, race winner Jacques Villeneuve (right), and moral winner Damon Hill, reunite on the podium to spray the champagne following Hill's supreme if ultimately fruitless drive

**Race 608** Round 11/17

**1997 HUNGARIAN GP** Hungaroring 10 August 1997

**JACQUES VILLENEUVE** Williams-Renault FW19 173.295kph, 107.681mph

Two miles short of a famous victory, the reigning champion's Arrows-Yamaha was overtaken by former Williams teammate Villeneuve. Hill's underpowered car was superbly set-up and beautifully driven. Once hobbled by hydraulics failure, his 35s lead was enough to keep him ahead for two laps, but not the very last one. Hill had brilliantly qualified his Bridgestone-shod car third, closely pursued pole-man Schumacher for ten laps, then barged past into the lead. His only challenger after that was the driver who had replaced him at Williams, but after taking the lead on lap 26, Heinz-Harald Frentzen was out soon after. It left Damon pulling away out front to post an historic maiden victory for both Arrows and Yamaha, and a poke in the eye for his erstwhile team. But it wasn't to be.

| Pos | Driver | Car | Time/gap | Grid | Stops | Tyres |
|---|---|---|---|---|---|---|
| 1 | Jacques Villeneuve | Williams-Renault | 1h 45m 47.149s | 2 | 2 | G |
| 2 | Damon Hill | Arrows-Yamaha | -9.079s | 3 | 2 | B |
| 3 | Johnny Herbert | Sauber-Petronas | -20.445s | 10 | 2 | G |
| 4 | Michael Schumacher | Ferrari | -30.501s | 1 | 3 | G |
| 5 | Ralf Schumacher | Jordan-Peugeot | -30.715s | 14 | 2 | G |
| 6 | Shinji Nakano | Prost-Mugen Honda | -41.512s | 16 | 2 | B |

**POLE POSITION** M Schumacher, Ferrari, 1m 14.672s (0.187s), 191.300kph, 118.869mph
**LAPS** 77 x 3.968 km, 2.466 miles
**DISTANCE** 305.536 km, 189.851 miles
**STARTERS/FINISHERS** 22/13
**WEATHER** Sunny, hot, dry
**LAP LEADERS** M Schumacher 1-10 (10); D Hill 11-25, 30-76 (62); Frentzen 26-29 (4); Villeneuve 77 (1)
**WINNER'S LAPS** 1-6 P5, 7-12 P4, 13 P3, 14-23 P2, 24 P3, 25-26 P4, 27-29 P3, 30-76 P2, 77 P1
**FASTEST LAP** H-H Frentzen, Williams-Renault, 1m 18.372s (lap 25), 182.269kph, 113.257mph
**CHAMPIONSHIP** M Schumacher 56, Villeneuve 53, Alesi 22, Berger 20, Frentzen 19

*RACE POD*

8 THRILLERS

# Ascari spun and Fangio dodged by for a last-gasp win for Maserati

This race epitomises the motorsport maxim, "To finish first, first you have to finish"! Here, winner Fangio (50) leads Ascari (4), who spun away victory on the final lap, with Farina (6) and a lapped Marimón (54)

## Race 32 — 1953 ITALIAN GP Monza

**Round 9/9** — **13 September 1953**

At the season's finale, Fangio's Maserati for a sixth time took its place alongside Ascari's pole-sitting and so far unbeatable Ferrari. The race was a classic Monza slipstreamer, up to six cars disputing the lead and 24 lead changes recorded on the lap chart. But Ascari held the initiative, repeatedly leading the gaggle of cars across the line on laps 53 to 79. But on the 80th and last lap, with Ascari, Fangio and Farina in a four-car bunch including the lapped Marimón, Alberto spun at the final corner causing chaos. Marimón T-boned Ascari, Farina took to the grass, while Fangio dodged by on the inside to seize a last-gasp Monza home win and maiden championship victory for the ecstatic Maserati team. But Ascari was Champion again, Fangio's victory lifting him to runner-up.

| Pos | Driver | Car | Time/gap | Grid | Stops | Tyres |
|---|---|---|---|---|---|---|
| 1 | Juan Manuel Fangio | Maserati | 2h 49m 45.9s | 2 | 0 | P |
| 2 | Nino Farina | Ferrari | –1.4s | 3 | 0 | P |
| 3 | Luigi Villoresi | Ferrari | –1 lap | 5 | 0 | P |
| 4 | Mike Hawthorn | Ferrari | –1 lap | 6 | 0 | P |
| 5 | Maurice Trintignant | Gordini | –1 lap | 8 | 0 | E |
| 6 | Roberto Mières | Gordini | –3 laps | 7 | 0 | E |

## JUAN MANUEL FANGIO

**Maserati A6GCM** 178.129kph, 110.684mph

**POLE POSITION** Alberto Ascari, Ferrari, 2m 2.7s (0.5s), 184.841kph, 114.855mph
**LAPS** 80 x 6.300 km, 3.915 miles
**DISTANCE** 504.000 km, 313.171 miles
**STARTERS/FINISHERS** 30/16
**WEATHER** Sunny, warm, dry
**LAP LEADERS** Ascari 1-6, 9, 14-22, 27-31, 34-36, 39-40, 42, 44-45, 47-49, 53-79 (59); Fangio 7-8, 11, 23, 25-26, 32-33, 37, 41, 50-52, 80 (14); Farina 10, 12-13, 24, 38, 43, 46 (7)
**WINNER'S LAPS** NA
**FASTEST LAP** Fangio, Maserati, 2m 4.5s (lap 39), 182.169kph, 113.194mph
**CHAMPIONSHIP** Ascari 34.5, Fangio 27.5, Farina 26, Hawthorn 19, Villoresi 17

RACE POD

**7** THRILLERS

# On the final lap Kimi's front suspension broke, Alonso sweeping by

Within seconds of the defining moment in the destiny of the 2005 world championship, Alonso sweeps by to win at the Nürburgring

## Race 738 — 2005 EUROPEAN GP Nürburgring

**Round 7/19** — **29 May 2005**

## FERNANDO ALONSO

**Renault R25** 198.555kph, 123.377mph

Räikkönen comes to Germany on a hat-trick. After a dismal start to his Championship campaign, at last he's making inroads into Alonso's early points lead. He leads most of the race, starting the final ten laps 10s clear. Despite hindrance due to a worsening vibration from a flat-spotted tyre, Kimi spurns a tyre stop and a safe P2, retaining his fast-shrinking lead into the final lap. Sensationally, the front suspension breaks, the tethered wheel flailing violently, Kimi's gamble for outright victory has failed. Alonso sweeps by to win. Twelve points are lost, not four. If there was a defining moment in the destiny of the 2005 championship, this was it. Alonso is elated. His relentless race-long chase pushed the McLaren driver into the lock-up errors that led to Räikkönen's downfall.

| Pos | Driver | Car | Time/gap | Grid (pen) | Stops | Tyres |
|---|---|---|---|---|---|---|
| 1 | Fernando Alonso | Renault | 1h 31m 46.648s | 6 | 2 | M |
| 2 | Nick Heidfeld | Williams-BMW | −16.567s | 1 | 3 | M |
| 3 | Rubens Barrichello | Ferrari | −18.549s | 7 | 3 | B |
| 4 | David Coulthard | Red Bull-Cosworth | −31.588s | 12 | 3 | M |
| 5 | Michael Schumacher | Ferrari | −50.445s | 10 | 2 | B |
| 6 | Giancarlo Fisichella | Renault | −51.932s | 9 (PL) | 2 | M |

**POLE POSITION** Heidfeld, Williams-BMW, 1m 30.081s (0.116s), 205.734kph, 127.838mph
**LAPS** 59 x 5.148 km, 3.199 miles (Scheduled for 60 laps but reduced after aborted start)
**DISTANCE** 303.715 km, 188.730 miles
**STARTERS/FINISHERS** 20/18
**WEATHER** Cloudy with sunny intervals, hot, dry
**LAP LEADERS** K Räikkönen, McLaren-Mercedes 1-18, 24-29, 31-43, 48-58 (48); Coulthard 19 (1); Alonso 20-23, 44-47, 59 (9); Heidfeld 30 (1)
**WINNER'S LAPS** 1-7 P5, 8-12 P4, 13-18 P3, 19 P2, 20-23 P1, 24-31 P3, 32-43 P2, 44-47 P1, 48 P4, 49-50 P3, 51-58 P2, 59 P1
**FASTEST LAP** Alonso, Renault, 1m 30.711s (lap 44), 204.305kph, 126.950mph
**CHAMPIONSHIP** Alonso 59, Räikkönen 27, Trulli 27, Heidfeld 25, Webber 18

**RACE POD**

6

THRILLERS

# The first four cars crossed the line separated by less than 0.2 seconds

Lap one, the leading group comprises, left to right: Rindt (Lotus), Courage (Williams Brabham), Stewart (Matra), Siffert (Walker Lotus, screened by Stewart), Beltoise (Matra), McLaren (McLaren). 99 minutes later, four of them were still at it, wheel-to-wheel!

## Race 181 1969 ITALIAN GP Monza

**Round 8/11** **7 September 1969**

## JACKIE STEWART

**Matra-Ford MS80** 236.521kph, 146.968mph

The race quickly developed into a classic Monza slipstreamer, six or more cars tied together, vying for the lead lap after lap, ducking and diving to gain any small advantage. Gradually the leading bunch thinned out as some retired – Graham Hill on lap 63, driveshaft; Jo Siffert lap 65, piston – while others fell back, notably the Frank Williams Brabham, the tiny team nevertheless elated to have led a GP for the first time. But Stewart, aided by a long fourth gear, seemed to hold the ascendency, leading 58 laps including the final 30. But it was all desperately close, the first four cars crossing the line less than 0.2s apart – Stewart, Rindt, Beltoise, McLaren. Stewart's sixth win from eight races gave him an unassailable points lead. He was the new World Champion and with victory at Monza he had won the title in style.

| Pos | Driver | Car | Time/gap | Grid | Stops | Tyres |
|---|---|---|---|---|---|---|
| 1 | Jackie Stewart | Matra-Ford | 1h 39m 11.26s | 3 | 0 | D |
| 2 | Jochen Rindt | Lotus-Ford | –0.08s | 1 | 0 | F |
| 3 | Jean-Pierre Beltoise | Matra-Ford | –0.17s | 6 | 0 | D |
| 4 | Bruce McLaren | McLaren-Ford | –0.19s | 5 | 0 | G |
| 5 | Piers Courage | Brabham-Ford | –33.44s | 4 | 0 | D |
| 6 | Pedro Rodríguez | Ferrari | –2 laps | 12 | 0 | F |

**POLE POSITION** Rindt, Lotus-Ford, 1m 25.48s (0.21s), 242.162kph, 150.472mph
**LAPS** 68 x 5.750 km, 3.573 miles
**DISTANCE** 391.000 km, 242.956 miles
**STARTERS/FINISHERS** 15/10
**WEATHER** Sunny, warm, dry
**LAP LEADERS** Stewart 1-6, 9-17, 19-24, 28-30, 33, 35-36, 38-68 (58); Rindt 7, 25-27, 31, 34, 37 (7); D Hulme, McLaren-Ford 8 (1); Courage 18, 32 (2)
**WINNER'S LAPS** 1-6 P1, 7-8 P2, 9-17 P1, 18 P2, 19-24 P1, 25-26 P3, 27 P2, 28-30 P1, 31-32 P2, 33 P1, 34 P2, 35-36 P1, 37 P2, 38-68 P1
**FASTEST LAP** Beltoise, Matra-Ford, 1m 25.20s (lap 64), 242.958kph, 150.967mph
**CHAMPIONSHIP** Stewart 60, McLaren 24, Ickx 22, G Hill 19, Beltoise 16

RACE POD

## 5 THRILLERS

# For lap after lap the two cars closed, Rosberg failing by just 0.050 seconds

The chase was brief, but incredibly exciting, Keke Rosberg (6) closing 3s in 5 laps on de Angelis (11), to fall short by just 0.050s at the line, the fourth-closest GP finish of all time

## Race 370
**Round 13/16**

## 1982 AUSTRIAN GP Österreichring
**15 August 1982**

## ELIO DE ANGELIS
**Lotus-Ford 91** 222.204kph, 138.071mph

The Brabham-BMW pair dominated qualifying and, employing their unique one-stop race strategy, rushed off into the distance. But this time at least the pit stops were enacted before the BMWs broke, fuel and tyres on Riccardo Patrese's leading car replenished in 14s. Now Alain Prost's Renault, the last turbo runner in with a chance, held a commanding lead from de Angelis, his Lotus leading the non-turbo brigade, normally the province of Rosberg's Williams. With just five laps remaining the Renault fuel injection packed up, leaving de Angelis 3s ahead of Rosberg. For lap after thrilling lap the two cars closed, Rosberg failing by just 0.050s at the line, the fourth-closest GP finish of all time. After four seasons, Lotus was a winner again.

| Pos | Driver | Car | Time/gap | Grid | Stops | Tyres |
|---|---|---|---|---|---|---|
| 1 | Elio de Angelis | Lotus-Ford | 1h 25m 2.212s | 7 | 0 | G |
| 2 | Keke Rosberg | Williams-Ford | –0.050s | 6 | 0 | G |
| 3 | Jacques Laffite | Ligier-Matra | –1 lap | 14 | 0 | M |
| 4 | Patrick Tambay | Ferrari | –1 lap | 4 | 1 | G |
| 5 | Niki Lauda | McLaren-Ford | –1 lap | 10 | 0 | M |
| 6 | Mauro Baldi | Arrows-Ford | –1 lap | 23 | 0 | P |

**POLE POSITION** N Piquet, Brabham-BMW, 1m 27.612s (0.359s), 244.158kph, 151.713mph
**LAPS** 53 x 5.942 km, 3.692 miles
**DISTANCE** 314.926 km, 195.686 miles
**STARTERS/FINISHERS** 26/8
**WEATHER** Sunny, hot, dry
**LAP LEADERS** Piquet 1 (1); R Patrese, Brabham-BMW 2-27 (26); A Prost, Renault 28-48 (21); de Angelis 49-53 (5)
**WINNER'S LAPS** 1 P6, 2-14 P5, 15-17 P4, 18-27 P3, 28-48 P2, 49-53 P1
**FASTEST LAP** N Piquet, Brabham-BMW, 1m 33.699s (lap 5), 228.297kph, 141.857mph
**CHAMPIONSHIP** Pironi 39, Rosberg 33, Watson 30, Lauda 26, Prost 25

**RACE POD**

4 THRILLERS

# It was a thrilling chase, both drivers at ten-tenths lap after lap

**Over the final nine laps Mansell caught Senna by 20 seconds, an incredible 2.2s per lap. For the first five of those laps, before being held up by Prost fighting for P2, Mansell had closed the gap by 2.9s per lap! But that's motor racing!**

## Race 422 — 1986 SPANISH GP Jerez

**Round 2/16** — **13 April 1986**

Senna on pole from the Williams pair then the two McLarens, these five breaking clear from the start. The race was all about fuel and tyre management. Senna led the first half from Nelson Piquet's Williams until it's retirement on lap 39. The following lap Mansell, never far adrift, took the lead and held it until he began to run out of rubber, pitting on lap 63. On fresh tyres the Williams driver rejoined with nine laps to go and 20s to make up. It was a thrilling chase, both drivers ten-tenths lap after lap, Mansell carving great slices from the gap to Senna. But in the drag race from the final corner to the line he fell short by just .014s. The race was actually decided with four laps to go, Mansell losing crucial time passing Prost, the McLarens finishing 3-4, slowed by pessimistic fuel readouts.

| Pos | Driver | Car | Time/gap | Grid | Stops | Tyres |
|---|---|---|---|---|---|---|
| 1 | Ayrton Senna | Lotus-Renault | 1h 48m 47.735s | 1 | 0 | G |
| 2 | Nigel Mansell | Williams-Honda | –0.014s | 3 | 1 | G |
| 3 | Alain Prost | McLaren-TAG | –21.552s | 4 | 0 | G |
| 4 | Keke Rosberg | McLaren-TAG | –1 lap | 5 | 1 | G |
| 5 | Teo Fabi | Benetton-BMW | –1 lap | 9 | 1 | P |
| 6 | Gerhard Berger | Benetton-BMW | –1 lap | 7 | 1 | P |

## AYRTON SENNA

**Lotus-Renault 98T** 167.486kph, 104.071mph

**POLE POSITION** Senna, Lotus-Renault, 1m 21.605s (0.826s), 186.077kph, 115.623mph
**LAPS** 72 x 4.218 km, 2.621 miles
**DISTANCE** 303.696 km, 188.708 miles
**STARTERS/FINISHERS** 24/8
**WEATHER** Sunny, warm, dry
**LAP LEADERS** Senna 1-39, 63-72 (49); Mansell 40-62 (23)
**WINNER'S LAPS** 1-39 P1, 40-62 P2, 63-72 P1
**FASTEST LAP** Mansell, Williams-Honda, 1m 27.176s (lap 65), 174.186kph, 108.234mph
**CHAMPIONSHIP** Senna 15, Piquet 9, Mansell 6, Laffite 4, Prost 4

*RACE POD*

**What a finish! What a race! First Clark looked the likely winner, then Hulme, then Hill, then Clark again. In the end it was Surtees (14) passing Braham (16) at the exit to Parabolica, then that drag race to the line on *giri 68***

THRILLERS

# 3 Surtees pips Brabham as extraordinary Clark is denied

As thrillers go, the 1967 Italian Grand Prix has few equals. In a race of changing fortunes, it was not only the thrilling finish between Surtees and Brabham that marks it out, but it is often cited as Jim Clark's finest drive.

Clark himself did not believe the drive was his best. In *'Jim Clark – Portrait of a Great Driver'* by Graham Gauld, journalist Gerard Crombac, who was a close friend of Clark's, even suggested that he was irritated the race was held in such high regard. "One thing which upset him was all the fuss, and the praise he got, after his fruitless 1967 Italian GP," said Crombac. "He was hailed as the world's greatest then, but in his mind he had done nothing exceptional in this race. He did not think that Monza is a driver's circuit; if his team-mate hadn't blown up he could not have caught up with him, and in any case, he knew that he just had a better car than anybody else."

This 1967 Monza contest still stands as testament to Clark's determination – any time someone comes from a lap down to lead a GP is remarkable. But this particular classic probably says more about the way the Lotus 49 moved the goalposts in grand prix racing than it does about Clark's exceptional ability.

## Race 159 1967 ITALIAN GP Monza

**Round 9/11** **10 September 1967**

Leading a four-car slipstreaming gaggle of Lotuses and Brabhams, a deflating tyre forced Clark to pit on lap 13, losing a lap in the process. On lap 61 he retook the lead from Brabham, having made up 100s in 46 laps, one of the most incredible comeback drives in the annals of F1. Regrettably, fuel pump failure on the very last lap ruined one fairy tale yet wrote quite another. Surtees overtook a very sideways Brabham on the exit to Parabolica to win by 0.2s, the new 'Hondola' only leading the race on the final lap, but critically for those final few hundred metres. In truth, if Graham Hill's engine had not broken ten laps from the end when 75s ahead of Brabham, Clark could not have retaken the lead, but it takes nothing from his feat or the myth surrounding it.

| Pos | Driver | Car | Time/gap | Grid | Stops | Tyres |
|---|---|---|---|---|---|---|
| 1 | John Surtees | Honda | 1h 43m 45.0s | 9 | 0 | F |
| 2 | Jack Brabham | Brabham-Repco | –0.2s | 2 | 0 | G |
| 3 | Jim Clark | Lotus-Ford | –23.1s | 1 | 1 | F |
| 4 | Jochen Rindt | Cooper-Maserati | –56.6s | 11 | 0 | F |
| 5 | Mike Spence | BRM | –1 lap | 12 | 0 | G |
| 6 | Jacky Ickx | Cooper-Maserati | –2 laps | 15 | 0 | F |

## JOHN SURTEES

**Honda RA300** 226.120kph, 140.505mph

**POLE POSITION** Clark, Lotus-Ford, 1m 28.5s (0.3s), 233.898kph, 145.338mph
**LAPS** 68 x 5.750 km, 3.573 miles
**DISTANCE** 391.000 km, 242.956 miles
**STARTERS/FINISHERS** 18/7
**WEATHER** Sunny, warm, dry
**LAP LEADERS** D Gurney, Eagle-Weslake 1-2 (2); Clark 3-9, 11-12, 61-67 (16); D Hulme, Brabham-Repco 10, 13-15, 17, 24-27 (9); Brabham 16, 59-60 (3); G Hill, Lotus-Ford 18-23, 28-58 (37); Surtees 68 (1)
**WINNER'S LAPS** 1 P10, 2-4 P9, 5-6 P8, 7 P7, 8 P6, 9 P5, 10 P6, 11-12 P5, 13-30 P4, 31-36 P3, 37 P4, 38-41 P3, 42 P4, 43-64 P3, 65-67 P2, 68 P1
**FASTEST LAP** Clark, Lotus-Ford, 1m 28.5s (lap 26), 233.898kph, 145.338mph
**CHAMPIONSHIP** Hulme 43, Brabham 40, Clark 23, Amon 20, Surtees 17

RACE POD

Suddenly scenting an improbable victory, Rindt closed in on Brabham at an incredible rate, on his final lap posting a new track record around the Monte Carlo street circuit

**2** THRILLERS

# Rindt danced his Lotus around the streets, forcing a famous Brabham error

In his autobiography *'When the Flag Drops'* Brabham wrote: "When I got to the braking area I found Piers Courage apparently coasting with a dead engine. While I was trying to decide how to cope with this, I passed my braking point by just a few yards. One thing must be said for Jochen after all my misfortunes. His last two lap times were 1m23.3s and 1m23.2s – and that was simply fabulous driving on that track under any circumstances."

And here's Rindt's perspective, taken from a post-race TV interview: "Well I was catching Jack slightly and something must have gone wrong for him in the last five laps because he wasn't quite as quick and I was catching him more and more and more and then it was two seconds and then it was one second. I was (still) following him into the last lap and he just overcooked (his) last braking for the last corner and he went straight on and I went round the last corner and won. I can't believe it myself."

And in closing the interview Jochen was to make a prophetic and, with hindsight, highly poignant remark when told that his Monaco victory had put him into Championship contention: "Well it's good news for me especially when the new 72 Lotus comes out which is supposed to be a lot quicker and we should have a better chance then."

Rindt in his Lotus 72 would win four of the following six Grands Prix, but lost his life in the seventh to become Formula 1's only posthumous Champion.

**Race 187** **1970 MONACO GP** Monte Carlo

**Round 3/13** **10 May 1970**

**JOCHEN RINDT**

**Lotus-Ford 49C** 131.716kph, 81.845mph

For 27 laps Stewart ran away with it from pole, but once he pitted with ignition trouble it was Brabham leading Amon. Rindt meanwhile had moved up through the field from his P8 grid spot, overtaking Hulme for third on lap 41, which became second 20 laps later when Amon dropped out. For ten laps Brabham held the gap to Rindt at a comfortable 10s, but with only four to go lost a big chunk of time to a backmarker. Suddenly scenting an improbable victory, Rindt literally danced his Lotus 49C around the classic street circuit, his final lap 0.8s faster than pole – and 2.7s quicker than his own grid time! Little wonder he pressured the Australian into a braking error at the final corner, sweeping past to a famous victory.

| Pos | Driver | Car | Time/gap | Grid | Stops | Tyres |
|---|---|---|---|---|---|---|
| 1 | Jochen Rindt | Lotus-Ford | 1h 54m 36.6s | 8 | 0 | F |
| 2 | Jack Brabham | Brabham-Ford | –23.1s | 4 | 0 | G |
| 3 | Henri Pescarolo | Matra | –51.4s | 7 | 0 | G |
| 4 | Denny Hulme | McLaren-Ford | –1m 28.3s | 3 | 0 | G |
| 5 | Graham Hill | Lotus-Ford | –1 lap | 12 | 0 | F |
| 6 | Pedro Rodríguez | BRM | –2 laps | 16 | 0 | D |

**POLE POSITION** J Stewart, March-Ford, 1m 24.0s (0.6s), 134.786kph, 83.752mph
**LAPS** 80 x 3.145km, 1.954 miles
**DISTANCE** 251.600 km, 156.337 miles
**STARTERS/FINISHERS** 16/8
**WEATHER** Sunny, warm, dry
**LAP LEADERS** Stewart 1-27 (27); Brabham 28-79 (52); Rindt 80 (1)
**WINNER'S LAPS** 1-2 P7, 3-11 P8, 12-21 P7, 22-27 P6, 28-35 P5, 36-40 P4, 41-60 P3, 61-79 P2, 80 P1
**FASTEST LAP** Rindt, Lotus-Ford, 1m 23.2s (lap 80), 136.082kph, 84.557mph
**CHAMPIONSHIP** Brabham 15, Stewart 13, Rindt 9, Hulme 9, McLaren 6

***RACE POD***

THRILLERS

1

# In the closest finish in Grand Prix history, 0.61 seconds covered five cars

Gethin's BRM crosses the finish line just a wheel ahead of Peterson's March, Gethin raising his arm to ensure the timekeepers awarded him the victory

# Race 206 — 1971 ITALIAN GP Monza — PETER GETHIN

**Round 9/11** — **5 September 1971** — **BRM P160** 242.616kph, 150.755mph

The 1971 Italian Grand Prix was the final and greatest Monza slipstreamer, with 25 lead changes and five cars spectacularly hurtling over the line covered by 0.61s. This race was and remains the closest finish in World Championship Grand Prix history, Peter Gethin's winning margin over Ronnie Peterson officially 0.01s or about 70cm, a couple of feet. Peterson led by far the most laps, 23, Gethin just three. On lap 20 Gethin was 10s adrift of the leaders but caught up brilliantly to first take the lead with three to go. On the final lap, the BRM driver made a tyre-smoking inside pass on Peterson and Cevert under braking for Parabolica to snatch victory. The race, the fastest at that time and the first run at over 150mph, also topped the then list for the most race leaders, eight.

| Pos | Driver | Car | Time/gap | Grid | Stops | Tyres |
|---|---|---|---|---|---|---|
| 1 | Peter Gethin | BRM | 1h 18m 12.60s | 11 | 0 | F |
| 2 | Ronnie Peterson | March-Ford | –0.01s | 6 | 0 | F |
| 3 | François Cevert | Tyrrell-Ford | –0.09s | 5 | 0 | G |
| 4 | Mike Hailwood | Surtees-Ford | –0.18s | 17 | 0 | F |
| 5 | Howden Ganley | BRM | –0.61s | 4 | 0 | F |
| 6 | Chris Amon | Matra | –32.36s | 1 | 0 | G |

**POLE POSITION** Amon, Matra, 1m 24.40s (0.42s), 251.214kph, 156.097mph
**LAPS** 55 x 5.750 km, 3.573 miles
**DISTANCE** 316.250 km, 196.509 miles
**STARTERS/FINISHERS** 23/10
**WEATHER** Sunny, hot, dry
**LAP LEADERS** C Regazzoni, Ferrari 1-3, 9 (4); Peterson 4-7, 10-14, 17-22, 24, 26, 33, 47-50, 54 (23); J Stewart, Tyrrell-Ford 8 (1); Cevert 15-16, 23, 31-32, 34, 36 (7); Hailwood 25, 27, 35, 42, 51 (5); Siffert, BRM 28-30 (3); Amon 37-41, 43-46 (9); Gethin 52-53, 55 (3)
**WINNER'S LAPS** 1 P9, 2 P8, 3 P10, 4-11 P8, 12 P9, 13 P10, 14 P9, 15 P10, 16-17 P8, 18 P7, 19 P8, 20-31 P7, 32-47 P6, 48-49 P5, 50-51 P3, 52-53 P1, 54 P4, 55 P1
**FASTEST LAP** H Pescarolo, March-Ford, 1m 23.80s (lap 9), 247.017kph, 153.489mph
**CHAMPIONSHIP** Stewart 51, Peterson 23, Ickx 19, Cevert 16, Fittipaldi 16

*RACE POD*

In *Autosport*'s Race of My Life series in 1990, Peter Gethin recalled: "I made a reasonable start, and I was in the first 10 cars. Then, lapping some backmarkers, I got a fair way behind the leading pack. I was cut off from them, but the reason I think the race was a good one for me is because, from about half distance when I lost contact until the end of the race, I had to drive every lap absolutely flat out.

"I felt I drove very well. I didn't make any mistakes and with seven laps to go I caught them. When I got to 4.5s behind them that was enough to get a tow!

"As it happened, I went into Parabolica in third on the last lap. Cevert was outbraked by Peterson, and Ronnie slid a bit wide. I was right behind him and got inside him perfectly. I was a bit locked up, but I felt it was under control!

"I was sideways, but I got the power on early, and it was a race between me and Ronnie. We got to the line and he was very close to me – we were alongside each other. So to try and convince them that I was the winner I put my hand up on the line, so they would think I'd won!"

## CHAPTER 2

# DUELS

## FIRST AMONG EQUALS

Head-to-head duels in evenly matched machinery create some of Formula 1's most gripping racing. In all but one of the ten uncompromising encounters in this collection, outright victory is on the line. To triumph, a driver must outthink, outmanoeuvre, and outlast their rival in this *mano e mano* struggle to be first among equals.

A true duel is more than just an overtake or a fleeting skirmish. It's when two drivers become locked in combat so fierce that the rest of the field fades into irrelevance. Each is driven by an unshakable belief that they are the better racer, the rightful victor. Sometimes, these duels unfold over an entire Grand Prix distance, a game of cat and mouse played at 300kph. The hunter relentlessly stalks their prey, applying persistent pressure, searching for the slightest weakness, a half-chance to strike. The hunted, knowing escape is impossible, fights to maintain control, desperate to break free but forced to defend with precision. Every move must be calculated, every reaction flawless, because one misstep could mean the difference between victory and defeat.

Some duels unfold with the two combatants chopping and changing for the lead, intent on trying to break away to find some breathing space and their racing rhythm. Others are brief but blistering, settled in a handful of breathtaking laps.

Every great duel tells a story of mutual respect or deep-seated rivalry, of risk and defiance, of two competitors pushing themselves and each other to the absolute limit. And when the dust settles, only one emerges victorious – the first among equals.

**TO TRIUMPH, A DRIVER MUST OUTTHINK, OUTMANOEUVRE, AND OUTLAST THEIR RIVAL IN THIS *MANO E MANO* STRUGGLE TO BE FIRST AMONG EQUALS**

10 DUELS

# Chris Amon shadowed the Mexican but could never fully get to grips

This photo superbly captures the intensity of the duel between the Yardley BRM of Pedro Rodríguez (1) and Chris Amon's STP March-Ford (10). Here they exit Eau Rouge to head up the hill to Raidillon

## Race 188 — 1970 BELGIAN GP Spa-Francorchamps

**Round 4/13** — **7 June 1970**

## PEDRO RODRÍGUEZ

**BRM P153** 241.308kph, 149.942mph

The McLaren team was absent in deference to the death of its founder five days earlier. World Champion Jackie Stewart was in sparkling qualifying form with pole, and in the race he and Amon, both in Marches, disputed the lead initially. Pedro Rodríguez, driving the Yardley BRM P153, took Jochen Rindt's Lotus 49C for third on lap three, then Stewart and Amon on successive laps to lead by lap five. Amon's works March shadowed the Mexican all the way but could never fully get to grips with the swift V12, just 1.1s behind at the line. The Spa circuit, always good to unleash V12 power, had two Matras and a Ferrari joining the BRM in the top six, Rodríguez bringing victory to the Bourne team for the first time since 1966. Stewart retired with engine trouble on lap 14.

| Pos | Driver | Car | Time/gap | Grid | Stops | Tyres |
|---|---|---|---|---|---|---|
| 1 | Pedro Rodríguez | BRM | 1h 38m 9.9s | 6 | 0 | D |
| 2 | Chris Amon | March-Ford | –1.1s | 3 | 0 | F |
| 3 | Jean-Pierre Beltoise | Matra | –1m 43.7s | 11 | 0 | G |
| 4 | Ignazio Giunti | Ferrari | –2m 38.5s | 8 | 1 | F |
| 5 | Rolf Stommelen | Brabham-Ford | –3m 31.8s | 7 | 0 | G |
| 6r | Henri Pescarolo | Matra | –1 lap | 17 | 1 | G |

**POLE POSITION** J Stewart, March-Ford, 3m 28.0s (2.1s), 244.038kph, 151.638mph
**LAPS** 28 x 14.100 km, 8.761 miles
**DISTANCE** 394.800 km, 245.317 miles
**STARTERS/FINISHERS** 17/8
**WEATHER** Sunny, warm, dry
**LAP LEADERS** Amon 1, 3-4 (3); Stewart 2 (1); Rodríguez 5-28 (24)
**WINNER'S LAPS** 1-2 P4, 3 P3, 4 P2, 5-28 P 1
**FASTEST LAP** Amon, March-Ford 3m 27.4s (lap 27), 244.744kph, 152.077mph
**CHAMPIONSHIP** Brabham 15, Stewart 13, Rodríguez 10, Rindt 9, Hulme 9

*RACE POD*

DUELS

# Alonso and Schumacher engaged in an enthralling opening-race duel

Alonso and Schumacher kicked off their epic 2006 title battle with a duel so closely matched that it was decided by very fine margins

## Race 751 — 2006 BAHRAIN GP Sakhir

**Round 1/18** — **12 March 2006**

At the opening round, seven-time Champion Schumacher's Bridgestone-shod Ferrari sat on pole, reigning Champion Alonso's Renault behind on row two, on Michelins, before the pair engaged in an enthralling race-long duel. In a storming first stint, Schumacher drew out a 6s gap, but by going four laps longer, Alonso was within 1s of the Ferrari by the end of lap 24. There he remained until Michael's second stop on lap 36, Fernando again employing the overcut. Exiting the pits on the inside line approaching turn 1, Alonso's track positioning just thwarted Schumacher from retaking the lead as he hurtled down the pits straight and turned into the corner. The rivals were so closely matched that, once behind, Schumacher couldn't dislodge Alonso for the remaining 17 laps, just as Fernando had been similarly frustrated earlier.

| Pos | Driver | Car | Time/gap | Grid (pen) | Stops | Tyres |
|---|---|---|---|---|---|---|
| 1 | Fernando Alonso | Renault | 1h 29m 46.205s | 4 | 2 | M |
| 2 | Michael Schumacher | Ferrari | −1.246s | 1 | 2 | B |
| 3 | Kimi Räikkönen | McLaren-Mercedes | −19.360s | 22 | 1 | M |
| 4 | Jenson Button | Honda | −19.992s | 3 | 2 | M |
| 5 | Juan Pablo Montoya | McLaren-Mercedes | −37.048s | 5 | 2 | M |
| 6 | Mark Webber | Williams-Cosworth | −41.932s | 7 | 2 | B |

## FERNANDO ALONSO

**Renault R26** 206.018kph, 128.014mph

**POLE POSITION** M Schumacher, Ferrari, 1m 31.431s (0.047s), 213.091kph, 132.408mph
**LAPS** 57 x 5.412 km, 3.363 miles
**DISTANCE** 308.238 km, 191.530 miles
**STARTERS/FINISHERS** 22/18
**WEATHER** Sunny, warm, dry, breezy
**LAP LEADERS** M Schumacher 1-15, 24-35 (27); Alonso 16-19, 36-39, 41-57 (25); Montoya 20-23 (4); Button 40 (1)
**WINNER'S LAPS** 1-15 P2, 16-19 P1, 20-23 P3, 24-35 P2, 36-39 P1, 40 P2, 41-57 P1
**FASTEST LAP** N Rosberg, Williams-Cosworth, 1m 32.408s (lap 42), 210.838kph, 131.009mph
**CHAMPIONSHIP** Alonso 10, M Schumacher 8, Räikkönen 6, Button 5, Montoya 4

*RACE POD*

DUELS

# Two rain aces in identical cars, both McLarens gripless by the line

**It was gutsy for Button to go up against Hamilton at McLaren from 2010-2012. This was the only genuine head-to-head race Jenson won, but he will also be quietly proud of beating Lewis on points in 2011**

## Race 824 — 2010 CHINESE GP Shanghai

**Round 4/19** — **18 April 2010**

With rain threatening, most used a first lap SC to switch to inters. Rosberg, Button and Kubica did not, leading at the restart and extending it when the rest had to switch back to slicks. On lap 19, as rain finally fell, Button took the lead and led the charge for inters. During that first stint, Hamilton had been more than a minute behind but had recovered to P7 when a second SC slashed Jenson's massive advantage. Hamilton then charged past the Renaults and Rosberg to get Button in his sights 3s ahead. Making their final stops almost together set up a 18-lap duel between two rain aces in identical cars on the same intermediate tyres. Initially Button pulled a 10s gap, but over the final seven riveting laps Lewis closed to 1.5s, both McLarens gripless by the time they crossed the line for a resounding 1-2.

| Pos | Driver | Car | Time/gap | Grid (pen) | Stops | Tyres (h/s) |
|---|---|---|---|---|---|---|
| 1 | Jenson Button | McLaren-Mercedes | 1h 46m 42.163s | 5 | 2 | oii |
| 2 | Lewis Hamilton | McLaren-Mercedes | –1.530s | 6 | 4 | oipii |
| 3 | Nico Rosberg | Mercedes | –9.484s | 4 | 2 | oii |
| 4 | Fernando Alonso | Ferrari | –11.869s | 3 | 4 | oiioi |
| 5 | Robert Kubica | Renault | –22.213s | 8 | 2 | oii |
| 6 | Sebastian Vettel | Red Bull-Renault | –33.310s | 1 | 4 | oipii |

## JENSON BUTTON

**McLaren-Mercedes MP4-25** 171.541kph, 106.591mph

**POLE POSITION** Vettel, Red Bull-Renault, 1m 34.558s (0.248s), 207.529kph, 128.952mph
**LAPS** 56 x 5.451 km, 3.387 miles
**DISTANCE** 305.066 km, 189.559 miles
**STARTERS/FINISHERS** 24/17
**WEATHER** Overcast, warm, dry start then showers
**LAP LEADERS** Alonso 1-2 (2); Rosberg 3-18 (16); Button 19-56 (38); SC 1-3, 22-25 (7)
**WINNER'S LAPS** 1 P5, 2 P4, 3-18 P2, 19-56 P1
**FASTEST LAP** Hamilton, McLaren-Mercedes, 1m 42.061s (lap 13), 192.273kph, 119.473mph
**CHAMPIONSHIP** Button 60, Rosberg 50, Alonso 49, Hamilton 49, Vettel 45

*RACE POD*

DUELS

# In their high-speed duel, Lotus chassis/aero overcame Ferrari horsepower/grunt

Here, Rindt leads Ickx, Clay Regazzoni and Amon. Rindt's victory was ultimately enough to give him an unassailable lead in the 1970 championship despite Ickx winning three of the remaining five rounds

## Race 192 — 1970 GERMAN GP Hockenheim

**Round 8/13** — **2 August 1970**

## JOCHEN RINDT

**Lotus-Ford 72C** 199.667kph, 124.067mph

For his fourth consecutive victory in what would become his posthumously awarded championship year, Rindt had to work hard to beat Ickx in the ever-improving Ferrari 312B. These two filled the front row, the Ferrari on pole. From the off a five-car slipstreaming battle ensued between Rindt, the two Ferraris, and the works March pair of Chris Amon and Jo Siffert. As the flat-out pace took its toll on engines, just two remained by two-thirds distance, never more than a car's length between them, chopping and changing over those closing laps: lap 45-46 Ickx, 47 Rindt, 48 Ickx, 49 Rindt and finally 50 Rindt, to win by 0.7s. In their high-speed duel, Lotus chassis/aero had overcome Ferrari horsepower/grunt, but only just. It was a fascinating encounter and Jochen's final victory before the Monza tragedy.

| Pos | Driver | Car | Time/gap | Grid | Stops | Tyres |
|---|---|---|---|---|---|---|
| 1 | Jochen Rindt | Lotus-Ford | 1h 42m 0.3s | 2 | 0 | F |
| 2 | Jacky Ickx | Ferrari | –0.7s | 1 | 0 | F |
| 3 | Denny Hulme | McLaren-Ford | –1m 21.8s | 16 | 0 | G |
| 4 | Emerson Fittipaldi | Lotus-Ford | –1m 55.1s | 13 | 0 | F |
| 5 | Rolf Stommelen | Brabham-Ford | –1 lap | 11 | 0 | G |
| 6 | Henri Pescarolo | Matra | –1 lap | 5 | 1 | G |

**POLE POSITION** Ickx, Ferrari, 1m 59.5s (0.2s), 204.522kph, 127.084mph
**LAPS** 50 x 6.789 km, 4.218 miles
**DISTANCE** 339.450 km, 210.924 miles
**STARTERS/FINISHERS** 21/9
**WEATHER** Sunny, hot, dry
**LAP LEADERS** Ickx 1-6, 10-17, 26-31, 36-43, 45-46, 48 (31); Rindt 7-9, 18-21, 24-25, 32-35, 44, 47, 49-50 (17); C Regazzoni, Ferrari 22-23 (2)
**WINNER'S LAPS** 1-6 P2, 7-9 P1, 10-11 P2, 12 P3, 13-17 P2, 18-21 P1, 22-23 P2, 24-25 P1, 26-28 P2, 29 P3, 30-31 P2, 32-35 P1, 36-43 P2, 44 P1, 45-46 P2, 47 P1, 48 P2, 49-50 P1
**FASTEST LAP** Ickx, Ferrari, 2m 00.5s (lap 50), 202.825kph, 126.030mph
**CHAMPIONSHIP** Rindt 45, Brabham 25, Hulme 20, Stewart 19, Amon 14

RACE POD

## 6 DUELS

# Classy Piastri beats Leclerc in Baku street-fight classic

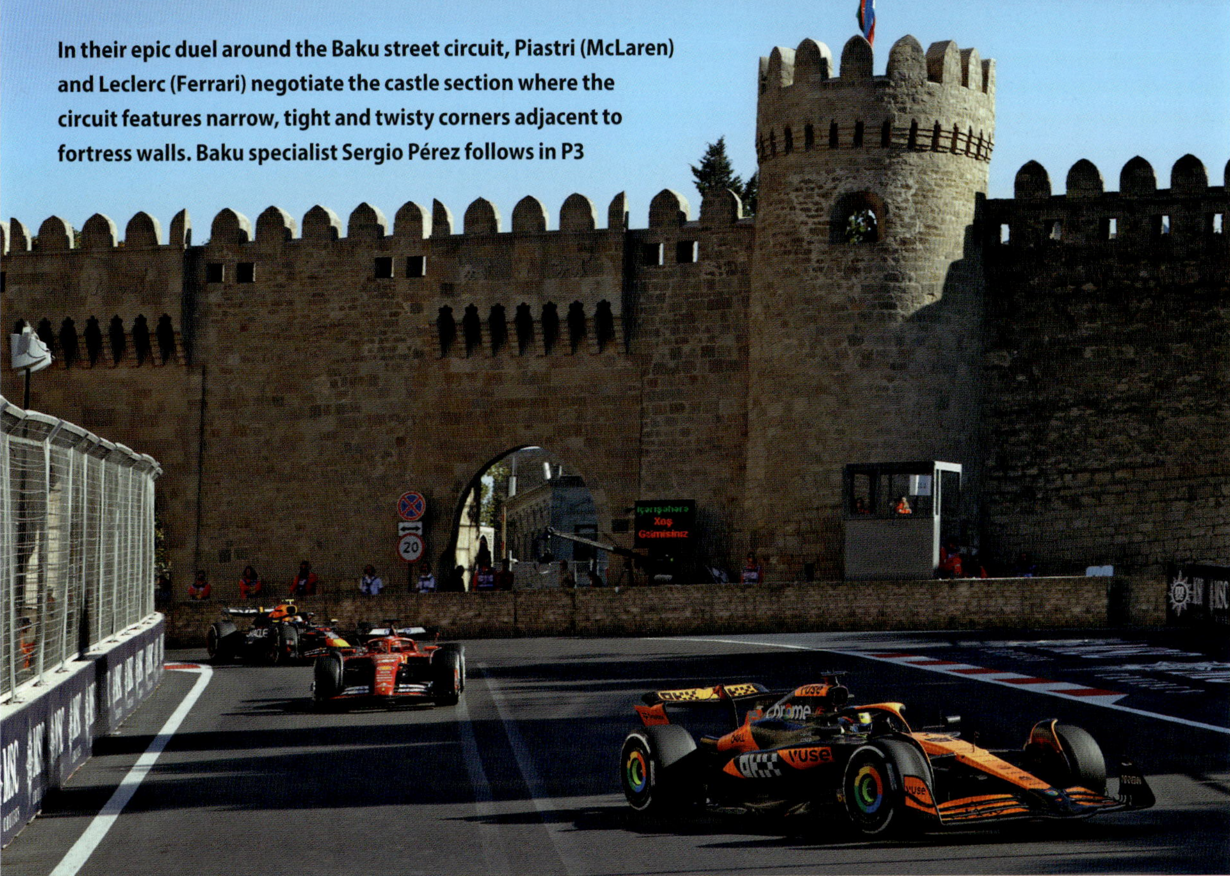

In their epic duel around the Baku street circuit, Piastri (McLaren) and Leclerc (Ferrari) negotiate the castle section where the circuit features narrow, tight and twisty corners adjacent to fortress walls. Baku specialist Sergio Pérez follows in P3

## Race 1118 2024 AZERBAIJAN GP Baku

**Round 17/24** **15 September 2024**

In a spellbinding race-long battle, Piastri defeated Leclerc in a classic F1 duel between closely matched cars. From pole, Leclerc pulled out almost 6s by lap 15, when the young Australian, starting from P2, made a tyre stop. Ferrari responded next lap but lost crucial time, Leclerc rejoining only 1.3s ahead. Piastri sensed the moment and on lap 20 at turn 1 made his move. Coming from a long way back, he surprised the Ferrari driver, Leclerc failing to defend the inside line, Oscar's bold pass impeccable. Over the next 26 laps the pair duelled relentlessly separated by 0.5s or less, Leclerc grasping every attack opportunity, Piastri soaking up the pressure, both fair, both flawless. Suddenly, with five laps to go, it was over. Leclerc, his rear tyres shot, began to fall back, Piastri taking an outstanding victory.

| Pos | Driver | Car | Time/gap | Grid | Stops | Tyres |
|---|---|---|---|---|---|---|
| 1 | Oscar Piastri | McLaren-Mercedes | 1h 32m 58.007s | 2 | 1 | mh |
| 2 | Charles Leclerc | Ferrari | –10.910s | 1 | 1 | mh |
| 3 | George Russell | Mercedes | –31.328s | 5 | 1 | mh |
| 4 | Lando Norris | McLaren-Mercedes | –36.143s | 15 | 1 | hm |
| 5 | Max Verstappen | Red Bull-Honda RBPT | –1m 17.098s | 6 | 2 | mhs |
| 6 | Fernando Alonso | Aston Martin-Mercedes | –1m 25.468s | 7 | 1 | mh |

## OSCAR PIASTRI

**McLaren-Mercedes MCL38** 197.521kph, 122.733mph

**POLE POSITION** Leclerc, Ferrari, 1m 41.365s (0.321s), 213.197kph, 132.474mph
**LAPS** 51 x 6.003 km, 3.730 miles
**DISTANCE** 306.049 km, 190.170 miles
**STARTERS/FINISHERS** 20/16
**WEATHER** Sunny, hot, dry
**LAP LEADERS** Leclerc 1-16, 18-19 (18); Sainz 17 (1); Piastri 20-51 (32); VSC 51 (1)
**WINNER'S LAPS** 1-14 P2, 15 P3, 16 P4, 17 P3, 18-19 P2, 20-51 P1
**FASTEST LAP** Norris, McLaren-Mercedes, 1m 45.255s (Lap 42), 205.318kph, 127.578mph
**CHAMPIONSHIP** Verstappen 313, Norris 254, Leclerc 235, Piastri 222, Sainz 184

*RACE POD*

**5** DUELS

# Fangio and Hawthorn played out a spellbinding duel

Hawthorn narrowly beat Fangio in their intense duel to become the first British winner of a World Championship race

## Race 28 1953 FRENCH GP Reims

**Round 5/9** **5 July 1953**

Pole suggested Ascari's Ferrari would continue to dominate the season, but qualifying pointed to a closer race, the top six covered by just 1.3s. González on low fuel rocketed his Maserati into the lead, pulling out 20s before making his fuel stop on lap 30. This left Fangio's Maserati leading from Hawthorn's Ferrari, these two beginning to pull away slightly from Ascari and the rest. Thereafter Fangio and Hawthorn played out an enthralling duel, passing one another 11 times over the final 30 laps, Hawthorn finally winning by 'a nose' to save Ferrari's blushes. There was little to choose between the top speed of the two cars, but Ferrari had grunt out of corners, making the crucial difference from the Thillois hairpin to the finishing line. González finished third, Ascari fourth.

| Pos | Driver | Car | Time/gap | Grid | Stops | Tyres |
|---|---|---|---|---|---|---|
| 1 | Mike Hawthorn | Ferrari | 2h 44m 18.6s | 7 | 0 | P |
| 2 | Juan Manuel Fangio | Maserati | –1.0s | 4 | 0 | P |
| 3 | Froilán González | Maserati | –1.4s | 5 | 1 | P |
| 4 | Alberto Ascari | Ferrari | –4.6s | 1 | 0 | P |
| 5 | Nino Farina | Ferrari | –1m 7.6s | 6 | 0 | P |
| 6 | Luigi Villoresi | Ferrari | –1m 15.9s | 3 | 0 | P |

## MIKE HAWTHORN

**Ferrari 500** 182.881kph, 113.637mph

**POLE POSITION** Ascari, Ferrari, 2m 41.2s (1.4s), 186.409kph, 115.829mph
**LAPS** 60 x 8.347 km, 5.187 miles
**DISTANCE** 500.820 km, 311.195 miles
**STARTERS/FINISHERS** 25/15
**WEATHER** Sunny, hot, dry
**LAP LEADERS** González 1-29 (29); Fangio 30-31, 35-36, 39-41, 45-47, 49-53, 55-56 (17); Hawthorn 32-34, 37-38, 42-44, 48, 54, 57-60 (14)
**WINNER'S LAPS** 1-2 P5, 3 P4, 4 P3, 5 P4, 6 P3, 7 P4, 8 P3, 9-13 P2, 14-16 P3, 17-18 P4, 19 P3, 20 P2, 21 P3, 22 P2, 23 P4, 24 P3, 25 P4, 26 P6, 27 P5, 28-29 P4, 30-31 P2, 32-34 P1, 35-36 P2, 37-38 P1, 39-41 P2, 42-44 P1, 45-47 P2, 48 P1, 49-53 P2, 54 P1, 55-56 P2, 57-60 P1
**FASTEST LAP** Fangio, Maserati/Ascari, Ferrari, 2m 41.1s (laps 25/37), 186.525kph, 115.901mph
**CHAMPIONSHIP** Ascari 28.5, Hawthorn 14, Villoresi 13, González 11, Vukovich 9

*RACE POD*

4 DUELS

# Their heart-in-mouth, wheel-to-wheel duel for victory was intense

Post-race revealed quite how much each had striven for victory, the elation of one, the anguish of the other

## Race 900 — 2014 BAHRAIN GP Sakhir

**Round 3/19** — **6 April 2014**

Pole at Bahrain's first night race unexpectedly went to Rosberg, Nico honing a quicker package that weekend. But Hamilton's fightback began instantly the lights went out, taking the lead and resolutely defending from Nico's determined attack just before his lap 19 first stop. This gave him tyre-selection precedence, staying on options, while Nico's switch to harder primes enabled Lewis to pull out 9.5s, still far less than expected. And with tyre advantage reversing in their final stint, Rosberg was clear favourite, especially when a late SC closed up the field. Surely Hamilton couldn't resist Rosberg's underlying pace and on faster rubber? But Hamilton wouldn't be denied, cutting back repeatedly on his teammate in their heart-in-mouth wheel-to-wheel duel to come home the narrow winner.

| Pos | Driver | Car | Time/gap | Grid (pen) | Stops | Tyres (h/s) |
|---|---|---|---|---|---|---|
| 1 | Lewis Hamilton | Mercedes | 1h 39m 42.743s | 2 | 2 | oop |
| 2 | Nico Rosberg | Mercedes | –1.085s | 1 | 2 | opo |
| 3 | Sergio Pérez | Force India-Mercedes | –24.067s | 4 | 2 | oop |
| 4 | Daniel Ricciardo | Red Bull-Renault | –24.489s | 13 (–10) | 2 | opo |
| 5 | Nico Hülkenberg | Force India-Mercedes | –28.654s | 11 | 2 | oop |
| 6 | Sebastian Vettel | Red Bull-Renault | –29.879s | 10 | 2 | poo |

## LEWIS HAMILTON

**Mercedes F1 W05** 185.476kph, 115.249mph

**POLE POSITION** Rosberg, Mercedes, 1m 33.185s (0.279s), 209.080kph, 129.916mph
**LAPS** 57 x 5.412 km, 3.362 miles
**DISTANCE** 308.238 km, 191.530 miles
**STARTERS/FINISHERS** 22/17
**WEATHER** Dark, hot, dry
**LAP LEADERS** Hamilton 1-18, 22-57 (54); Rosberg 19-21 (3); SC 42-46 (5)
**WINNER'S LAPS** 1-18 P1, 19-21 P2, 22-57 P1
**FASTEST LAP** Rosberg, Mercedes, 1m 37.020s (lap 49), 200.816kph, 124.781mph
**CHAMPIONSHIP** Rosberg 61, Hamilton 50, Hülkenberg 28, Alonso 26, Button 23

*RACE POD*

Despite a hefty practice prang due to loose kerbing at Woodcote, Stewart (3) lined up beside Rindt (2) on pole. Their mesmerising duel lasted over 60 laps before Rindt was forced to make a pitstop

3 DUELS

# Stewart and Rindt put on a titanic duel, head and shoulders above the rest

"The 1969 British Grand Prix was one of the most exciting and enjoyable Formula 1 races that I ever had," recalled Stewart. "Jochen was one of my best friends. The cooperation we had in not trying to block each other allowed us to definitively run away from the rest of the field. We knew, because in those days there was no aerodynamic sophistication, that we could draft each other and pass if we were not blocked. Almost every lap, we exchanged the lead on the Hangar Straight and going into the 155mph Woodcote corner, which in those days had no chicane. We pointed to each other which side to be passed on, to avoid reducing our lead from the rest of the pack. We exchanged the lead more than 30 times and it was a fantastic race for both of us.

"The Matra MS80 was a wonderful car to drive and the Lotus 49 was also exceptional, in addition to which we were such good friends that there were no nasty circumstances during the entire race, until the unfortunate point at which Jochen's rear wing came loose. I was sure he was going to blow a tyre so I passed him and pointed. He then saw it in his mirror and went into the pits. And then they didn't have enough fuel in the car…

"My father and my brother were there to see me win. It was a big day in my life."

## Race 179 — 1969 BRITISH GP Silverstone

**Round 6/11** — **19 July 1969**

Rindt's first season with Team Lotus wasn't going to plan. He'd captured poles but no points and Stewart was running away with the title with four wins from the first five rounds. Stewart lined up beside Rindt on pole and at last their long overdue duel looked on. This time a titanic struggle ensued between the Lotus 49 and the blue Matra MS80. Rindt led the first five laps, Stewart the next nine, after which Rindt did most of the leading, Stewart never more than a few car lengths behind, their pace so fast they lapped the entire field by the end of lap 56. But on lap 63 of 84 the spell was broken, Rindt pitting to fix a rear-wing endplate which threatened to puncture his rear tyre. Later, a further stop for fuel dropped Jochen to fourth, but at least he'd scored his first points of the season.

| Pos | Driver | Car | Time/gap | Grid | Stops | Tyres |
|---|---|---|---|---|---|---|
| 1 | Jackie Stewart | Matra-Ford | 1h 55m 55.6s | 2 | 0 | D |
| 2 | Jacky Ickx | Brabham-Ford | –1 lap | 4 | 0 | G |
| 3 | Bruce McLaren | McLaren-Ford | –1 lap | 7 | 0 | G |
| 4 | Jochen Rindt | Lotus-Ford | –1 lap | 1 | 2 | F |
| 5 | Piers Courage | Brabham-Ford | –1 lap | 10 | 0 | D |
| 6 | Vic Elford | McLaren-Ford | –2 laps | 11 | 0 | G |

### JACKIE STEWART

**Matra-Ford MS80** 204.795kph, 127.254mph

**POLE POSITION** Rindt, Lotus-Ford, 1m 20.8s (0.4s), 209.876kph, 130.411mph
**LAPS** 84 x 4.711 km, 2.927 miles
**DISTANCE** 395.686 km, 245.868 miles
**STARTERS/FINISHERS** 17/10
**WEATHER** Overcast, dry
**LAP LEADERS** Rindt 1-5, 16-61 (51); Stewart 6-15, 62-84 (33)
**WINNER'S LAPS** 1-5 P2, 6-15 P1, 16-61 P2, 62-84 P1
**FASTEST LAP** Stewart, Matra-Ford, 1m 21.3s (laps 57 & 60), 208.585kph, 129.609mph
**CHAMPIONSHIP** Stewart 45, McLaren 17, G Hill 16, Siffert 13, Ickx 13

*RACE POD*

DUELS

# Hill's greatest victory set up an unexpected Adelaide showdown

Damon Hill, who selected the Japanese GP as his greatest drive when asked about his best performances by *Autosport*, recalled: "With the deaths of Roland Ratzenberger and Ayrton Senna, 1994 was a highly stressful and dramatic year.

"To stay in the championship fight I had to win. Off we went and Michael was in front of me. I just had to hang onto his gearbox – I had a really good view of his driving style in the wet. We were both driving at a very high level. It was incredibly hard. The level of concentration needed in those conditions – it demands a lot. I love driving in the wet, even though it terrifies the shit out of me! When you do it, you test all your instincts. It's the most enjoyable, satisfying experience – it's so incredibly otherworldish!

"On the last lap I had to pull out all the stops to maintain the advantage. I said, 'Ayrton, if you're up there, I could do with a hand!'. The next thing I know, I'm flying around the Esses, like someone has got my foot and stuck it on the throttle, to the bulkhead.

"I got as far as Degner 2 or the hairpin and I thought, 'I can't keep this up'. I came back to being a bit more cautious and had to hope it was enough. It was almost as though I had let my instinct drive the car. It was an astonishing experience, driven by the championship situation. All my energy went into that performance. I had to go way beyond what I previously thought I was capable of."

## Race 563 1994 JAPANESE GP Suzuka

**Round 15/16** **6 November 1994**

## DAMON HILL

**Williams-Renault FW16B** 151.796kph, 94.322mph

Atrocious rain, accidents and injury to a marshal eventually produced a red flag after 13 laps, Hill 7s behind Schumacher. From a SC rolling start the race resumed over 37 laps, the results to be decided on aggregate. After five laps Schumacher dived for the pits, Hill continuing for another seven and keeping the lead during his stop. It took Schumacher ten laps to narrow the 7s gap and regain the net lead, but after a further five, lap 40, he made a second stop. It soon became clear Hill would not stop again and on rejoining Schumacher needed to gain 15s in ten laps. On the still-wet track Hill skilfully and resolutely defended his shrinking lead, even gaining time on the final lap. Against the odds, and in the face of monumental pressure, Hill beat Schumacher to the damp chequered flag by a net 3.365s after a fantastic duel.

| Pos | Driver | Car | Time/gap | Grid | Stops | Tyres |
|---|---|---|---|---|---|---|
| 1 | Damon Hill | Williams-Renault | 1h 55m 53.532s | 2 | 1 | G |
| 2 | Michael Schumacher | Benetton-Ford | –3.365s | 1 | 2 | G |
| 3 | Jean Alesi | Ferrari | –52.045s | 7 | 1 | G |
| 4 | Nigel Mansell | Williams-Renault | –56.074s | 4 | 1 | G |
| 5 | Eddie Irvine | Jordan-Hart | –1m 42.107s | 6 | 1 | G |
| 6 | Heinz-Harald Frentzen | Sauber-Mercedes | –1m 59.863s | 3 | 1 | G |

**POLE POSITION** Schumacher, Benetton-Ford, 1m 37.209s (0.487s), 217.165kph, 134.940mph
**LAPS** 50 x 5.864 km, 3.644 miles (53 lap race interrupted due to accident. Result aggregate of 13 + 37 laps)
**DISTANCE** 293.200 km, 182.186 miles
**STARTERS/FINISHERS** 26/13
**WEATHER** Overcast, cold, very wet
**LAP LEADERS** (On the road) Schumacher 1-18, 36-40 (23); Hill 19-35, 41-50 (27); SC 3-9, 14-15 (9)
**WINNER'S LAPS** 1-18 P2, 19-35 P1, 36-40 P2, 41-50 P1
**FASTEST LAP** Hill, Williams-Renault, 1m 56.597s (lap 24), 181.054kph, 112.502mph
**CHAMPIONSHIP** Schumacher 92, Hill 91, Berger 35, Häkkinen 26, Alesi 23

Over the years Damon Hill frequently won against more highly vaunted teammates and rivals. Here Michael Schumacher offers a sporting hand after Hill beat him in their gripping duel at Suzuka in 1994

1 DUELS

# Arnoux and Villeneuve duelled unyieldingly, passing and repassing

In *Gilles Villeneuve: The life of the legendary racing driver* by Gerald Donaldson, Villeneuve, speaking about the 1979 French Grand Prix said: "I tell you that was really fun! I thought for sure we were going to get on our heads, you know, because when you start interlocking wheels it's very easy for one car to climb over another. But we didn't crash and it's okay. I enjoyed myself amazingly!"

"I always considered him my best friend in Formula 1," said Arnoux many years later talking to Hungarian journalist Károly Méhes in *Gilles Villeneuve: His Untold Life from Berthierville to Zolder* (2018). "To me, the name Gilles Villeneuve symbolises a real acrobat behind the wheel; someone who drives at the limit on every corner, every time… Gilles didn't understand the meaning of the word 'danger'. One time he said to me, 'René, if you have a steering wheel and brakes, you can achieve everything!'

"Dijon 1979 was the best race in the world! It was possible only because Gilles and I knew each other very well. Yes, it was quite dangerous, especially the wheel banging, but I knew we could control the situation. I wanted to finish second, but I was experiencing some fuel pick up problems and I always feared that in the big corner before the start-finish line the car would stop or hesitate. I kept pushing and trying. In the end, it wasn't that important, coming second or third. The best was the fight between us."

## Race 321 — 1979 FRENCH GP Dijon-Prenois — JEAN-PIERRE JABOUILLE

**Round 8/15** — **1 July 1979** — **Renault RS10** 191.315kph, 118.877mph

An all-Renault front row but Arnoux almost stalled, dropping to ninth, and Jabouille was outgunned by Villeneuve from row two. On lap 47 Jabouille finally powered by the Ferrari, now on worn tyres, which began falling into the grasp of the quickly recovering Arnoux, intent on a glorious Renault 1-2. On lap 77, urged on by the patriotic crowd, he took Villeneuve for second, but Gilles was having none of it. Over those final three crazy, awe-inspiring, wheel-banging laps, Arnoux and Villeneuve fought uncompromisingly over second place, passing and repassing, the epitome of motor racing. Their famous duel has always overshadowed the amazing feat that, two years after Renault's debut, Jabouille's historic first turbo victory was an extraordinary French triumph: driver, car, engine, tyres, fuel, and at Dijon.

| Pos | Driver | Car | Time/gap | Grid | Stops | Tyres |
|---|---|---|---|---|---|---|
| 1 | Jean-Pierre Jabouille | Renault | 1h 35m 20.42 | 1 | 0 | M |
| 2 | Gilles Villeneuve | Ferrari | –14.59s | 3 | 0 | M |
| 3 | René Arnoux | Renault | –14.83s | 2 | 0 | M |
| 4 | Alan Jones | Williams-Ford | –36.61s | 7 | 0 | G |
| 5 | Jean-Pierre Jarier | Tyrrell-Ford | –1m 4.51s | 10 | 0 | G |
| 6 | Clay Regazzoni | Williams-Ford | –1m 5.51s | 9 | 0 | G |

**POLE POSITION** Jabouille, Renault, 1m 07.19s (0.26s), 203.602kph, 126.512mph
**LAPS** 80 x 3.800 km, 2.361 miles
**DISTANCE** 304.000 km, 188.897 miles
**STARTERS/FINISHERS** 24/18
**WEATHER** Overcast, dry
**LAP LEADERS** Villeneuve 1-46 (46); Jabouille 47-80 (34)
**WINNER'S LAPS** 1-46 P2, 47-80 P1
**FASTEST LAP** Arnoux, Renault, 1m 09.16s (lap 71), 197.802kph, 122.909mph
**CHAMPIONSHIP** Scheckter 30, Villeneuve 26, Laffite 24, Depailler 20, Reutemann 20

**RACE POD**

**Behind Renault's historic first turbo victory, Gilles Villeneuve's Ferrari and René Arnoux's Renault memorably duelled over second place at Dijon**

CHAPTER 3

# COMEBACKS

## THROUGH THE FIELD

When a driver in a competitive car encounters a setback, it can set the stage for the electrifying drama of a recovery drive. As they carve their way through the field, overtaking car after car in their pursuit of redemption or possible victory, each bold move becomes captivating entertainment.

The Formula 1 starting grid rewards speed. Those who excel in qualifying gain the advantage of track position, with the fastest qualifier earning pole position at the very front of the grid. Given that the fastest driver-car combinations typically secure the front spots, it's no surprise that around 43% of races are won from pole, with two-thirds of victories coming from the 'front row'. Conversely, the odds of winning from deeper in the pack are far slimmer: less than one-third of victories come from beyond the front row, and the chances from outside the top ten are little more than two-in-a-hundred! Yet, in the rarest of cases, a driver defies those odds with a breathtaking comeback, carving through the field to snatch victory against all expectations.

This collection of races highlights three astonishing comeback drives where misfortune in qualifying or grid penalties left exceptional drivers starting out of position. In a fourth race, the driver stalled on the starting grid, dropping to the very back, yet staged an incredible charge to seize the lead.

The remaining six races showcase a different kind of comeback drive, one where a mid-race setback, often a tyre issue, forces a driver into a furious charge to claim or regain the lead. In ranking these performances and identifying the most exceptional among them, it is crucial to consider the specific circumstances that shaped each victory.

Since the introduction of the Safety Car in 1993, its role in reshaping races has been significant, erasing a leader's hard-earned advantage or giving a chasing driver an unexpected lifeline. Also from the 1990s onward, radical improvements in car reliability, driven by better quality control and regulatory changes, have altered the dynamics of comeback drives. In earlier eras, mechanical attrition could just as easily snatch victory away from a race leading driver as it could hand a recovering driver an unexpected triumph. Yet, regardless of era or circumstance, comeback drives remain among the most exhilarating spectacles in Formula 1. Fans anxiously watch the timing screens as the gap shrinks, stopwatches in hand, while the grandstands erupt on every lap as the charging driver comes from behind, slicing through the field in pursuit of glory.

**AS THEY CARVE THEIR WAY THROUGH THE FIELD, OVERTAKING CAR AFTER CAR IN THEIR PURSUIT OF REDEMPTION OR POSSIBLE VICTORY, EACH BOLD MOVE BECOMES CAPTIVATING ENTERTAINMENT**

COMEBACKS

# A superb comeback drive saw Prost retake the lead on lap 68

Arnoux streaked into the lead from pole chased closely by Prost, the Renault pair leaving the rest in their wake. Prost ultimately won after a scintillating recovery drive

## Race 358 — 1982 SOUTH AFRICAN GP Kyalami — ALAIN PROST

**Round 1/16** — **23 January 1982** — **Renault RE30B** 205.779kph, 127.865mph

At the season's opening round during Thursday practice, Niki Lauda, returning with McLaren, was the ringleader in a drivers' strike over super licences. Rosberg, replacing Alan Jones at Williams, qualified P7, the fastest non-turbo now that Brabham-BMW had joined the turbo brigade. The Renaults took command from the off, pole-man Arnoux leading until a backmarker helped Prost ahead on lap 14. On lap 41, holding an 11s lead, Prost suffered a puncture and had to pit, falling to eighth and a lap behind Arnoux. A superb comeback drive on fresh rubber saw Prost first unlap himself then pass his slowing teammate a second time on lap 68 of 77 to retake the lead. Arnoux's tyre problems, vibration caused by rubber pick-up, became so acute he lost second to Reutemann. Lauda finished fourth, the Ferraris and Brabhams failing.

| Pos | Driver | Car | Time/gap | Grid | Stops | Tyres |
|---|---|---|---|---|---|---|
| 1 | Alain Prost | Renault | 1h 32m 8.401s | 5 | 1 | M |
| 2 | Carlos Reutemann | Williams-Ford | –14.946s | 8 | 0 | G |
| 3 | René Arnoux | Renault | –27.900s | 1 | 0 | M |
| 4 | Niki Lauda | McLaren-Ford | –32.133s | 13 | 0 | M |
| 5 | Keke Rosberg | Williams-Ford | –46.139s | 7 | 0 | G |
| 6 | John Watson | McLaren-Ford | –50.993s | 9 | 0 | M |

**POLE POSITION** Arnoux, Renault, 1m 06.351s (0.274s), 222.670kph, 138.361mph
**LAPS** 77 x 4.104 km, 2.550 miles
**DISTANCE** 316.008 km, 196.358 miles
**STARTERS/FINISHERS** 26/18
**WEATHER** Sunny, hot, dry
**LAP LEADERS** Arnoux 1-13, 41-67 (40); Prost 14-40, 68-77 (37)
**WINNER'S LAPS** 1-13 P2, 14-40 P1, 41-43 P8, 44-50 P7, 51-53 P6, 54 P5, 55-60 P4, 61 P3, 62-67 P2, 68-77 P1
**FASTEST LAP** Prost, Renault, 1m 08.278s (lap 49), 216.386kph, 134.456mph
**CHAMPIONSHIP** Prost 9, Reutemann 6, Arnoux 4, Lauda 3, Rosberg 2

*RACE POD*

9 COMEBACKS

# Hamilton miraculously wins from P14 as Vettel throws away home victory

On lap 52 with a 9s lead, Vettel crashed out of his home GP at the slippery Sachskurve. The photo superbly captures the moment of impact and the dismay of the partisan crowd

## Race 987 2018 GERMAN GP Hockenheim

**Round 11/21** **22 July 2018**

Late rain produced a sensational race of two distinct phases. The first saw pole-sitter Vettel on course for a comfortable win from Bottas, while Hamilton, condemned to start P14 due to a technical failure, carved through the field to P5 by the end of lap 14, 25.6s behind Vettel. When Ferrari pitted Vettel on lap 25, he rejoined between the flying Kimi and Lewis. Rather than wave past the faster Seb, Kimi stayed ahead for 13 laps until a belated lap 39 'pass' order. On lap 43 it rained, but being localised and sporadic, any switch to 'inters' a gamble. The top four tiptoed around on slicks until incredibly, on lap 52 with a 9s lead, Vettel crashed out at the slippery Sachskurve. Bottas and Räikkönen pitted whereas Hamilton stayed out, miraculously taking the lead on lap 53 and defending resolutely against Bottas until the pit-wall intervened.

| Pos | Driver | Car | Time/gap | Grid (pen) | Stops | Tyres |
|---|---|---|---|---|---|---|
| 1 | Lewis Hamilton | Mercedes | 1h 32m 29.845s | 14 | 1 | su |
| 2 | Valtteri Bottas | Mercedes | -4.535s | 2 | 2 | usu |
| 3 | Kimi Räikkönen | Ferrari | -6.732s | 3 | 2 | usu |
| 4 | Max Verstappen | Red Bull-TAG Heuer | -7.654s | 4 | 3 | usiu |
| 5 | Nico Hülkenberg | Renault | -26.609s | 7 | 3 | umiu |
| 6 | Romain Grosjean | Haas-Ferrari | -28.871s | 6 | 3 | umiu |

## LEWIS HAMILTON

**Mercedes F1 W09** 198.789kph, 123.521mph

**POLE POSITION** Vettel, Ferrari, 1m 11.212s (0.204s), 231.230kph, 143.679mph
**LAPS** 67 x 4.574 km, 2.842 miles
**DISTANCE** 306.458 km, 190.424 miles
**STARTERS/FINISHERS** 20/16
**WEATHER** Initially cloudy, warm, dry, showers later.
**LAP LEADERS** Vettel 1-25, 39-51 (38); Bottas 26-28, 52 (4); Räikkönen 29-38 (10); Hamilton 53-67 (15); SC 52-57 (6)
**WINNER'S LAPS** 1 P13, 2 P12, 3 P11, 4-5 P10, 6-7 P9, 8 P8, 9-10 P7, 11-13 P6, 14-28 P5, 29 P4, 30-41 P3, 42 P4, 43-46 P5, 47-51 P4, 52 P3, 53-67 P1
**FASTEST LAP** Hamilton, Mercedes, 1m 15.545s (lap 66), 217.968kph, 135.439mph
**CHAMPIONSHIP** Hamilton 188, Vettel 171, Räikkönen 131, Bottas 122, Ricciardo 106

RACE POD

8

COMEBACKS

# In a 16-lap green-flag period, Button charged from 21st and last to P4

**The longest race on record was excessively wet, suspended for over two hours and five SCs deployed. Yet Vettel led 68 of 70 laps. Nevertheless, victory went to Button (shown here) after six pit stops including a drive-through penalty!**

## Race 846 — 2011 CANADIAN GP Montréal

**Round 7/19** — **12 June 2011**

## JENSON BUTTON

**McLaren-Mercedes MP4-26** 74.864kph, 46.518mph

Vettel beat the Ferraris to pole, leading all the way until the final lap when he half-spun under pressure from Button. Anticipating rain, the McLarens qualified P5 and P7, and wet it was with a two-hour delay mid-race and numerous SC outings, the start included. Once released, Hamilton clashed first with Webber and then with teammate Button, race over for the rash Lewis. Button's damage check was the first of six pit visits, his second a SC speeding drive-through on lap 13, the fifth a lap 36 puncture after tangling with Fernando Alonso, who spun out. Now, in a 16-lap green-flag period, Button charged from 21st and last to P4, a final SC then closing up the field. Jenson, on option slicks as the racing line dried, passed Webber, Schumacher and finally Vettel for P1 when Seb slid wide on that final lap.

| Pos | Driver | Car | Time/gap | Grid (pen) | Stops | Tyres (-/ss) |
|---|---|---|---|---|---|---|
| 1 | Jenson Button | McLaren-Mercedes | 4h 4m 39.537s | 7 | 5 | wiwwiio |
| 2 | Sebastian Vettel | Red Bull-Renault | -2.709s | 1 | 3 | wwwio |
| 3 | Mark Webber | Red Bull-Renault | -13.828s | 4 | 3 | wwwio |
| 4 | Michael Schumacher | Mercedes | -14.219s | 8 | 4 | wiwwio |
| 5 | Vitaly Petrov | Renault | -20.395s | 10 | 2 | wwio |
| 6 | Felipe Massa | Ferrari | -33.225s | 3 | 4 | wwwioo |

**POLE POSITION** Vettel, Red Bull-Renault, 1m 13.014s (0.185s), 215.021kph, 133.608mph
**LAPS** 70 x 4.361 km, 2.710 miles (Race stopped by rain on lap 24 and suspended for 2h 4m 3s)
**DISTANCE** 305.270 km, 189.686 miles
**STARTERS/FINISHERS** 24/18
**WEATHER** Overcast, cool, wet then drying
**LAP LEADERS** Vettel 1-19, 21-69 (68); Massa 20 (1); Button 70 (1); SC 1-4, 8-12, 20-34, 37-40, 57-60 (32)
**WINNER'S LAPS** 1-5 P4, 6-7 P6, 8 P14, 9-12 P12, 13 P15, 14 P14, 15-16 P11, 17 P10, 18 P8, 19-20 P11, 21-24 P10, 25 P11, 26-33 P10, 34 P9, 35 P15, 36 P11, 37-40 P21, 41 P20, 42 P18, 43 P15, 44 P14, 45-48 P12, 49 P10, 50 P8, 51 P10, 52 P9, 53 P7, 54 P5, 55-63 P4, 64 P3, 65-69 P2, 70 P1
**FASTEST LAP** Button, McLaren-Mercedes, 1m 16.956s (lap 69), 204.007kph, 126.764mph
**CHAMPIONSHIP** Vettel 161, Button 101, Webber 94, Hamilton 85, Alonso 69

RACE POD

## 7 COMEBACKS

# Having completed lap one in 22nd place, Hill took the lead on lap 55

Graham Hill's BRM closes on Jack Brabham's Cooper-Climax before taking the lead on lap 55. But his mighty recovery drive was all in vain as with six laps remaining, hounded by Brabham, Hill spun off at Copse

## Race 91 — 1960 BRITISH GP Silverstone

**Round 7/10** — **16 July 1960**

A race all about Graham Hill. As Stirling Moss, recuperating from his Spa injuries, dropped the flag, Hill stalled his BRM. From P2 alongside pole-man Brabham on the four-across front row, he completed lap one in 22nd place, two from last. After ten laps he had recovered to eighth, but further progress meant passing his faster rivals starting with von Trips on lap 11. From there he dispensed with Jo Bonnier (lap 20), McLaren (lap 25), Jim Clark (lap 30), Surtees (lap 32), and Ireland (lap 37). Leader Brabham posed a tougher challenge, but on lap 55 he made the pass, holding P1 for the next 17 but unable to shake off the wily Australian. But there was to be no fairy tale ending. With just six laps remaining, hounded by Brabham, Hill spun-off at Copse while lapping the Ferraris, Brabham going on to receive the chequered flag.

| Pos | Driver | Car | Time/gap | Grid | Stops | Tyres |
|---|---|---|---|---|---|---|
| 1 | Jack Brabham | Cooper-Climax | 2h 4m 24.6s | 1 | 0 | D |
| 2 | John Surtees | Lotus-Climax | –49.6s | 11 | 0 | D |
| 3 | Innes Ireland | Lotus-Climax | –1m 29.6s | 5 | 0 | D |
| 4 | Bruce McLaren | Cooper-Climax | –1 lap | 3 | 0 | D |
| 5 | Tony Brooks | Cooper-Climax | –1 lap | 9 | 0 | D |
| 6 | Wolfgang von Trips | Ferrari | –2 laps | 7 | 0 | D |

## JACK BRABHAM

**Cooper-Climax T53** 174.928kph, 108.695mph

**POLE POSITION** Brabham, Cooper-Climax, 1m 34.6s (1.0s), 179.260kph, 111.387mph
**LAPS** 77 x 4.711 km, 2.927 miles
**DISTANCE** 362.712 km, 225.379 miles
**STARTERS/FINISHERS** 24/16
**WEATHER** Overcast, warm, dry
**LAP LEADERS** Brabham 1-54, 72-77 (60); G Hill 55-71 (17)
**WINNER'S LAPS** 1-54 P1, 55-71 P2, 72-77 P1
**FASTEST LAP** G Hill, BRM, 1m 34.4s (lap 56), 179.640kph, 111.623mph
**CHAMPIONSHIP** Brabham 32, McLaren 27, Moss 11, Ireland 11, Gendebien 10

*RACE POD*

6 COMEBACKS

# Another 20 sizzling laps brought Moss into contention for victory

Flanked by Tony Brooks and Stirling Moss (right), Tony Vandervell raises the victor's trophy at Aintree in 1957 to celebrate the first World Championship Grand Prix win by a British car

## Race 61 — 1957 BRITISH GP Aintree

**Round 5/8** — **20 July 1957**

## TONY BROOKS/STIRLING MOSS

**Vanwall VW (57)** 139.696kph, 86.803mph

Fittingly at the British GP, Vanwall became the first British car to win a championship race, and with British drivers too. Moss led easily until engine trouble intervened, the Vanwall team then deciding to bring in Brooks' car, the driver still suffering from his Le Mans injuries, Moss rejoining ninth on lap 28 in Tony's car. Battling through the field and gaining on race leader Jean Behra, Moss was still some 50s in arrears at half-distance. Another 20 sizzling laps brought him into contention, then on lap 70 the clutch on the leading Maserati exploded, the debris punctured the tyre of Hawthorn's following Lancia Ferrari, and suddenly Vanwalls were leading 1-2. Stuart Lewis-Evans' Vanwall stopped soon afterwards but Stirling sailed on to an historic victory, time even for a precautionary fuel stop.

| Pos | Driver | Car | Time/gap | Grid | Stops | Tyres |
|---|---|---|---|---|---|---|
| 1 | Tony Brooks/Stirling Moss | Vanwall | 3h 6m 37.8s | 3 | 2 | P |
| 2 | Luigi Musso | Lancia Ferrari | –25.6s | 10 | 0 | E |
| 3 | Mike Hawthorn | Lancia Ferrari | –42.8s | 5 | 1 | E |
| 4 | Maurice Trintignant/Peter Collins | Lancia Ferrari | –2 laps | 9 | 2 | E |
| 5 | Roy Salvadori | Cooper-Climax | –5 laps | 15 | NA | E |
| 6 | Bob Gerard | Cooper-Bristol | –8 laps | 18 | NA | E |

**POLE POSITION** Moss, Vanwall, 2m 0.2s (0.0s), 144.600kph, 89.850mph
**LAPS** 90 x 4.828 km, 3.000 miles
**DISTANCE** 434.523 km, 270.000 miles
**STARTERS/FINISHERS** 18/8
**WEATHER** Overcast, warm, dry
**LAP LEADERS** Moss 1-21, 70-90 (42); J Behra, Maserati 22-69 (48)
**WINNER'S LAPS** 1-21 P1, 22 P7, 28 P9, 30-34 P7, 35-39 P6, 40-46 P5, 47-69 P4, 70-90 P1
**FASTEST LAP** Moss, Vanwall, 1m 59.2s (lap 66), 145.813kph, 90.604mph
**CHAMPIONSHIP** Fangio 25, Musso 13, Brooks 10, Hanks 8, Rathmann 7

*RACE POD*

## 5 COMEBACKS

# Over half a minute was lost as Hill pushed his BRM back onto the circuit

It was now Hill's flying BRM (3) versus the Ferrari pair, the Londoner catching and passing Surtees (18) on lap 53 and Bandini (17) on lap 65

## Race 133 — 1965 MONACO GP Monte Carlo

**Round 2/10** — **30 May 1965**

### GRAHAM HILL

**BRM P261** 119.688kph, 74.371mph

Graham Hill scored a remarkable Monte Carlo hat-trick for BRM. The absence of Jim Clark and Dan Gurney at Indianapolis eased his task, but from pole position he was in irrepressible form. At the start he led comfortably but on exiting the tunnel on lap 25 he encountered a stricken car approaching the chicane and was forced to take to the escape road. Over half a minute was lost as Hill pushed his BRM back onto the circuit, Stewart, Bandini, Surtees and Jack Brabham all going by. On lap 30 Stewart spun away his lead, then Brabham overtook new leader Bandini until his engine blew. It was now Hill's flying BRM versus the Ferrari pair, the Londoner catching and passing Surtees on lap 53 and Bandini on lap 65. Surtees ran out of fuel, elevating Bandini and Stewart to the podium, albeit over a minute behind the triumphant Hill.

| Pos | Driver | Car | Time/gap | Grid | Stops | Tyres |
|---|---|---|---|---|---|---|
| 1 | Graham Hill | BRM | 2h 37m 39.6s | 1 | 0 | D |
| 2 | Lorenzo Bandini | Ferrari | –1m 4.0s | 4 | 0 | D |
| 3 | Jackie Stewart | BRM | –1m 41.9s | 3 | 0 | D |
| 4r | John Surtees | Ferrari | –1 lap | 5 | 0 | D |
| 5 | Bruce McLaren | Cooper-Climax | –2 laps | 7 | 0 | D |
| 6 | Jo Siffert | Brabham-BRM | –2 laps | 10 | 0 | D |

**POLE POSITION** G Hill, BRM, 1m 32.5s (0.1s), 122.400kph, 76.056mph
**LAPS** 100 x 3.145km, 1.954 miles
**DISTANCE** 314.500 km, 195.421 miles
**STARTERS/FINISHERS** 16/10
**WEATHER** Overcast, dry
**LAP LEADERS** G Hill 1-24, 65-100 (60); Stewart 25-29 (5); Bandini 30-33, 43-64 (26); J Brabham, Brabham-Climax 34-42 (9)
**WINNER'S LAPS** 1-24 P1, 25-33 P5, 34-42 P4, 43-52 P3, 53-64 P2, 65-100 P1
**FASTEST LAP** G Hill, BRM 1m 31.7s (lap 82), 123.468kph, 76.719mph
**CHAMPIONSHIP** G Hill 13, Clark 9, Surtees 9, Bandini 6, Stewart 5

*RACE POD*

4

COMEBACKS

# Mansell's comeback began with 30 laps to go, exiting the pits 28s in arrears

Mansell, in 'Red 5', lining up Piquet to execute one of the great passing moves of all time, selling the perfect dummy then slicing past the sister car at Stowe

## Race 443 1987 BRITISH GP Silverstone

**Round 7/16** **12 July 1987**

## NIGEL MANSELL

**Williams-Honda FW11B** 235.298kph, 146.208mph

From a Williams-Honda front row lock out, Nelson led from pole chased closely by Mansell until Nigel unexpectedly dived for the pits on lap 35. A tyre stop had been forced on him by extreme vibrations due to the loss of a front wheel balance weight. Mansell exited the pits 28s in arrears with 30 laps to go; even with fresh rubber surely it was an impossible task? But driving at ten-tenths and urged on by the frenzied, partisan crowd, Mansell lowered the lap record nine times, his recovery drive taking great chunks out of Nelson's lead. With 2½ laps remaining, Mansell sold Piquet the perfect dummy then sliced past the sister car on the inside at Stowe. Later, on his victory lap, showman Mansell stopped at Stowe to kiss the Tarmac where he had executed one of the great passing moves of all time.

| Pos | Driver | Car | Time/gap | Grid | Stops | Tyres |
|---|---|---|---|---|---|---|
| 1 | Nigel Mansell | Williams-Honda | 1h 19m 11.780s | 2 | 1 | G |
| 2 | Nelson Piquet | Williams-Honda | –1.918s | 1 | 0 | G |
| 3 | Ayrton Senna | Lotus-Honda | –1 lap | 3 | 0 | G |
| 4 | Satoru Nakajima | Lotus-Honda | –2 laps | 12 | 0 | G |
| 5 | Derek Warwick | Arrows-Megatron | –2 laps | 13 | 0 | G |
| 6 | Teo Fabi | Benetton-Ford | –2 laps | 6 | 0 | G |

**POLE POSITION** Piquet, Williams-Honda, 1m 07.110s (0.070s), 256.315kph, 159.267mph
**LAPS** 65 x 4.778 km, 2.969 miles
**DISTANCE** 310.579 km, 192.985 miles
**STARTERS/FINISHERS** 25/9
**WEATHER** Cloudy with sunny intervals, warm, dry
**LAP LEADERS** Piquet 1-62 (62); Mansell 63-65 (3)
**WINNER'S LAPS** 1-62 P2, 63-65 P1
**FASTEST LAP** Mansell, Williams-Honda, 1m 09.832s (lap 58), 246.324kph, 153.059mph
**CHAMPIONSHIP** Senna 31, Mansell 30, Piquet 30, Prost 26, Johansson 13

RACE POD

3

COMEBACKS

# Mansell, from 12th, was now somehow hounding Senna's leading McLaren

More than 20 years later, when asked about his best races and finest overtaking moves by *Autosport*, Mansell said: "This was one of my greatest drives for many reasons. My engineer, Maurizio Nardon, and I just couldn't get rid of terrible understeer, so we decided the best thing was just to work on the race set-up. We needed more downforce on the front wing. We had these sheet metal extensions with Gurney flaps made overnight. [Designer] John Barnard went mad and ordered us to take off 'those Mickey Mouse ears'. But when I went a second a lap faster in the morning warm-up, I said they were staying on!

"I knew Ayrton was going to make it very difficult to get by and I had to await my chance. I saw Stefan Johansson ahead but we didn't know he was struggling to select gears. It was very rare that Ayrton put himself in a position that he just got a little bit too close and, before he knew it, there was nowhere for him to go. Stefan saw us coming and moved left but Senna misjudged the speed of the Onyx, backed off slightly and got boxed in as I darted right and passed them both. You can't plan things like that. You've got to be ready and I was there to take full advantage of it.

"Of all the races I've won and the moves I've pulled, that's one of the most satisfying. Twelfth to first at the Hungaroring is not something we see every day."

## Race 478 — 1989 HUNGARIAN GP Hungaroring — NIGEL MANSELL

**Round 10/16** **13 August 1989** **Ferrari 640** 167.197kph, 103.891mph

From the first non-McLaren pole in over 12 months, Riccardo Patrese's Williams-Renault kept Senna, Gerhard Berger and Prost at bay for 52 laps until a holed radiator ended it. Senna now led from Mansell, having carved his way up from a P12 grid slot. In qualifying Nigel's Ferrari had been hopeless so he had spent the final practice session honing race-day set-up. Now the strategy was paying dividends, the Ferrari handling beautifully if not the measure of the McLaren on the straights. On his way to the front Mansell had made up four places on lap one, but had then then held up by Alex Caffi, relinquishing 20s to the leaders. Once past he closed the gap to the leaders in 15 laps and was now hounding Senna. The endgame was sheer poetry: a backmarker; Senna hesitated; Mansell swooped; game over on lap 58.

| Pos | Driver | Car | Time/gap | Grid | Stops | Tyres |
|---|---|---|---|---|---|---|
| 1 | Nigel Mansell | Ferrari | 1h 49m 38.650s | 12 | 0 | G |
| 2 | Ayrton Senna | McLaren-Honda | –25.967s | 2 | 0 | G |
| 3 | Thierry Boutsen | Williams-Renault | –38.354s | 4 | 1 | G |
| 4 | Alain Prost | McLaren-Honda | –44.177s | 5 | 1 | G |
| 5 | Eddie Cheever | Arrows-Ford | –45.106s | 16 | 0 | G |
| 6 | Nelson Piquet | Lotus-Judd | –1m 12.039s | 17 | 1 | G |

**POLE POSITION** R Patrese, Williams-Renault, 1m 19.726s (0.313s), 179.174kph, 111.333mph
**LAPS** 77 x 3.968 km, 2.466 miles
**DISTANCE** 305.536 km, 189.851 miles
**STARTERS/FINISHERS** 26/13
**WEATHER** Sunny, hot, dry
**LAP LEADERS** Patrese 1-52 (52); Senna 53-57 (5); Mansell 58-77 (20)
**WINNER'S LAPS** 1-11 P8, 12-19 P7, 20-21 P6, 22-29 P5, 30-40 P4, 41-52 P3, 53-57 P2, 58-77 P1
**FASTEST LAP** Mansell, Ferrari, 1m 22.637s (lap 66), 172.862kph, 107.411mph
**CHAMPIONSHIP** Prost 56, Senna 42, Mansell 34, Patrese 25, Boutsen 17

RACE POD

Mansell's Ferrari, not the measure of Senna's McLaren on the straights, was handling beautifully. The endgame was sheer poetry: a backmarker, Senna hesitated, Mansell swooped, game over

# 2 COMEBACKS

## The McLarens started 22nd and 23rd. Two hours later Watson led in a 1-2

Watson told *Autosport* years later: "Principally what I wanted was a race car that was useable. Maybe Niki was better at achieving a single fast-lap car. I felt I had a better car with the need to overtake, because we weren't starting at the front.

"I could hustle my car under brakes. If I had to go offline to do things, I could do it. I had worked with my engineers to achieve a lot of stability at the rear of the car. I didn't depend on the front wheels to give me entry into a corner. I would come into a corner, do my braking, give it a fairly quick initial turn to get the car to rotate, so that by the time I got to the apex my steering input was very little.

"When it came to catching and overtaking Niki, we'd been running nose to tail throughout the race, and I knew that if we let a car get between the two of us it was going to be hard to get back on his tail. Every time he passed, I was doppelganger and followed him through.

"Eventually I made a bit of a late move into the chicane and the car just flinched a bit, but it got the job done and on I went. I did a similar thing to [Jacques] Laffite for the lead midway round the circuit, with a momentary little lock-up on the left-rear, but got through and I was on my way."

**Race 375** **1983 UNITED STATES GP WEST** Long Beach **JOHN WATSON**

**Round 2/15** **27 March 1983** **McLaren-Ford MP4/1C** 129.753kph, 80.625mph

Two Ferraris then two Williamses filled the sharp end of the grid. Near the back, the McLarens started P22 and P23. Around two hours later Watson led in a McLaren 1-2. To prove this extraordinary result was about drivers and Michelins rather than reliability and attrition, a Ferrari finished third, a Williams fourth. True, around lap 25 the McLarens were assisted by the elimination of three of a front-running quartet. In a failed overtaking attempt, Keke Rosberg punted out leader Patrick Tambay while at the very next corner Jean-Pierre Jarier paid Rosberg a similar compliment, both out. The survivor, Laffite's Williams, led until the remarkable Watson overtook him on lap 45 of 75. Watson made numerous passes that day, most crucially teammate Lauda on lap 33.

| Pos | Driver | Car | Time/gap | Grid | Stops | Tyres |
|---|---|---|---|---|---|---|
| 1 | John Watson | McLaren-Ford | 1h 53m 34.889s | 22 | 0 | M |
| 2 | Niki Lauda | McLaren-Ford | –27.993s | 23 | 0 | M |
| 3 | René Arnoux | Ferrari | –1m 13.638s | 2 | 2 | G |
| 4 | Jacques Laffite | Williams-Ford | –1 lap | 4 | 0 | G |
| 5 | Marc Surer | Arrows-Ford | –1 lap | 16 | 0 | G |
| 6 | Johnny Cecotto | Theodore-Ford | –1 lap | 17 | 0 | G |

**POLE POSITION** P Tambay, Ferrari, 1m 26.117s (0.818s), 136.907kph, 85.070mph
**LAPS** 75 x 3.275 km, 2.035 miles
**DISTANCE** 245.626 km, 152.625 miles
**STARTERS/FINISHERS** 26/12
**WEATHER** Sunny, hot, dry
**LAP LEADERS** Tambay 1-25 (25); Laffite 26-44 (19); Watson 45-75 (31)
**WINNER'S LAPS** 1-3 P20, 4-5 P21, 6 P20, 7-10 P19, 11 P18, 12, P17, 13-14 P16, 15 P15, 16-23 P13, 24 P12, 25 P10, 26 P7, 27 P5, 28-32 P4, 33-43 P3, 44 P2, 45-75 P1
**FASTEST LAP** Lauda, McLaren-Ford, 1m 28.330s (lap 42), 133.477kph, 82.939mph
**CHAMPIONSHIP** Lauda 10, Piquet 9, Watson 9, Laffite 6, Arnoux 4

**RACE POD**

Starting P22, Watson made multiple passes that day, most crucially teammate Lauda on lap 33

On the penultimate lap Fangio took Collins (7) at the North Curve and Hawthorn (8) at Breidscheid to win his final and greatest victory and to seal his fifth drivers' crown

COMEBACKS

# 1 Fangio's final victory was the greatest drive of his illustrious career

In *'Fangio, A Pirelli Album'* by Stirling Moss with Doug Nye, the maestro said: "I then began to use higher gears through the corners. This gave less precise control of the car's attitude when it was sliding, but as long as I entered the corners absolutely right, I knew I could reach higher revs along the following straight. There was a lack of grip in the higher gears but it was worth the risk for the time I could make up.

"The swerves through the dip beneath the bridge at the end of the main straight offered a great time saving. I normally took it in fifth gear, just lifting off the throttle a little, trying to skim the crest rather than to jump over it so as not to upset the car on landing. In that race I did not lift my foot at all.

"I kept as far to the inside as I could and just let the car take off. It soared along and landed way across on the right of the track right up against the fence, and I could see the dust cloud I raised there when I glanced in my mirror. But I knew right then that I'd saved seconds, treating those two separate sections of straight absolutely as one. It was not something I would consider doing every lap of every race there, but that year was special.

"I believe I was inspired that day. I never drove quite like that before, and I never drove quite like that ever again."

**Race 62** **1957 GERMAN GP** Nürburgring **JUAN MANUEL FANGIO**

**Round 6/8** **4 August 1957** **Maserati 250F** 142.943kph, 88.820mph

With the Vanwalls unsuited to the Nordschleife, Italian machinery occupied the four-across front row. Fuelled light, Fangio planned to build a lead over the non-stopping Lancia Ferraris, but spent the first two laps behind them. Once by he pulled away, but slow pit work on lap 12 turned his 30s lead into a 48s deficit to new leaders Collins and Hawthorn. As he reeled in the Lancia Ferrari pair, engaged in their own victory duel, Fangio exhibited what is regarded as the greatest drive of his illustrious career. On lap 19 he stole 11s from them, leaving the lap record in shreds. On lap 21, the penultimate, he took Collins at the North Curve and Hawthorn at Breidscheid to win by 3.6s and seal his fifth drivers' crown. Fangio's final victory was truly his greatest.

| Pos | Driver | Car | Time/gap | Grid | Stops | Tyres |
|---|---|---|---|---|---|---|
| 1 | Juan Manuel Fangio | Maserati | 3h 30m 38.3s | 1 | 1 | P |
| 2 | Mike Hawthorn | Lancia Ferrari | –3.6s | 2 | 0 | E |
| 3 | Peter Collins | Lancia Ferrari | –35.6s | 4 | 0 | E |
| 4 | Luigi Musso | Lancia Ferrari | –3m 37.6s | 8 | 0 | E |
| 5 | Stirling Moss | Vanwall | –4m 37.5s | 7 | 0 | P |
| 6 | Jean Behra | Maserati | –4m 38.5s | 3 | 1 | P |

**POLE POSITION** Fangio, Maserati, 9m 25.6s (2.8s), 145.184kph, 90.213mph
**LAPS** 22 x 22.810 km, 14.173 miles
**DISTANCE** 501.820 km, 311.816 miles
**STARTERS/FINISHERS** 24/15 (Including F2 cars)
**WEATHER** Sunny, hot, dry
**LAP LEADERS** Hawthorn 1-2, 15-20 (8); Fangio 3-11, 21-22 (11); Collins 12-14 (3)
**WINNER'S LAPS** 1-2 P3, 3-11 P1, 12-20 P3, 21-22 P1
**FASTEST LAP** Fangio, Maserati, 9m 17.4s (lap 20), 147.320kph, 91.540mph
**CHAMPIONSHIP** Fangio 34, Musso 16, Hawthorn 13, Brooks 10, Moss 8

RACE POD

CHAPTER 4

# WHAT THE...

## BIZARRE HAPPENINGS

Some races leave onlookers struggling to process what just unfolded. These unpredictable spectacles often feature sudden reversals of fortune, chaotic crashes, or multiple lead changes, all wrapped up in an edgy undercurrent of mayhem. This is the raw, unscripted drama of Formula 1, where happenstance, luck, and driver brilliance converge in unexpected ways.

Several factors can cause a Grand Prix to spiral into a wild, unpredictable affair. The most common culprit is rain, or at least a sudden, violent downpour that catches drivers on the wrong tyres in the rapidly changing track conditions, creating a skating rink of car carnage. Then there's driver error, an overambitious move or misjudgement that triggers a multi-car pileup leaving half the field wiped out in the chain reaction. There have also even been weird events where car reliability seems to collapse across the board and the winner is 'the last man standing' in a seriously depleted field.

Some bizarre happenings haven't made it into this top ten collection, such as track invasions by rogue fans or by unexpected wildlife, the latter still dangerous if adding a level of levity. Controversial stewarding calls, or even disqualifications, can play a decisive role too, turning races upside down and sometimes leaving the final result in limbo long after the chequered flag.

Many of these whacky races, as some might call them, have become legendary, standing the test of time and living on through magazines and fan discussion for decades. They provide some of the most unexpected and unforgettable moments in the sport where conventional wisdom is thrown out the window to leave fans and pundits alike shaking their heads in disbelief. These races aren't just entertaining; they form a crucial part of folklore, reminding us that in Formula 1, as Murray Walker once put it, "Anything can happen, and it usually does!"

**THESE RACES AREN'T JUST ENTERTAINING; THEY FORM A CRUCIAL PART OF FOLKLORE, REMINDING US THAT IN FORMULA 1, AS MURRAY WALKER ONCE PUT IT, "ANYTHING CAN HAPPEN... AND IT USUALLY DOES!"**

## 10 WHAT THE...

# 'Bulls'-dozer Bottas wreaks freak result as Ocon wins with Alonso's help

With a little help from his friend, Esteban Ocon crosses the line for his maiden victory

## Race 1046 2021 HUNGARIAN GP Hungaroring

**Round 11/22** **1 August 2021**

Misjudging his braking into turn 1, Valtteri Bottas triggered a pile-up that included the Red Bulls and eliminated four of the top seven cars. Red flag! On the formation lap for the grid restart, Hamilton led Ocon, Sebastian Vettel, and the rest with sun drying the track rapidly. Fearing he'd be baulked when the field pitted for slicks, Hamilton, on inters, took the restart alone but still fell to last place, P14, when he switched next lap. Pitstops aside, Ocon's Alpine then led from lap five until the flag. He was relentlessly chased by Vettel's quicker Aston Martin, later disqualified, but Esteban handled the pressure well. Now P5, Lewis made a final tyre stop, needing to catch Ocon by 1s per lap over 23 laps for the win. He quickly caught Alonso but the wily Fernando held him up for 11 laps, assuring victory for teammate Ocon by 2.7s.

| Pos | Driver | Car | Time/gap | Grid | Stops† | Tyres |
|---|---|---|---|---|---|---|
| 1 | Esteban Ocon | Alpine-Renault | 2h 4m 43.199s | 8 | 3 | iimh |
| 2 | Lewis Hamilton | Mercedes | –2.736s | 1 | 4 | iimhm |
| 3 | Carlos Sainz | Ferrari | –15.018s | 15 | 3 | iimh |
| 4 | Fernando Alonso | Alpine-Renault | –15.651s | 9 | 3 | iimh |
| 5 | Pierre Gasly | AlphaTauri-Honda | –1m 3.614s | 5 | 4 | iimhs |
| 6 | Yuki Tsunoda | AlphaTauri-Honda | –1m 15.803s | 16 | 3 | iimh |

† Including red flag stop

## ESTEBAN OCON

**Alpine-Renault A521** 147.512kph, 91.659mph

**POLE POSITION** Hamilton, Mercedes, 1m 15.419s (0.315s), 209.119kph, 129.940mph
**LAPS** 70 x 4.381 km, 2.722 miles (Race red flagged on lap 1 for accident; suspended for approximately 30 minutes)
**DISTANCE** 306.630 km, 190.531 miles
**STARTERS/FINISHERS** 20/13 (S Vettel, Aston Martin-Mercedes, 2h 4m 45.058s, DSQ from P2)
**WEATHER** Rain before start, sunny at restart, temperature rising, rainclouds building later
**LAP LEADERS** Hamilton 1-2, 4 (3); Ocon 3, 5-70 (65); Alonso 38-39 (2); SC 1-3 (3)
**WINNER'S LAPS** 1-2 P2, 3 P1, 4 P2, 5-70 P1
**FASTEST LAP** Gasly, AlphaTauri-Honda, 1m 18.394s (lap 70), 201.183kph, 125.009mph
**CHAMPIONSHIP** Hamilton 195, Verstappen 187, Norris 113, Bottas 108, Pérez 104

***RACE POD***

9 WHAT THE...

# Collision between Red Bull teammates gifts 1-2 victory to McLaren pair

Vettel lunged, leader Webber held his line, the two Red Bulls collided. In the subsequent blame game, Webber was left feeling isolated by his own team

## Race 827 — 2010 TURKISH GP Istanbul

**Round 7/19** — **30 May 2010**

The context of this bizarre collision between teammates was that after Webber's back-to-back wins, he and Sebastian Vettel came to Istanbul leading the championship tied on points. Then, for the third race in a row, Webber took pole. The order remained unchanged until lap 16 when Vettel undercut Hamilton for P2 at the stops. To guarantee fuel to finish, Webber was instructed to turn down his engine whereas Vettel, now following, curiously was not, and on lap 40 attacked, edging right, towards his teammate, as he came alongside. Webber held his line, they collided and spun, Vettel out but Webber, after a nosecone replacement, regaining P3 behind the astonished McLaren pair. Later, inferring unfair treatment, Webber wrote, "Having a washed-up old Australian dog take the title was not part of Red Bull Racing's plans."

| Pos | Driver | Car | Time/gap | Grid (pen) | Stops | Tyres (h/s) |
|---|---|---|---|---|---|---|
| 1 | Lewis Hamilton | McLaren-Mercedes | 1h 28m 47.620s | 2 | 1 | op |
| 2 | Jenson Button | McLaren-Mercedes | -2.645s | 4 | 1 | op |
| 3 | Mark Webber | Red Bull-Renault | -24.285s | 1 | 2 | opp |
| 4 | Michael Schumacher | Mercedes | -31.110s | 5 | 1 | op |
| 5 | Nico Rosberg | Mercedes | -32.226s | 6 | 1 | op |
| 6 | Robert Kubica | Renault | -32.824s | 7 | 1 | op |

## LEWIS HAMILTON

**McLaren-Mercedes MP4-25** 209.066kph, 129.908mph

**POLE POSITION** Webber, Red Bull-Renault, 1m 26.295s (0.138s), 222.687kph, 138.371mph
**LAPS** 58 x 5.338 km, 3.317 miles
**DISTANCE** 309.396 km, 192.250 miles
**STARTERS/FINISHERS** 24/20
**WEATHER** Cloudy with sunny intervals, hot, dry, spitting rain
**LAP LEADERS** Webber 1-15, 18-39 (37); Button 16-17, 48 (3); Hamilton 40-47, 49-58 (18)
**WINNER'S LAPS** 1-15 P2, 16-17 P4, 18-39 P3, 40-47 P1, 48 P2, 49-58 P1
**FASTEST LAP** V Petrov, Renault, 1m 29.165s (lap 57), 215.519kph, 133.918mph
**CHAMPIONSHIP** Webber 93, Button 88, Hamilton 84, Alonso 79, Vettel 78

RACE POD

## 8 WHAT THE...

# A scrambled grid produced four separate race leaders and six lead changes

The expressions on the podium exemplify their race fortunes: Coulthard (centre), winner from a P11 start; Montoya (left) P2 after spinning 11 laps from the end when leading; Raikkonen P3 from P15

**Race 698** Round 1/16

**2003 AUSTRALIAN GP** Melbourne
9 March 2003

**DAVID COULTHARD**
**McLaren-Mercedes MP4-17D** 194.868kph, 121.086mph

The first 20 laps were breathtaking. Single-shot qualifying had scrambled the grid, together with a wet track and differing tyre choices and fuel loads. Additionally, two SC periods assisted some, hindered others. Once things settled down, Räikkönen, Montoya and Schumacher all led but each lost time to costly error: Kimi pitlane speeding, Michael kerb damage, but most notably, Juan Pablo spun away the lead on worn tyres with just 11 laps to go. So Coulthard, starting P11 and plain last on lap two, won by 8.7s from Montoya-Räikkönen-Schumacher, these three covered by less than a second. It was not Coulthard's finest win, but unlike his rivals for victory, his drive was mistake-free. It was his 13th and last Grand Prix triumph and his seventh victorious season in succession.

| Pos | Driver | Car | Time/gap | Grid | Stops | Tyres |
|---|---|---|---|---|---|---|
| 1 | David Coulthard | McLaren-Mercedes | 1h 34m 42.124s | 11 | 2 | M |
| 2 | Juan Pablo Montoya | Williams-BMW | -8.675s | 3 | 2 | M |
| 3 | Kimi Räikkönen | McLaren-Mercedes | -9.192s | 15 | 2 | M |
| 4 | Michael Schumacher | Ferrari | -9.482s | 1 | 2 | B |
| 5 | Jarno Trulli | Renault | -38.801s | 12 | 2 | M |
| 6 | Heinz-Harald Frentzen | Sauber-Petronas | -43.928s | 4 | 2 | B |

**POLE POSITION** M Schumacher, Ferrari, 1m 27.173s (0.245s), 218.999kph, 136.080mph
**LAPS** 58 x 5.303 km, 3.295 miles
**DISTANCE** 307.574 km, 191.117 miles
**STARTERS/FINISHERS** 20/13
**WEATHER** Overcast, warm, wet then drying
**LAP LEADERS** M Schumacher 1-6, 42-45 (10); Montoya 7-16, 33-41, 46-47 (21); Räikkönen 17-32 (16); Coulthard 48-58 (11); SC 9-11, 18-20 (6)
**WINNER'S LAPS** 1 P10, 2-3 P20, 4 P18, 5 P17, 6 P15, 7 P12, 8-9 P8, 10-15 P7, 16 P6, 17-28 P3, 29-31 P2, 32-35 P5, 36-38 P4, 39-45 P3, 46-47 P2, 48-58 P1
**FASTEST LAP** Räikkönen, McLaren-Mercedes, 1m 27.724s (lap 32), 217.623kph, 135.225mph
**CHAMPIONSHIP** Coulthard 10, Montoya 8, Räikkönen 6, M Schumacher 5, Trulli 4

RACE POD

7 WHAT THE...

# On their final wheel-banging lap, Depailler lost out to Peterson

Again, not difficult to pick out winner and loser in this photo of Ronnie Peterson (right) and Patrick Depailler. Also notice, in this bizarre race, that none of the top six finishers came from the top four rows in qualifying!

## Race 300 — 1978 SOUTH AFRICAN GP Kyalami — RONNIE PETERSON

**Round 3/16** — **4 March 1978** — **Lotus-Ford 78** 187.817kph, 116.704mph

A thrilling race with five leaders and two memorable happenings. The first was that in only its second appearance, the controversial new Arrows of Riccardo Patrese looked odds-on to win on merit until its Ford Cosworth engine expired with just 15 of 78 laps to go. Then Depailler led in the new Tyrrell 008 – and now the second happening – only to run short of fuel and lose out to Peterson by 0.466s on their final wheel-banging lap. Initial race leaders were Mario Andretti and Jody Scheckter until they both had to back off to conserve tyres, and then for 37 extraordinary laps the race was Patrese's to lose. His wretched luck left Depailler leading Andretti, Watson and Peterson. Watson spun on oil, Andretti pitted for fuel, leaving Patrick and Ronnie to engage in an unforgettable final lap race for the flag.

| Pos | Driver | Car | Time/gap | Grid | Stops | Tyres |
|---|---|---|---|---|---|---|
| 1 | Ronnie Peterson | Lotus-Ford | 1h 42m 15.767s | 11 | 0 | G |
| 2 | Patrick Depailler | Tyrrell-Ford | –0.466s | 12 | 0 | G |
| 3 | John Watson | Brabham-Alfa | –4.442s | 10 | 0 | G |
| 4 | Alan Jones | Williams-Ford | –38.986s | 18 | 0 | G |
| 5 | Jacques Laffite | Ligier-Matra | –1m 9.218s | 14 | 0 | G |
| 6 | Didier Pironi | Tyrrell-Ford | –1 lap | 13 | 0 | G |

**POLE POSITION** N Lauda, Brabham-Alfa, 1m 14.65s (0.25s), 197.916kph, 122.979mph
**LAPS** 78 x 4.104 km, 2.550 miles
**DISTANCE** 320.112 km, 198.908 miles
**STARTERS/FINISHERS** 26/12
**WEATHER** Sunny, hot, dry
**LAP LEADERS** Andretti 1-20 (20); J Scheckter, Wolf-Ford 21-26 (6); R Patrese, Arrows-Ford 27-63 (37); Depailler 64-77 (14); Peterson 78 (1)
**WINNER'S LAPS** 1 P10, 2 P9, 3-4 P10, 5 P9, 6-14 P10, 15-22 P11, 23-29 P10, 30-33 P9, 34 P8, 35-51 P7, 52 P6, 53-54 P5, 55-63 P4, 64-74 P3, 75-77 P2, 78 P1
**FASTEST LAP** M Andretti, Lotus-Ford, 1m 17.09s (lap 2), 191.651kph, 119.087mph
**CHAMPIONSHIP** Andretti 12, Peterson 11, Lauda 10, Depailler 10, Reutemann 9

RACE POD

## 6 WHAT THE...

# The result of the race was announced nine weeks after it took place!

At turn 1, Paddock Hill Bend, fast starting Regazzoni from row two spun when he collided with Ferrari teammate and pole-sitter Lauda. Here, Regazzoni's Ferrari has collected Hunt's McLaren (11) with Andretti's Lotus (5) taking avoiding action

## Race 273 — 1976 BRITISH GP Brands Hatch

**Round 9/16** — **18 July 1976**

## NIKI LAUDA

**Ferrari 312T2** 183.874kph, 114.254mph

A Hunt-Lauda front row, but the two Ferraris led into Paddock and touched. Bedlam, red flag. When it was announced that Hunt would not be allowed to restart because his damaged car had not completed the red-flag lap, spectator people-power – jeering, clapping, stamping – reversed the stewards' decision. For 44 laps of the rerun race Lauda led James, pulling a 6s gap that then shrank back to nothing. On lap 45 Hunt took the lead at Druids, the crowd ecstatic, to win by almost one minute. Hunt's race car had been repaired in time to take the restart, whereas Regazzoni was disqualified for using his spare Ferrari. This led to various protests following the race, the question at issue being, should Hunt's car have been allowed to take the restart? On 25th September an FIA Court disqualified Hunt and instated Lauda as winner.

| Pos | Driver | Car | Time/gap | Grid | Stops | Tyres |
|---|---|---|---|---|---|---|
| 1 | Niki Lauda | Ferrari | 1h 44m 19.66s | 1 | 0 | G |
| 2 | Jody Scheckter | Tyrrell-Ford | –16.18s | 8 | 0 | G |
| 3 | John Watson | Penske-Ford | –1 lap | 11 | 1 | G |
| 4 | Tom Pryce | Shadow-Ford | –1 lap | 20 | 0 | G |
| 5 | Alan Jones | Surtees-Ford | –1 lap | 19 | 0 | G |
| 6 | Emerson Fittipaldi | Fittipaldi-Ford | –2 laps | 21 | 0 | G |

**POLE POSITION** Lauda, Ferrari, 1m 19.35s (0.06s), 190.858kph, 118.594mph
**LAPS** 76 x 4.207 km, 2.614 miles (Race restarted for scheduled 76 laps following accident)
**DISTANCE** 319.719 km, 198.664 miles
**STARTERS/FINISHERS** 26/9
**WEATHER** Sunny, warm, dry
**LAP LEADERS** (On the road) Lauda 1-44 (44); J Hunt, McLaren-Ford 45-76 (32)
**WINNER'S LAPS** 1-44 P1, 45-76 P2 (Hunt disqualified from first place)
**FASTEST LAP** Hunt, McLaren-Ford, 1m 19.82s (lap 44), 189.520kph, 117.762mph
**CHAMPIONSHIP** Lauda 61, Scheckter 30, Hunt 26, Depailler 26, Regazzoni 16 (Points reflect final results)

RACE POD

# 5 WHAT THE...

## Two laps out, a bizarre sequence occurred that involved four race leaders

Bruce McLaren's Cooper-Climax coasts down the hill from La Source with a dead engine only to see Jim Clark's green and yellow Lotus flash by and take the flag

## Race 124 — 1964 BELGIAN GP Spa-Francorchamps — JIM CLARK

**Round 3/10** — **14 June 1964** — **Lotus-Climax 25** 213.712kph, 132.795mph

Despite a staggering pole time, an even quicker fastest lap and leading 28 of the 32 laps race-distance, Dan Gurney still couldn't bring the Brabham team its deserved maiden victory. Behind Gurney, Hill, McLaren and Clark – until delayed by a pit stop to top up the water radiator – closely contested second place. Then, two laps out, a bizarre sequence of events occurred. Leading by 40s, Gurney pitted for fuel but found his team were ill-prepared to give him the required 'splash and dash'. This handed the lead to Hill, but during his final lap the Bendix fuel system failed on the BRM. Now McLaren's Cooper led, but his battery died at La Source. Coasting down the hill, 100 yards from the finish line, Bruce saw a flash of green and yellow as Clark's Lotus snatched victory… then promptly ran out of fuel.

| Pos | Driver | Car | Time/gap | Grid | Stops | Tyres |
|---|---|---|---|---|---|---|
| 1 | Jim Clark | Lotus-Climax | 2h 6m 40.5s | 6 | 1 | D |
| 2 | Bruce McLaren | Cooper-Climax | –3.4s | 7 | 0 | D |
| 3 | Jack Brabham | Brabham-Climax | –48.1s | 3 | 0 | D |
| 4 | Richie Ginther | BRM | –1m 58.6s | 8 | 0 | D |
| 5r | Graham Hill | BRM | –1 lap | 2 | 0 | D |
| 6r | Dan Gurney | Brabham-Climax | –1 lap | 1 | 1 | D |

**POLE POSITION** Gurney, Brabham-Climax, 3m 50.9s (1.8s), 219.835kph, 136.599mph
**LAPS** 32 x 14.100 km, 8.761 miles
**DISTANCE** 451.200 km, 280.363 miles
**STARTERS/FINISHERS** 18/10
**WEATHER** Overcast, dry
**LAP LEADERS** Gurney 1-2,4-29 (28); J Surtees, Ferrari 3 (1); G Hill 30-31 (2); Clark 32 (1)
**WINNER'S LAPS** 1-3 P3, 4-6 P2, 7-8 P3, 9-11 P4, 12 P2, 13-14 P3, 15 P2, 16, P3, 17-19 P2, 20-22 P3, 23 P4, 24-27 P3, 28-31 P4, 32 P1
**FASTEST LAP** Gurney, Brabham-Climax, 3m 49.2s (lap 27), 221.466kph, 137.613mph
**CHAMPIONSHIP** Clark 21, G Hill 14, Ginther 9, Arundell 8, Surtees 6

RACE POD

# 4 WHAT THE...

# Showers shaped a bizarre event with seven different race leaders

Carnage at Club Corner. Wilson Fittipaldi, standing centre, was the last of the eight cars to aquaplane into the pile-up. His Copersucar (30), Hunt's Hesketh (24), Scheckter's Elf Tyrrell and Crawford's JPS Lotus are clearly visible, Morgan's Surtees and the rest in there somewhere

## Race 260 — 1975 BRITISH GP Silverstone

**Round 10/14** — **19 July 1975**

Tom Pryce's Shadow was on pole, but, in a bizarre event, it was the reigning World Champion who returned to the winner's circle. Showers shaped the race, sweeping through on separate occasions, sometimes localised to different parts of the Silverstone circuit. Some drivers switched to wets, others not, producing seven different race leaders. Although there was disappointment for the partisan crowd when Pryce crashed out on lap 20 within two laps of taking the lead, there was excitement later when Hunt's Hesketh led the race for eight laps until first Emerson Fittipaldi and then Carlos Pace got by. But the skies were darkening again, and when 12 cars – eight a multiple pile-up at Club corner – failed to negotiate lap 56, the race was stopped, winner Fittipaldi one of very few not to physically leave the track.

| Pos | Driver | Car | Time/gap | Grid | Stops | Tyres |
|---|---|---|---|---|---|---|
| 1 | Emerson Fittipaldi | McLaren-Ford | 1h 22m 5.0s | 7 | 1 | G |
| 2r | Carlos Pace | Brabham-Ford | –1 lap | 2 | 0 | G |
| 3r | Jody Scheckter | Tyrrell-Ford | –1 lap | 6 | 2 | G |
| 4r | James Hunt | Hesketh-Ford | –1 lap | 9 | 0 | G |
| 5r | Mark Donohue | March-Ford | –1 lap | 15 | 0 | G |
| 6 | Vittorio Brambilla | March-Ford | –1 lap | 5 | 1 | G |

## EMERSON FITTIPALDI

**McLaren-Ford M23** 193.151kph, 120.019mph

**POLE POSITION** T Pryce, Shadow-Ford, 1m 19.36s (0.14s), 214.049kph, 133.004mph
**LAPS** 56 x 4.719 km, 2.932 miles (Scheduled for 67 laps but stopped due to rain)
**DISTANCE** 264.241 km, 164.192 miles
**STARTERS/FINISHERS** 26/19
**WEATHER** Showers, heavy later
**LAP LEADERS** Pace 1-12, 22-26 (17); Regazzoni 13-18 (6); Pryce 19-20 (2); Scheckter 21, 27-32 (7); J-P Jarier, Shadow-Ford 33-34 (2); Hunt 35-42 (8); Fittipaldi 43-56 (14)
**WINNER'S LAPS** 1 P8, 2-8 P7, 9-18 P6, 19-20 P5, 21 P4, 22-26 P2, 27-28 P5, 29-32 P4, 33-34 P3, 35-42 P2, 43-56 P1
**FASTEST LAP** C Regazzoni, Ferrari, 1m 20.90s (lap 16), 209.975kph, 130.472mph
**CHAMPIONSHIP** Lauda 47, Fittipaldi 33, Hunt 25, Reutemann 25, Pace 24

RACE POD

**The lasting image was a champagne-soaked podium, Jackie Stewart flanked by drivers Herbert (left) and Barrichello**

3

WHAT THE...

## Many drivers *could* have won this bizarre race but Herbert *did* – from 14th

When selecting his greatest races with *Autosport* in 2024, Herbert said: "Normally when you talk about rain you don't see it coming, it just appears. But on this occasion going down to the hairpin I'd seen this wide, teardrop cloud coming from Spa. I watched this cloud and, as it came, it never deviated and was coming dead straight over the track. It was quite a dark colour and I thought, 'When that hits it's going to be an absolute deluge'.

"I was very lucky because I got the radio call to pit and as I got down to the hairpin it absolutely chucked it down, so I got on the radio and said, 'Wets'. When Rubens came in [two laps later] the team decided to leave him on slicks.

"It was absolutely sodden, slicks almost impossible and cars whizzing off all over the place. It was a crazy race to be in! I was just hoping and praying towards the end that everything would hold together. I had quite a gap, so I was able to change the gears earlier and brake earlier and just concentrate on not putting too much strain on the car.

"I'm glad I was able to make that call to put wets on at exactly the right time. If I hadn't, I'd never have been in that position. It was a special one because it was Sir Jackie [Stewart] and Paul's only win, and it was at the venue where Jackie took his last F1 win."

**Race 644** **1999 EUROPEAN GP** Nürburgring **JOHNNY HERBERT**

**Round 14/16** **26 September 1999** **Stewart-Ford SF-3** 177.034kph, 110.004mph

Pedro Diniz's horrifying, somersaulting first lap crash released the SC for six laps. Then, Heinz-Harald Frentzen's title bid for Jordan, which had begun with pole, continued by leading the opening 32 laps. But having successfully beaten the chasing David Coulthard away from their concurrent pit stop, electrical failure ended it. Changeable weather and resultant team blunders eliminated Häkkinen and Eddie Irvine from serious contention, while Coulthard and Giancarlo Fisichella spun out, and Ralf Schumacher punctured, the latter three while leading. This, plus a timely call for wet tyres, set up victory for Herbert from a P14 start, the first and only win for the team. Trulli brought Prost-Peugeot P2, but the lasting image was a champagne-soaked podium, Jackie Stewart flanked by drivers Herbert and Barrichello.

| Pos | Driver | Car | Time/gap | Grid | Stops | Tyres |
|---|---|---|---|---|---|---|
| 1 | Johnny Herbert | Stewart-Ford | 1h 41m 54.314s | 14 | 2 | B |
| 2 | Jarno Trulli | Prost-Peugeot | –22.619s | 10 | 3 | B |
| 3 | Rubens Barrichello | Stewart-Ford | –22.866s | 15 | 1 | B |
| 4 | Ralf Schumacher | Williams-Supertec | –39.508s | 4 | 3 | B |
| 5 | Mika Häkkinen | McLaren-Mercedes | –1m 2.950s | 3 | 2 | B |
| 6 | Marc Gené | Minardi-Ford | –1m 5.154s | 20 | 1 | B |

**POLE POSITION** H-H Frentzen, Jordan-Mugen Honda, 1m 19.910s (0.266s), 205.250kph, 127.537mph
**LAPS** 66 x 4.556 km, 2.831 miles (67 lap race interrupted due to accident. Restarted over 66 laps)
**DISTANCE** 300.679 km, 186.833 miles
**STARTERS/FINISHERS** 22/10
**WEATHER** Overcast, cold, dry then showers
**LAP LEADERS** Frentzen 1-32 (32); D Coulthard, McLaren-Mercedes 33-37 (5); R Schumacher 38-44, 49 (8); G Fisichella, Benetton-Playlife 45-48 (4); Herbert 50-66 (17); SC 2-7 (6)
**WINNER'S LAPS** 1-10 P13, 11-19 P12, 20 P9, 21 P8, 22-24 P7, 25-27 P8, 28 P7, 29-32 P6, 33-37 P5, 38-44 P3, 45-46 P2, 47 P3, 48 P4, 49 P2, 50-66 P1
**FASTEST LAP** Häkkinen, McLaren-Mercedes, 1m 21.282s (lap 64), 201.786kph, 125.384mph
**CHAMPIONSHIP** Häkkinen 62, Irvine 60, Frentzen 50, Coulthard 48, R Schumacher 33

**RACE POD**

**The three drivers on the podium – left to right, de Angelis (mistakenly), de Cesaris and winner Patrese – appear slightly bemused by the bizarre events of those final two laps. Prince Rainier stands centre stage, the lady in red to his right, Princess Grace Kelly**

**WHAT THE...**

# 2 Prost's late crash triggered five minutes of F1 madness

Speaking with Jonathan Phillips for a forthcoming biography of the Italian, due in 2026, Patrese said: "I was going very, very, slowly but after Mirabeau I lost the car. So, the marshals were pulling me away from the road because I was stuck in the middle. I saw an Alfa Romeo, then Pironi come by. I knew Rosberg was fifth and I saw a Williams. So I started to shake inside the car, because the nose was pointing downhill. And by luck or Saint Anthony [patron saint of Padova] the car started to roll and I could engage second gear. It was the last lap and I saw de Cesaris stopped. Then the tunnel and Pironi stopped. So I crossed the line and thought Rosberg is the winner. I was going along with a lot of clouds in my mind. Shit! I lost the Monaco GP. They said in the briefing only the winner's car goes to the podium. I was ready to go into the pits but they stop me: 'Go to the podium!' Maybe they changed the rule? I arrive and no other cars. Strange. Then an Italian guy came to me and say 'Riccardo! You won the race!' So I realised I was the winner. Then the big ball. I was at the table with Princess Grace when suddenly she says, 'We are going to open the dancing with a waltz.' 'But Princess, I'm not able to dance a waltz.' 'Don't worry' she replied. 'For once I will drive. I lead, you follow.' She was very nice, but oh my God, that was much more difficult than winning the GP. But I remember this with big pleasure because it was the last time she was there [before her fatal accident in October].

## Race 363 — 1982 MONACO GP Monte Carlo

**Round 6/16** — **23 May 1982**

When pole-man René Arnoux spun away his lead on lap 15, teammate Alain Prost's Renault looked the certain winner until two-and-a-half laps from glory. Heading towards Tabac, the track surface greasy from drizzle, he lost control as he negotiated a backmarker and struck the barriers hard. For Patrese, his Brabham running within a few seconds of Prost for much of the race, a maiden victory seemed assured. But approaching the hairpin he too spun away the lead, allowing Pironi's Ferrari and the Alfa Romeo of de Cesaris by. But fate granted Patrese another chance. First, although push-started, he escaped disqualification as his car was in a dangerous position; then de Cesaris ran out of fuel, and finally Pironi's battery failed, Patrese the only driver to complete the full distance. Prost's late crash had triggered five minutes of F1 madness.

| Pos | Driver | Car | Time/gap | Grid | Stops | Tyres |
|---|---|---|---|---|---|---|
| 1 | Riccardo Patrese | Brabham-Ford | 1h 54m 11.259s | 2 | 0 | G |
| 2r | Didier Pironi | Ferrari | –1 lap | 5 | 0 | G |
| 3r | Andrea de Cesaris | Alfa Romeo | –1 lap | 7 | 0 | M |
| 4 | Nigel Mansell | Lotus-Ford | –1 lap | 11 | 1 | G |
| 5 | Elio de Angelis | Lotus-Ford | –1 lap | 15 | 0 | G |
| 6r | Derek Daly | Williams-Ford | –2 laps | 8 | 0 | G |

## RICCARDO PATRESE

**Brabham-Ford BT49D** 132.262kph, 82.184mph

**POLE POSITION** R Arnoux, Renault, 1m 23.281s (0.510s), 143.168kph, 88.961mph
**LAPS** 76 x 3.312 km, 2.058 miles
**DISTANCE** 251.712 km, 156.407 miles
**STARTERS/FINISHERS** 20/10
**WEATHER** Warm and dry, rain in closing laps
**LAP LEADERS** Arnoux 1-14 (14); A Prost, Renault 15-73 (59); Patrese 74, 76 (2); Pironi 75 (1)
**WINNER'S LAPS** 1-4 P4, 5-15 P3, 16-73 P2, 74 P1, 75 P3, 76 P1
**FASTEST LAP** Patrese, Brabham-Ford, 1m 26.354s (lap 69), 138.074kph, 85.795mph
**CHAMPIONSHIP** Prost 18, Watson 17, Pironi 16, Rosberg 14, Patrese 13

**RACE POD**

**1**

**WHAT THE...**

# Beginning with a pile-up, then a punch-up, it ended with joy for Jordan

Eddie Jordan on the 1998 Belgian GP, from the Unlikely Lads documentary and *Autosport*:

The 1998 Belgian Grand Prix was chaotic from the start, yet it became a defining moment for both Damon Hill and Eddie Jordan. As torrential rain drenched Spa, Hill brought his Jordan crew together before the race. "You [Hill] said listen, the forecast is really poor, we have a great chance here," Eddie Jordan later recalled. "You gave us the inspiration, the belief… I shall never forget that."

Hill's foresight paid off. He avoided the first-lap pile-up that eliminated half the grid and seized the lead at the second start. Michael Schumacher surged ahead, only to collide spectacularly with David Coulthard while lapping him.

With Michael out, Ralf Schumacher chased down Hill thanks to a Safety Car, putting Jordan's first-ever victory, and a potential 1–2, on the line. But Hill again stepped up. "If we race, we could end up with nothing," he radioed. "It's your choice."

Jordan was hesitant. "I was in the middle of a deal with Ralf," he admitted later. "But Damon spoke to me like he'd never spoken to me before – 'I am a world champion, I know how to win'." That message swung the call: team orders were issued, and Ralf reluctantly obeyed.

Hill crossed the line delivering Jordan's maiden win, Eddie Jordan danced a wild jig, and a Formula 1 classic was born as much from leadership off-track as from drama on it.

## Race 627 — 1998 BELGIAN GP Spa-Francorchamps — DAMON HILL

**Round 13/16** — **30 August 1998** — **Jordan-Mugen Honda 198** 177.229kph, 110.125mph

This wet-race classic began with a terrifying 13-car first-corner pile-up triggered by David Coulthard's spin. At the restart Hill, having qualified P3, nabbed the lead for seven laps until Michael Schumacher went by to establish an apparently unassailable 37s lead. On lap 25 in zero visibility he shunted Coulthard in the process of lapping him, which restored Hill to the front. Fascinatingly, this race exposed the collective Schumacher mindset. Michael was livid with Coulthard for getting in his way, needing to be physically restained, while Ralf, only in contention due to a second SC, was livid with his team, anxiously on the verge of its maiden victory, for not allowing him to race his team leader. There was unbounded joy in the Jordan pit and at Sauber too for Alesi's P3.

| Pos | Driver | Car | Time/gap | Grid | Stops | Tyres |
|---|---|---|---|---|---|---|
| 1 | Damon Hill | Jordan-Mugen Honda | 1h 43m 47.407s | 3 | 2 | G |
| 2 | Ralf Schumacher | Jordan-Mugen Honda | –0.932s | 8 | 2 | G |
| 3 | Jean Alesi | Sauber-Petronas | –7.240s | 10 | 2 | G |
| 4 | Heinz-Harald Frentzen | Williams-Mecachrome | –32.243s | 9 | 2 | G |
| 5 | Pedro Diniz | Arrows | –51.682s | 16 | 1 | B |
| 6 | Jarno Trulli | Prost-Peugeot | –2 laps | 13 | 1 | B |

**POLE POSITION** M Häkkinen, McLaren-Mercedes, 1m 48.682s (0.163s), 230.809kph, 143.418mph
**LAPS** 44 x 6.968 km, 4.330 miles (Race restarted for scheduled 44 laps following multiple accident)
**DISTANCE** 306.577 km, 190.498 miles
**STARTERS/FINISHERS** 22/8
**WEATHER** Overcast, cold, heavy rain
**LAP LEADERS** Hill 1-7, 26-44 (26); M Schumacher 8-25 (18); SC 1-2, 29-32 (6)
**WINNER'S LAPS** 1-7 P1, 8-25 P2, 26-44 P1
**FASTEST LAP** M Schumacher, Ferrari, 2m 03.766s (lap 9), 202.679kph, 125.939mph
**CHAMPIONSHIP** Häkkinen 77, M Schumacher 70, Coulthard 48, Irvine 32, Villeneuve 20

*RACE POD*

There was unbounded joy on the Jordan pit wall when Damon Hill (out of shot) delivered the team's very first GP victory, the first new constructor to win in 12 seasons

CHAPTER 5

# EPICS

## AGAINST THE ODDS

Some drivers defy the odds by conquering adversity or triumphing in a less-than-dominant car. Such victories often exhibit their exceptional race craft, that ability to read the unfolding pattern of the race, seize fleeting opportunities, or turn setback into victory. Such legendary performances are the true mark of the champion, those who can transcend the hand they've been dealt that day, or the limitations of their machinery.

Raw speed may be the fundamental trait of the Formula 1 driver, but it takes more than pace to pull off the extraordinary, when the script is torn apart by sheer brilliance behind the wheel. Some victories are routine, the inevitable outcome of a dominant car and a well-executed strategy. Others are remarkable triumphs when a driver rises above it all, produces a performance so extraordinary that it defies logic. These are the against-the-odds victories that define the legacy of champions. It requires an almost intangible, extra sensory quality that enables the great drivers to do what appears impossible.

Race craft is often what sets the greats apart. It's the ability to sense the race's rhythm, anticipate gaps before they open, or force a car to seemingly perform beyond its limits. Race craft is a blend of instinct, adaptability, and ruthless execution under pressure, together with unwavering self-belief. It's knowing when to attack, when to defend or when to play the waiting game. It's making the car do things that others cannot, like managing tyres to the brink of destruction, or nursing a failing car to the finish. A driver with superior race craft can negotiate 'traffic' (lapped backmarkers) to steal precious seconds on a chasing rival by executing daring overtakes that others wouldn't risk, threading the needle in moments of pure racing brilliance.

This collection of remarkable against-the-odds drives showcases the very essence of what makes a champion, the ability to do the impossible when it matters the most. These races stay alive in the annals of motorsport, reminding us that while Formula 1 is a battle of engineering, it is ultimately a battle of willpower.

**AGAINST-THE-ODDS VICTORIES REQUIRE AN ALMOST INTANGIBLE, EXTRA SENSORY QUALITY THAT ENABLES THE GREAT DRIVERS TO DO WHAT APPEARS IMPOSSIBLE**

10 EPICS

# Clark kept his sick motor running by switching it off in the corners

A garlanded Jim Clark accepts the plaudits after his against-the-odds win. It was his fourth successive British GP victory

## Race 136 — 1965 BRITISH GP Silverstone

**Round 5/10** — **10 July 1965**

The British GP grid had five Brits in the top six, with Clark on pole and Hill alongside on the four-wide front row. Clark catapulted into the lead and although Hill gave relentless pursuit, he steadily fell back having mistakenly chosen rear 'wets'. But with around 20 of the 80 laps to go, the latest 32-valve Climax engine installed in the back of Clark's Lotus ran short of oil, sounding very sick indeed. Clark, with a 34s lead, then demonstrated masterly mechanical sympathy by switching the engine off while cornering to prevent oil-surge damage, sometimes losing 3s in a lap. The crowd began to urge Hill to reduce the deficit, but with his own brakes failing, and despite fastest lap on the final circuit, the BRM was thwarted by 3.2s. 'Can't go beats can't stop' the sports headlines shrieked the following day.

| Pos | Driver | Car | Time/gap | Grid | Stops | Tyres |
|---|---|---|---|---|---|---|
| 1 | Jim Clark | Lotus-Climax | 2h 5m 25.4s | 1 | 0 | D |
| 2 | Graham Hill | BRM | –3.2s | 2 | 0 | D |
| 3 | John Surtees | Ferrari | –27.6s | 5 | 0 | D |
| 4 | Mike Spence | Lotus-Climax | –39.6s | 6 | 0 | D |
| 5 | Jackie Stewart | BRM | –1m 14.6s | 4 | 0 | D |
| 6 | Dan Gurney | Brabham-Climax | –1 lap | 7 | 0 | G |

## JIM CLARK

**Lotus-Climax 33** 180.275kph, 112.017mph

**POLE POSITION** Clark, Lotus-Climax, 1m 30.8s (0.2s), 186.762kph, 116.048mph
**LAPS** 80 x 4.711 km, 2.927 miles
**DISTANCE** 376.844 km, 234.160 miles
**STARTERS/FINISHERS** 20/14
**WEATHER** Overcast, dry
**LAP LEADERS** Clark 1-80 (80)
**WINNER'S LAPS** 1-80 P1
**FASTEST LAP** G Hill, BRM, 1m 32.2s (lap 80), 183.926kph, 114.286mph
**CHAMPIONSHIP** Clark 36, G Hill 23, Stewart 19, Surtees 17, McLaren 8

*RACE POD*

EPICS

# 9 A classic victory by the tiny Hesketh team over the might of Maranello

In what turned out to be a rehearsal for their titanic championship duel the following year, James Hunt (24) beat Niki Lauda (12) fair and square at Zandvoort, but by a mere 1.06 seconds

## Race 258 1975 DUTCH GP Zandvoort

**Round 8/14** **22 June 1975**

With Lauda on pole and on a three-race winning roll, was there no one to defy the might of Maranello? Enter James Hunt. This was a classic victory by the Englishman and the tiny Hesketh team as well as the first skirmish in the fabled Hunt versus Lauda saga to be played out the following year. Hunt qualified best of the rest behind the Ferrari pair but the key moment was the canny tyre change from wets to dries. Running fourth, Hunt was the first of the leaders on the still slick track to pit, a full six laps sooner than leader Lauda, and dropping to P19 in the process. But as Lauda rejoined Hunt had gone by, and worse still Jean-Pierre Jarier in the Shadow pushed him back to third for 28 laps until he spun out with a tyre burst. Once released, still with over 30 laps to go, Lauda did close the 10s gap to Hunt, but pass he could not.

| Pos | Driver | Car | Time/gap | Grid | Stops | Tyres |
|---|---|---|---|---|---|---|
| 1 | James Hunt | Hesketh-Ford | 1h 46m 57.40s | 3 | 1 | G |
| 2 | Niki Lauda | Ferrari | –1.06s | 1 | 1 | G |
| 3 | Clay Regazzoni | Ferrari | –55.06s | 2 | 1 | G |
| 4 | Carlos Reutemann | Brabham-Ford | –1 lap | 5 | 1 | G |
| 5 | Carlos Pace | Brabham-Ford | –1 lap | 9 | 1 | G |
| 6 | Tom Pryce | Shadow-Ford | –1 lap | 12 | 1 | G |

## JAMES HUNT

**Hesketh-Ford 308** 177.801kph, 110.480mph

**POLE POSITION** Lauda, Ferrari, 1m 20.29s (0.28s), 189.483kph, 117.739mph
**LAPS** 75 x 4.226 km, 2.626 miles
**DISTANCE** 316.950 km, 196.944 miles
**STARTERS/FINISHERS** 24/16
**WEATHER** Rain, then dry
**LAP LEADERS** Lauda 1-12 (12); Regazzoni 13-14 (2); Hunt 15-75 (61)
**WINNER'S LAPS** 1-7 P4, 8 P19, 9-10 P17, 11 P15, 12 P9, 13 P3, 14 P2, 15-75 P1
**FASTEST LAP** Lauda, Ferrari, 1m 21.54s (lap 55), 186.578kph, 115.934mph
**CHAMPIONSHIP** Lauda 38, Reutemann 25, Fittipaldi 21, Pace 18, Hunt 16

RACE POD

# In an epic drive, Rubens delivered the *coup de grâce* on leader Kimi

Rubens quaffs the champagne (well almost!) after stepping out of Schumacher's shadow with his epic Silverstone victory. Michael finished fourth

## Race 708 — 2003 BRITISH GP Silverstone

**Round 11/16** **20 July 2003**

Gambling on new-spec Bridgestones, Barrichello started from pole, Ferrari teammate Schumacher back in fifth. But the opening lap went badly and Rubens was still third after a brief early SC. And after the SC's second appearance to detain a deranged Irish priest sprinting up the Hangar Straight dressed in a brown kilt, he had lost further ground during the pit-stop scramble. When released on lap 16 Rubens found himself eighth in an SC-generated snake headed by two Toyotas. In an epic drive, overtaking in inspired fashion, he reached P2 by lap 31 but still lay 10s behind leader Räikkönen. On lap 42, following the second round of pit stops, Rubens had closed the gap to deliver the *coup de grâce* on Kimi, a sensational move that started at Stowe and finished at Bridge. An F1 classic.

| Pos | Driver | Car | Time/gap | Grid | Stops | Tyres |
|---|---|---|---|---|---|---|
| 1 | Rubens Barrichello | Ferrari | 1h 28m 37.554s | 1 | 2 | B |
| 2 | Juan Pablo Montoya | Williams-BMW | −5.462s | 7 | 2 | M |
| 3 | Kimi Räikkönen | McLaren-Mercedes | −10.656s | 3 | 2 | M |
| 4 | Michael Schumacher | Ferrari | −25.648s | 5 | 2 | B |
| 5 | David Coulthard | McLaren-Mercedes | −36.827s | 12 | 2 | M |
| 6 | Jarno Trulli | Renault | −43.067s | 2 | 2 | M |

## RUBENS BARRICHELLO

**Ferrari F2003-GA** 208.757kph, 129.716mph

**POLE POSITION** Barrichello, Ferrari, 1m 21.209s (0.172s), 227.900kph, 141.611mph
**LAPS** 60 x 5.141 km, 3.195 miles
**DISTANCE** 308.356 km, 191.604 miles
**STARTERS/FINISHERS** 20/17
**WEATHER** Cloudy, warm, dry
**LAP LEADERS** Trulli 1-12 (12); C da Matta, Toyota 13-29 (17); Räikkönen 30-35, 40-41 (8); Barrichello 36-39, 42-60 (23); SC 6-7, 12-15 (6)
**WINNER'S LAPS** 1-10 P3, 11-12 P2, 13-15 P8, 16 P7, 17-25 P6, 26-27 P5, 28-29 P4, 30 P3, 31-35 P2, 36-39 P1, 40-41 P2, 42-60 P1
**FASTEST LAP** Barrichello, Ferrari, 1m 22.236s (lap 38), 225.054kph, 139.843mph
**CHAMPIONSHIP** M Schumacher 69, Räikkönen 62, Montoya 55, R Schumacher 53, Barrichello 49

*RACE POD*

7 EPICS

# Hamilton thwarts Verstappen and 24 grid penalties for a famous win

**Following his sensational victory at Interlagos, Lewis Hamilton was handed a Brazilian flag which, much to the delight of the Paulistas in the Grandstands, he 'flew' on his victory lap**

## Race 1054 2021 SÃO PAULO GP Interlagos

**Round 19/22** **14 November 2021**

Instead of sprint-race pole, Hamilton was relegated to P20 for a DRS violation yet finished a sensational P5. For the GP grid, P5 became P10 due to a five-place engine penalty. In an astonishing display, Lewis passed Pérez for P2 on lap 19 and now the stage was set, race leader Verstappen 3.8s ahead. On lap 43 Lewis rejoined from his second stop 2s behind and absolutely flying. Attacking on lap 48, he got ahead approaching turn 4 but Max would not concede and controversially pushed Lewis wide. Both cars careered off track, Hamilton avoiding contact, Verstappen retaining P1. When it came on lap 59, the endgame was sheer poetry. Forced to defend an inside feint at turn 1, Verstappen's exit from the Senna 'S' was compromised, Hamilton passing before turn 4 to a mighty roar from the Paulistas to win by 10.5s.

| Pos | Driver | Car | Time/gap | QSR | GP | Stops | Tyres (c2/c3/c4) |
|---|---|---|---|---|---|---|---|
| 1 | Lewis Hamilton | Mercedes | 1h 32m 22.851s | 20 (-19) | 10 (-5) | 2 | mhh |
| 2 | Max Verstappen | Red Bull-Honda | –10.496s | 1 | 2 | 2 | mhh |
| 3 | Valtteri Bottas | Mercedes | –13.576s | 2 | 1 | 2 | mhh |
| 4 | Sergio Pérez | Red Bull-Honda | –39.940s | 3 | 4 | 3 | mhhs |
| 5 | Charles Leclerc | Ferrari | –49.517s | 6 | 6 | 2 | mmh |
| 6 | Carlos Sainz | Ferrari | –1 lap | 5 | 3 | 2 | mmh |

## LEWIS HAMILTON

**Mercedes F1 W12** 198.663kph, 123.443mph

**QSR POLE/Q1-3 FASTEST** Verstappen, Red Bull-Honda, 1m 8.372s (0.097s), 226.882kph, 140.977mph (Hamilton, Mercedes, won QSR pole in 1m 7.934s but was sent to the back of the grid for a rear-wing violation)
**GP POLE/QSR WINNER** Bottas, Mercedes 24 laps, 29m 9.559s, 212.671kph, 132.147mph
**LAPS** 71 x 4.309 km, 2.677
**DISTANCE** 305.879 km, 190.064 miles
**STARTERS/FINISHERS** 20/18
**WEATHER** Sunny, hot, dry, windy
**LAP LEADERS** Verstappen 1-27, 31-39, 44-58 (51); Bottas 28-30 (3); Hamilton 40-43, 59-71 (17); SC 6-9 (4); VSC 12-14, 30 (4)
**WINNER'S LAPS** 1-2 P6, 3-4 P4, 5-18 P3, 19-25 P2, 26 P3, 27 P6, 28 P4, 29-30 P3, 31-39 P2, 40-43 P1, 44-58 P2, 59-71 P1
**FASTEST LAP** Pérez, Red Bull-Honda, 1m 11.010s (lap 71), 218.453kph, 135.740mph
**CHAMPIONSHIP** Verstappen 332.5, Hamilton 318.5, Bottas 203, Pérez 178, Norris 151

RACE POD

## 6 EPICS

# Senna dispossessed Prost of the lead, and his title ambitions

Prost had to give best to Senna in the race, in the Championship, and on the podium in the champagne spraying contest!

## Race 467 1988 JAPANESE GP Suzuka

**Round 15/16** **30 October 1988**

From his 12th pole of the 16-race season, Senna stalled but found just enough momentum for a bump-start. He rounded the first corner P14 and completed the first lap P8. With Prost's lead over Senna more then 13s by lap five, the destiny of their titanic season-long championship battle would now surely await the Adelaide finale in two weeks. But it drizzled periodically, slicks on a damp surface meat and drink to Senna. Displaying uncanny skills, he sliced through the field, locking on to his McLaren teammate's tail on lap 20. Alain was no pushover, so it wasn't until lap 28 of 51 that Ayrton dispossessed him of the lead and his title ambitions. Game, set, match and championship to Senna. So, in the most intense intra-team rivalry of all time, the king versus the man who would be king, Senna had drawn first blood.

| Pos | Driver | Car | Time/gap | Grid | Stops | Tyres |
|---|---|---|---|---|---|---|
| 1 | Ayrton Senna | McLaren-Honda | 1h 33m 26.173s | 1 | 0 | G |
| 2 | Alain Prost | McLaren-Honda | –13.363s | 2 | 0 | G |
| 3 | Thierry Boutsen | Benetton-Ford | –36.109s | 10 | 0 | G |
| 4 | Gerhard Berger | Ferrari | –1m 26.714s | 3 | 0 | G |
| 5 | Alessandro Nannini | Benetton-Ford | –1m 30.603s | 12 | 0 | G |
| 6 | Riccardo Patrese | Williams-Judd | –1m 37.615s | 11 | 0 | G |

## AYRTON SENNA

**McLaren-Honda MP4/4** 191.880kph, 119.229mph

**POLE POSITION** Senna, McLaren- Honda, 1m 41.853s (0.324s), 207.087kph, 128.678mph
**LAPS** 51 x 5.859 km, 3.641 miles
**DISTANCE** 298.809 km, 185.671 miles
**STARTERS/FINISHERS** 26/17
**WEATHER** Overcast, cool, occasional light rain
**LAP LEADERS** Prost 1-15, 17-27 (26); I Capelli, March-Judd 16 (1); Senna 28-51 (24)
**WINNER'S LAPS** 1 P8, 2 P6, 3 P5, 4-10 P4, 11-19 P3, 20-27 P2, 28-51 P1
**FASTEST LAP** Senna, McLaren- Honda, 1m 46.326s (lap 33), 198.375kph, 123.264mph
**CHAMPIONSHIP** Senna 87, Prost 84, Berger 41, Boutsen 29, Alboreto 24

**RACE POD**

5 EPICS

# To the delight of the adoring grandstand, Alonso celebrated with them

Fernando Alonso gives Andrea Stella his race engineer a champagne shower as they celebrate a victory that propelled them into a 26-point championship lead over Vettel for the 2012 title. Twelve rounds later at the season finale in Brazil, they fell short of winning the crown by just three points

## Race 866 — 2012 EUROPEAN GP Valencia

**Round 8/20** — **24 June 2012**

## FERNANDO ALONSO

**Ferrari F2012** 177.727kph, 110.434mph

From another mighty pole, Vettel ran away with the race until shortly after half-distance. Then a Safety Car wiped out his 20s lead, and just as racing resumed on lap 34, the alternator in Seb's Renault broke. Remarkably, there to take over the lead, having mugged Grosjean for P2 at the SC restart, was Alonso's Ferrari. Qualifying a dismal P11, the local hero completed lap 1 P8, but through relentless lappery and assertive overtaking was there to take a lead which he comfortably held to the end once the Renault in Grosjean's Lotus, still threatening Alonso, suffered the same fate as Vettel's Red Bull. To ensure the prerequisite fuel sample, Fernando stopped his car around the back of the circuit on the slowing-down lap. To the delight of the adoring grandstand crowd, he celebrated with them, emotively waving the Spanish flag.

| Pos | Driver | Car | Time/gap | Grid (pen) | Stops | Tyres (m/s) |
|---|---|---|---|---|---|---|
| 1 | Fernando Alonso | Ferrari | 1h 44m 16.649s | 11 | 2 | oop |
| 2 | Kimi Räikkönen | Lotus-Renault | –6.421s | 5 | 2 | oop |
| 3 | Michael Schumacher | Mercedes | –12.639s | 12 | 2 | poo |
| 4 | Mark Webber | Red Bull-Renault | –13.628s | 19 | 2 | poo |
| 5 | Nico Hülkenberg | Force India-Mercedes | –19.993s | 8 | 2 | opp |
| 6 | Nico Rosberg | Mercedes | –21.176s | 6 | 2 | opo |

**POLE POSITION** S Vettel, Red Bull-Renault, 1m 38.086s (0.324s), 198.890kph, 123.584mph
**LAPS** 57 x 5.419 km, 3.367 miles
**DISTANCE** 308.883 km, 191.931 miles
**STARTERS/FINISHERS** 23/19
**WEATHER** Sunny, hot, dry
**LAP LEADERS** Vettel 1-33, (33); Alonso 34-57 (24); SC 29-33 (5)
**WINNER'S LAPS** 1-11 P8, 12 P7, 13 P6, 14 P3, 15 P4, 16-17 P9, 18 P7, 19 P6, 20-21 P5, 22-27 P4, 28-33 P3, 34-57 P1;
**FASTEST LAP** Rosberg, Mercedes, 1m 42.163s (lap 54), 190.953kph, 118.652mph
**CHAMPIONSHIP** Alonso 111, Webber 91, Hamilton 88, Vettel 85, Rosberg 75

RACE POD

EPICS

# Hamilton masterclass on worn inters cements seventh title

In the foreshortened season of the global pandemic, Hamilton and Mercedes were dominant, Lewis sewing up his seventh title by round 14 of 17. Note the Covid masks clutched by Lewis and Toto Wolff

## Race 1032 2020 TURKISH GP Istanbul

**Round 14/17** **15 November 2020**

Drastic swings in tyre performance served up a race of strikingly changing fortunes in the fickle conditions. Five race leaders each had their chance of victory. Shock pole-sitter Lance Stroll headed a splendid 1-2 as Racing Point surged ahead for over half the race. On lap 24 Alex Albon came within 4.3s of the lead as he attacked Pérez for P2, three potential 'new GP winners' leading the race for 15 laps. At half distance Hamilton was holding P5 behind these three and Vettel. On laps 33/34 Vettel pitted and Albon spun and now the flying Hamilton was P3, taking the lead from Pérez on lap 37 after Stroll's pitstop. By the finish 21 laps later, Hamilton on 50-lap-old treadless inters, had pulled out 31.6s on Pérez, struggling on similarly worn rubber. As Vettel put it, "It wasn't his race to win, and he still won it!"

| Pos | Driver | Car | Time/gap | Grid (pen) | Stops | Tyres (c1/c2/c3) |
|---|---|---|---|---|---|---|
| 1 | Lewis Hamilton | Mercedes | 1h 42m 19.313s | 6 | 1 | wi |
| 2 | Sergio Pérez | Racing Point-Mercedes | −31.633s | 3 | 1 | wi |
| 3 | Sebastian Vettel | Ferrari | −31.960s | 11 | 2 | wii |
| 4 | Charles Leclerc | Ferrari | −33.858s | 12 | 2 | wii |
| 5 | Carlos Sainz | McLaren-Renault | −34.363s | 15 (-3) | 2 | wii |
| 6 | Max Verstappen | Red Bull-Honda | −44.873s | 2 | 3 | wiii |

## LEWIS HAMILTON

**Mercedes F1 W11** 181.425kph, 112.732mph

**POLE POSITION** Stroll, Racing Point-Mercedes, 1m 47.765s (0.290s), 178.321kph, 110.803mph
**LAPS** 58 x 5.338 km, 3.317 miles
**DISTANCE** 309.396 km, 192.250 miles
**STARTERS/FINISHERS** 20/17
**WEATHER** Overcast, cool, wet track slowly drying, early poor spray visability, late threat of rain
**LAP LEADERS** Stroll 1-9, 13-35 (32); Pérez 10, 36 (2), Verstappen 11 (1), Albon 12 (1), Hamilton 37-58 (22), VSC 14 (1)
**WINNER'S LAPS** 1-8 P6, 9-10 P8, 11-12 P6, 13-14 P5, 15-17 P6, 18-32 P5, 33 P4, 34-36 P3, 37-58 P1
**FASTEST LAP** Norris, McLaren-Renault, 1m 36.806s (lap 58), 198.508kph, 123.347mph
**CHAMPIONSHIP** Hamilton 307, Bottas 197, Verstappen 170, Pérez 100, Leclerc 97

RACE POD

The 1980s were defined by the turbo era and le professeur, Alain Prost, the undoubted master of this F1 genre. But behind the wheel of a turbo, the driver who made the blood race was Gilles Villeneuve, here winning the second of his two remarkable 1981 victories

3 EPICS

# Gilles led a thrilling convoy of five cars covered by little more than 1s

In the June 25 1981 issue of *Autosport* magazine, Nigel Roebuck reported: "The last 20 laps were astonishing. Ferrari-Ligier-Williams-McLaren-Lotus ran the first five, all covered by less than two seconds. By now, the Ferrari's lack of grip was an embarrassment to its driver, the car crawling through the hairpins, with Laffite's Ligier all but climbing over it. But Gilles has this one worked out to perfection. He never chopped Laffite because he has no need. Simply, he covered the overtaking lines into the slow corners, made no driving errors and gave the 550 horsepower its head as often as possible – which, with Villeneuve, was often."

At the time, an understated Villeneuve said in *Autosport*:

"I was figuring to try and control the race. I knew that to make the tyres and brakes last I had to slow the pace, make use of my straight line speed to keep ahead and not make any mistakes anywhere. The engine was as good on the last lap as the first.

"This is my most public victory, I suppose. But I don't feel it was any better than others I've had. It's nice, of course, because I really didn't think I had much chance of winning here. I knew I had to go like hell from the start and of course it was lucky for me that Alan went off and Jacques made a bad start. There was a lot of pressure for sure. I feel I worked hard today!"

**Race 349** **1981 SPANISH GP** Jarama

**Round 7/15** **21 June 1981**

Laffite in the Ligier-Matra took pole but completed the first lap P11. As he finally finished P2, his botched start cost him dear. So Alan Jones' and Reutemann's Williams led from Villeneuve, who had made a blistering turbo-charged start from row four. On lap two Villeneuve passed Reutemann, the unwieldy Ferrari now acting as a mobile chicane that helped Jones disappear into the distance. But on lap 14, with a 10s lead, Jones unaccountably flew off the road. Famously, lap after lap for the next 67, Villeneuve defied the efforts of the potentially far quicker following cars. One slip and they were through, but Gilles was unconquerable in the corners and Ferrari turbo-power uncatchable on the straights. Towards the finish, Gilles was leading a thrilling convoy of five cars all within a second. His final victory was the stuff of legends.

| Pos | Driver | Car | Time/gap | Grid | Stops | Tyres |
|---|---|---|---|---|---|---|
| 1 | Gilles Villeneuve | Ferrari | 1h 46m 35.01s | 7 | 0 | M |
| 2 | Jacques Laffite | Ligier-Matra | –0.22s | 1 | 0 | M |
| 3 | John Watson | McLaren-Ford | –0.58s | 4 | 0 | M |
| 4 | Carlos Reutemann | Williams-Ford | –1.01s | 3 | 0 | M |
| 5 | Elio de Angelis | Lotus-Ford | –1.24s | 10 | 0 | M |
| 6 | Nigel Mansell | Lotus-Ford | –28.58s | 11 | 0 | M |

**GILLES VILLENEUVE**

**Ferrari 126CK** 149.156kph, 92.681mph

**POLE POSITION** Laffite, Ligier-Matra, 1m 13.754s (0.270s), 161.662kph, 100.452mph
**LAPS** 80 x 3.312 km, 2.058 miles
**DISTANCE** 264.960 km, 164.639 miles
**STARTERS/FINISHERS** 24/16
**WEATHER** Sunny, very hot, dry
**LAP LEADERS** Jones 1-13 (13); Villeneuve 14-80 (67)
**WINNER'S LAPS** 1 P3, 2-13 P2, 14-80 P1
**FASTEST LAP** A Jones, Williams-Ford, 1m 17.818s (lap 5), 153.219kph, 95.206mph
**CHAMPIONSHIP** Reutemann 37, Jones 24, Piquet 22, Villeneuve 21, Laffite 17

RACE POD

Moss was at the height of his powers in 1961, seen here in Rob Walker's privately entered Lotus 18 rounding Station Hairpin on his way to a famous victory

EPICS

# 2 In an epic two-hour chase, first one then the other Ferrari tried and failed to catch Moss

Moss selected the 1961 Monaco GP as his best drive for *Autosport*'s Race of My Life series:

"I started off in the leading battle, and I was in second by the end of lap two. I took the lead on the 14th lap, and between then and the finish the gap between myself and the Ferraris was never more than a few seconds.

"I got pole position, and if I had done 100 laps at the pace I did when I got pole, I would only have been 40 seconds quicker over the whole length of the race.

"The pressure was on so hard I was really hanging it out the whole race. At every corner I said to myself, 'I will try to do a faster lap from here' and of course I couldn't do it – I would get six inches off a kerb and have to say, 'I'll try again!'

It was relentless, and when there is that much pressure on you it is really difficult to keep up your concentration.

"After that race I was really elated – I was convinced the Ferraris were playing with me. I thought they were just going to come flying past on the last lap because I knew they had an extra 50 horsepower. It was only when I crossed the line that I knew I had won.

"It was the race in which I managed to do nearly 100% of the running flat out.

"Looking back, I've done over 500 races in my career and I've won 212, so it's quite hard to choose, but that one was the best."

## Race 95 — 1961 MONACO GP Monte Carlo — STIRLING MOSS

**Round 1/8** — **14 May 1961** — **Lotus-Climax 18** 113.788kph, 70.704mph

A famous against-the-odds victory by Moss, his Walker Lotus-Climax giving away over 30bhp to the Ferraris. Moss demonstrated the potential of his nimble Lotus by taking pole from Ginther's Ferrari and Jim Clark's works Lotus. But at the off, Ginther took an immediate lead, pulling out 7s in five laps until Moss began to reel him in. On lap 14 Moss went by and quickly built up a 10s lead. But then the superior Ferraris came back at him, the pursuit led by two Americans. In a tense and exciting two-hour chase, first Phil Hill then Ginther tried to catch Moss but his cornering speed and race craft, particularly cutting through the traffic, defied the might of Maranello. Soon after lap 70 the Ferrari pit signalled the faster Ginther to take up the attack from Hill, but at 100 laps Ginther finished still 3.6s short of the mighty Moss.

| Pos | Driver | Car | Time/gap | Grid | Stops | Tyres |
|---|---|---|---|---|---|---|
| 1 | Stirling Moss | Lotus-Climax | 2h 45m 50.1s | 1 | 0 | D |
| 2 | Richie Ginther | Ferrari | −3.6s | 2 | 0 | D |
| 3 | Phil Hill | Ferrari | −41.3s | 5 | 0 | D |
| 4r | Wolfgang von Trips | Ferrari | −2 laps | 6 | 0 | D |
| 5 | Dan Gurney | Porsche | −2 laps | 10 | 0 | D |
| 6 | Bruce McLaren | Cooper-Climax | −5 laps | 7 | 1 | D |

**POLE POSITION** Moss, Lotus-Climax, 1m 39.1s (0.2s), 114.248kph, 70.991mph
**LAPS** 100 x 3.145km, 1.954 miles
**DISTANCE** 314.500 km, 195.421 miles
**STARTERS/FINISHERS** 16/13
**WEATHER** Hazy, warm, dry
**LAP LEADERS** Ginther 1-13 (33); Moss 14-100 (100)
**WINNER'S LAPS** 1 P3, 2-13 P2, 14-100 P1
**FASTEST LAP** R Ginther, Ferrari/Moss, Lotus-Climax, 1m 36.3s (laps 84/85), 117.570kph, 73.055mph
**CHAMPIONSHIP** Moss 9, Ginther 6, P Hill 4, von Trips 3, Gurney 2

*RACE POD*

1 EPICS

# Senna annihilated the Williams pair, both well ahead in dry qualifying

Senna said: "Conditions were difficult. I don't know how many times we stopped for tyres. I think it's surely the record in any race, for pitstops. Driving with slicks in the damp and really slippery conditions was a tremendous effort, because you just don't get the feeling from the car. I had to gamble on this in some occasions because on wet tyres my car was a bit funny, with low water in the circuit. When there was a lot of water it was OK. But just light water or damp, my car was not working well so I had to gamble on the slicks, even on damp conditions. It paid off, and of course I'm over the moon with the result.

"If you try too hard you can be off the circuit. If you go too easy, they come and get you. In conditions like this it's gambling and taking chances that pay off, and we gambled well.

"The race told me everything about myself; it was what I wanted to prove to myself. A natural tendency for a driver, as long as he is able to do his job with a team, is to learn continuously. Experience only adds to your driving. Providing you can keep your motivation at a single level. I think that's been the case almost every year of my career from 1984, always just a little bit better – not necessarily faster, but more consistent, less susceptible to mistakes, think always, always, always. That experience allows you to be a step ahead all the time, ready to make the next move."

## Race 535 — 1993 EUROPEAN GP Donington — AYRTON SENNA

**Round 3/16** — **11 April 1993** — **McLaren-Ford MP4/8** 165.603kph, 102.901mph

Starting P4 in pouring rain, Senna fell to P5 off the grid but completed lap one in the lead. He dealt with Michael Schumacher at Redgate, fast-starting Karl Wendlinger around the outside of Craner Curves, Hill at Coppice and leader Prost at the Melbourne hairpin. Blending skill with strategy, Senna annihilated the Williams pair, both way ahead in dry qualifying. Track conditions fluctuated with each rain squall, a then record 63 pit stops as drivers switched between wets and slicks. Senna, optimally, made four stops plus, his pit crew unprepared, one drive-through. Hill made six stops to finish an unlapped second, while P3 went to the lapped Prost, who made seven on laps 19, 22, 33, 38, 48, 53 and 69. The other Brazilian star turn was rookie Barrichello, P3 with six to go when his Jordan failed.

| Pos | Driver | Car | Time/gap | Grid | Stops | Tyres |
|---|---|---|---|---|---|---|
| 1 | Ayrton Senna | McLaren-Ford | 1h 50m 46.570s | 4 | 4 | G |
| 2 | Damon Hill | Williams-Renault | –1m 23.199s | 2 | 6 | G |
| 3 | Alain Prost | Williams-Renault | –1 lap | 1 | 7 | G |
| 4 | Johnny Herbert | Lotus-Ford | –1 lap | 11 | 1 | G |
| 5 | Riccardo Patrese | Benetton-Ford | –2 laps | 10 | 4 | G |
| 6 | Fabrizio Barbazza | Minardi-Ford | –2 laps | 20 | 2 | G |

**POLE POSITION** Prost, Williams-Renault, 1m 10.458s (0.304s), 205.552kph, 127.724mph
**LAPS** 76 x 4.023 km, 2.500 miles
**DISTANCE** 305.748 km, 189.983 miles
**STARTERS/FINISHERS** 25/11
**WEATHER** Overcast, cool, persistent rain showers
**LAP LEADERS** Senna 1-18, 20-34, 39-76 (71); Prost 19, 35-38 (5)
**WINNER'S LAPS** 1-18 P1, 19 P2, 20-34 P1, 35-38 P2, 39-76 P1
**FASTEST LAP** Officially, A Senna, McLaren-Ford, 1m 18.029s (lap 57 via the pit-lane), 185.608kph, 115.331mph; best circuit lap was D Hill, Williams-Renault, 1m 19.379s (lap 55), 182.451kph, 113.370mph
**CHAMPIONSHIP** Senna 26, Prost 14, Hill 12, Blundell 6, Herbert 6

*RACE POD*

Track conditions at Donington fluctuated with each rain squall, but blending skill with strategy, Senna defeated the sophisticated Williams-Renaults

CHAPTER 6

# REGENMEISTERS

## WINNERS IN THE RAIN

Imagine driving down a motorway in torrential rain: rivulets forming across the asphalt, standing water pooling, the steering going disconcertingly light as the tyres come perilously close to aquaplaning, visibility impaired by an impenetrable fog of traffic spray, windscreen wipers scarcely coping with each burst of rain, the unnervingly close proximity of other vehicles.

Now visualise it amplified, hurtling at 300kph in an open cockpit with a misted-up helmet visor, racing wheel-to-wheel in a battle for victory. Tradition dictates that Formula 1 is not deterred by such conditions, a challenge necessitating a mindset somewhere between heroism and total folly. And to win, the special qualities needed are skill, concentration, willpower and immense courage. When the heavens open, a driver's talent is laid bare, with every twitch of the wheel and millimetre of throttle control separating triumph from disaster.

In the treacherous conditions described, with the unrelenting rain varying only in intensity throughout the race, the extraordinary ability of the Regenmeisters (Rainmasters) to dance on the knife-edge of control often results in breathtaking, virtuoso performances. Yet rain is also known as 'the great leveller', as it can elevate the underdog to hero as occasionally skill triumphs over superior machinery. This is underscored by the fact that just one of the ten wet-weather winners featured in this chapter was not a World Champion or title contender. His near 2½-hour triumph between the unforgiving barriers on a rain-soaked Monte Carlo circuit exemplifies some of the factors integral to determining the ranking of these resolute feats of skill.

Unlike other chapters, where comparison between 20th and 21st-century Grand Prix racing are reasonable to draw, the dynamic of rain profoundly alters that perspective. The title Regenmeisters pays homage to those who mastered the unique challenges of a soaking wet 14.2-mile Nürburgring, grappling with 1960s chassis and tyre technology, while racing for over two hours with no respite from a safety car, a red flag, and with a genuine spectre of death. These feats demand full recognition when evaluating the standing of the ten greatest wet-weather races. This chapter seeks to balance the remarkable artistry of the rainmasters with the evolving technology and track conditions that define Formula 1's wet-weather history.

**WHEN THE HEAVENS OPEN, A DRIVER'S TALENT IS LAID BARE, WITH EVERY TWITCH OF THE WHEEL AND MILLIMETRE OF THROTTLE CONTROL SEPARATING TRIUMPH FROM DISASTER**

## 10 REGENMEISTERS

# Hamilton won superbly, Rosberg did enough, while Verstappen defied physics

The gesture says it all. Verstappen accepts the plaudits after 'walking on water' during his charge from P14 to P3

## Race 955 2016 BRAZILIAN GP Interlagos

**Round 20/21** **13 November 2016**

On a streaming track, fast and flawless Hamilton led all the way to beat Rosberg by 11s, although SCs had negated previous leads of 3s and 18s. With five SCs and two red flags, the treacherous surface and atrocious visibility caught out many, even Verstappen losing control – broadside and heading for the barrier – before making the save of the day. Seven laps later, on lap 44, Rosberg half-spun leaving Juncao, a lost crown flashing before his eyes, but fortune smiled on Nico, the barrier avoided. In a mesmeric drive over the last 16 laps, Max on fresh tyres charged from P14 to P3, taking inside or outside lines at will. Braking later without locking, he passed car after car, including team-mate Daniel Ricciardo, to finish P3 behind rainmaster Hamilton, his first win in Brazil.

| Pos | Driver | Car | Time/gap | Grid (pen) | Stops[1] | Tyres (h/m/s) |
|---|---|---|---|---|---|---|
| 1 | Lewis Hamilton | Mercedes | 3h 1m 1.335s[2] | 1 | 2 | www |
| 2 | Nico Rosberg | Mercedes | –11.455s | 2 | 2 | www |
| 3 | Max Verstappen | Red Bull-TAG Heuer | –21.481s | 4 | 5 | wiwwiw |
| 4 | Sergio Pérez | Force India-Mercedes | –25.356s | 9 | 2 | www |
| 5 | Sebastian Vettel | Ferrari | –26.334s | 5 | 3 | wiww |
| 6 | Carlos Sainz | Toro Rosso-Ferrari | –29.160s | 15 | 2 | www |

[1]Including two red flags [2]Including stoppages of 1h 1m 17s

## LEWIS HAMILTON

**Mercedes F1 W07** 101.393kph, 63.002mph

**POLE POSITION** Hamilton, Mercedes, 1m 10.736s (0.102s), 219.299kph, 136.266mph
**LAPS** 71 x 4.309 km, 2.677 miles (SC start after 10m delay; red flag lap 20, 34m 37s stoppage, SC restart; red flag lap 28, 26m 40s stoppage, SC restart)
**DISTANCE** 305.909 km, 190.083 miles
**STARTERS/FINISHERS** 21/16
**WEATHER** Overcast, cool, continuous rain, wet or very wet
**LAP LEADERS** Hamilton 1-71 (71); SC 1-7, 13-20, 21-28, 29-31, 48-55 (34)
**WINNER'S LAPS** 1-71 P1
**FASTEST LAP** Verstappen, Red Bull-TAG Heuer, 1m 25.305s (lap 67), 181.846kph, 112.993mph
**CHAMPIONSHIP** Rosberg 367, Hamilton 355, Ricciardo 246, Vettel 197, Verstappen 192

RACE POD

9 REGENMEISTERS

# Ickx and Rodríguez put on a masterly display of wet-weather driving

Rodríguez in the BRM gets crossed up chasing Ickx's Ferrari, the duelling pair lapping the entire field in a race lasting close on two hours

## Race 201 — 1971 DUTCH GP Zandvoort

**Round 4/11** — **20 June 1971**

Ickx, Rodríguez and Jackie Stewart's Tyrrell on the front row, but in the very wet race-day conditions, championship leader Stewart was soon in trouble, as were most of the Goodyear runners, Firestone wets making a clean sweep of the available points. Ickx's Ferrari and Rodríguez in the BRM proceeded to put on a masterly display of wet-weather driving, leaving the rest spinning and sliding in their wake. Pole-sitter Ickx led until passed by Rodríguez on lap nine, to pull out 9s. Ickx fought back, retaking the lead on lap 30, losing it the next, then from lap 32 edging away as the rain eased, 15s up by lap 60. But as the rain intensified in the final ten laps, the BRM closed in again to finish 8s behind. The two rainmasters lapped Regazzoni in P3 once, the rest at least twice.

| Pos | Driver | Car | Time/gap | Grid | Stops | Tyres |
|---|---|---|---|---|---|---|
| 1 | Jacky Ickx | Ferrari | 1h 56m 20.09s | 1 | 0 | F |
| 2 | Pedro Rodríguez | BRM | –7.99s | 2 | 0 | F |
| 3 | Clay Regazzoni | Ferrari | –1 lap | 4 | 0 | F |
| 4 | Ronnie Peterson | March-Ford | –2 laps | 13 | 0 | F |
| 5 | John Surtees | Surtees-Ford | –2 laps | 7 | 0 | F |
| 6 | Jo Siffert | BRM | –2 laps | 8 | 0 | F |

## JACKY ICKX

**Ferrari 312B2** 151.379kph, 94.062mph

**POLE POSITION** Ickx, Ferrari, 1m 17.42s (0.04s), 194.973kph, 121.151mph
**LAPS** 70 x 4.193 km, 2.605 miles
**DISTANCE** 293.510 km, 182.379 miles
**STARTERS/FINISHERS** 24/12
**WEATHER** Overcast, rain
**LAP LEADERS** Ickx 1-8, 30, 32-70 (48); Rodríguez 9-29, 31 (22)
**WINNER'S LAPS** 1-8 P1, 9-29 P2, 30 P1, 31 P2, 32-70 P1
**FASTEST LAP** Ickx, Ferrari, 1m 34.95s (lap 49), 158.976kph, 98.783mph
**CHAMPIONSHIP** Stewart 24, Ickx 19, Andretti 9, Peterson 9, Rodríguez 9

*RACE POD*

# 8 REGENMEISTERS

## Verstappen was in a class of his own, winning from 17th spot on the grid

Racing resumed on lap 43, this time Verstappen (centre) immediately snatching the lead from Ocon at Turn 1. Norris (right) in P5 went off, denting his title ambitions

## Race 1122 2024 SÃO PAULO GP Interlagos

**Round 21/24** **3 November 2024**

In their title battle, Norris took a superb pole while Verstappen went out in Q2, and with an engine penalty would start P17. On the opening lap, Lando lost out to Russell while Verstappen rose to 11th. By lap 28 he'd reached P5 when the leading pair pitted under a SC, elevating Ocon, Verstappen and Gasly into the top three. Soon afterwards the rain intensified and another crash brought out the red flag. At the SC restart leader Ocon surprisingly pulled away from Verstappen until yet another SC intervention. Racing resumed on lap 43 for the final 27 laps, this time Verstappen immediately snatching the lead at turn 1. Pumping in lap after fastest lap on the still treacherous surface, Verstappen was in a class of his own, effectively clinching the title.

| Pos | Driver | Car | Time/gap | Grid † | Stops | Tyres |
|---|---|---|---|---|---|---|
| 1 | Max Verstappen | Red Bull-Honda RBPT | 2h 6m 54.430s | 17 (-5) | 1 | ii |
| 2 | Esteban Ocon | Alpine-Renault | –19.477s | 4 | 1 | ii |
| 3 | Pierre Gasly | Alpine-Renault | –22.532s | 13 | 1 | ii |
| 4 | George Russell | Mercedes | –23.265s | 2 | 2 | iii |
| 5 | Charles Leclerc | Ferrari | –30.177s | 6 | 2 | iii |
| 6 | Lando Norris | McLaren-Mercedes | –31.372s | 1 | 2 | iii |

† Including red flag stop

## MAX VERSTAPPEN

**Red Bull-Honda RBPT RB20** 140.540kph, 87.327mph

**POLE POSITION** Norris, McLaren-Mercedes, 1m 23.405s (0.173s), 185.988kph, 115.567mph
**LAPS** 69 x 4.309 km, 3.425 miles (Race red-flagged on lap 32 due to accidents, 25m delay, SC restart)
**DISTANCE** 297.261 km, 184.709 miles.
**STARTERS/FINISHERS** 18/15 (2 DNS)
**WEATHER** Overcast, cool, wet throughout. Intermittent rain then downpour mid race.
**LAP LEADERS** Russell 1-28 (28); Ocon 29-42 (14); Verstappen 43-69 (27); VSC 27 (1); SC 28-33, 40-42 (9)
**WINNER'S LAPS** 1 P11, 2-4 P10, 5 P9, 6-9 P8, 10 P7, 11-23 P6, 24-27 P5, 28 P4, 29-42 P2, 43-69 P1
**FASTEST LAP** Verstappen, Red Bull-Honda RBPT, 1m 20.472s (lap 67), 192.767kph, 119.779mph
**SPRINT RACE(SQ)** 1 Norris(2); 2 Piastri(1); 3 Leclerc(3); 4 Verstappen(4); 5 C Sainz(5); 6 Russell(6); 7 Gasly(7); 8 S Pérez(13)
**CHAMPIONSHIP** Verstappen 393, Norris 331, Leclerc 307, Piastri 262, Sainz 244

**RACE POD**

REGENMEISTERS

# 7 Graham Hill won brilliantly around the notorious Nordschleife circuit

In wet and demanding conditions Hill (11) won from Surtees and Gurney (7), all three displaying immense skill and courage

## Race 108 1962 GERMAN GP Nürburgring

**Round 6/9** **5 August 1962**

Gurney, Hill, Clark and Surtees made up the front row, and in wet and demanding conditions were to fill the first four positions by the close. The start was delayed by over an hour as the torrential rain had caused landslides but, once under way, the first three battled throughout the almost two hours and 40 minutes' duration, crossing the line just 4.4s apart. Pole-sitter Gurney led the opening two laps before conceding to first Hill and then Surtees on lap five. Clark's fourth place came after a fine recovery drive from a grid delay caused by failure to switch on his petrol pump. He then clawed his way back from tenth place, even catching the leaders until, after a particularly frightening slide in the treacherous conditions on lap 11, he wisely settled for fourth.

| Pos | Driver | Car | Time/gap | Grid | Stops | Tyres |
|---|---|---|---|---|---|---|
| 1 | Graham Hill | BRM | 2h 38m 45.3s | 2 | 0 | D |
| 2 | John Surtees | Lola-Climax | –2.5s | 4 | 0 | D |
| 3 | Dan Gurney | Porsche | –4.4s | 1 | 0 | D |
| 4 | Jim Clark | Lotus-Climax | –42.1s | 3 | 0 | D |
| 5 | Bruce McLaren | Cooper-Climax | –1m 19.6s | 5 | 0 | D |
| 6 | Ricardo Rodríguez | Ferrari | –1m 23.8s | 10 | 0 | D |

## GRAHAM HILL

**BRM P57** 129.312kph, 80.351mph

**POLE POSITION** Gurney, Porsche, 8m 47.2s (3.0s), 155.759kph, 96.784mph
**LAPS** 15 x 22.810 km, 14.173 miles
**DISTANCE** 342.150 km, 212.602 miles
**STARTERS/FINISHERS** 26/16
**WEATHER** Rain throughout, often heavy
**LAP LEADERS** Gurney 1-2 (2); G Hill 3-15 (13)
**WINNER'S LAPS** 1-2 P2, 3-15 P1
**FASTEST LAP** G Hill, BRM, 10m 12.2s (lap 3), 134.133kph, 83.346mph
**CHAMPIONSHIP** G Hill 28, J Clark 21, Surtees 19, McLaren 18, P Hill 14

RACE POD

## 6 REGENMEISTERS

# Finishing over a minute ahead, Hamilton made the rest look ordinary

Hamilton (left) passed teammate Kovalainen for the lead, the rest of the stuggling field slithering in his wake

## Race 794 — 2008 BRITISH GP Silverstone

**Round 9/18** — **6 July 2008**

Hamilton's imperious wet-weather performance made the rest look ordinary, championship rival Felipe Massa spinning repeatedly. A Kovalainen and Mark Webber front row was unusual, Räikkönen and Hamilton next. But dire race-day weather had Webber spinning on lap one and leader Kovalainen conceding to his faster teammate soon after. Räikkönen's strong early challenge fell way when Ferrari wrongly decided not to change his tyres at their lap 21 stop. Optimising his speed by using unique and varying lines, Hamilton finished over a minute ahead of the struggling field. That day there were many red faces, including the Ferrari pair and Robert Kubica, but not Heidfeld and Barrichello who shared Hamilton's podium. At mid-season, just two points separated the four championship contenders.

| Pos | Driver | Car | Time/gap | Grid (pen) | Stops | Tyres (h/m) |
|---|---|---|---|---|---|---|
| 1 | Lewis Hamilton | McLaren-Mercedes | 1h 39m 9.440s | 4 | 2 | www |
| 2 | Nick Heidfeld | BMW | –1m 8.577s | 5 | 2 | www |
| 3 | Rubens Barrichello | Honda | –1m 22.273s | 16 | 3 | wwxw |
| 4 | Kimi Räikkönen | Ferrari | –1 lap | 3 | 2 | www |
| 5 | Heikki Kovalainen | McLaren-Mercedes | –1 lap | 1 | 2 | www |
| 6 | Fernando Alonso | Renault | –1 lap | 6 | 2 | www |

## LEWIS HAMILTON

**McLaren-Mercedes MP4-23** 186.585kph, 115.939mph

**POLE POSITION** Kovalainen, McLaren-Mercedes, 1m 21.049s (0.505s), 228.350kph, 141.890mph
**LAPS** 60 x 5.141 km, 3.195 miles
**DISTANCE** 308.355 km, 191.603 miles
**STARTERS/FINISHERS** 20/13
**WEATHER** Overcast, cold, rain
**LAP LEADERS** Kovalainen 1-4 (4); Hamilton 5-21, 23-60 (55); Heidfeld 22 (1)
**WINNER'S LAPS** 1-4 P2, 5-21 P1, 22 P2, 23-60 P1
**FASTEST LAP** Räikkönen, Ferrari, 1m 32.150s (lap 18), 200.842kph, 124.797mph
**CHAMPIONSHIP** Hamilton 48, Massa 48, Räikkönen 48, Kubica 46, Heidfeld 36

*RACE POD*

5 REGENMEISTERS

# Even the sceptics had stopped waiting for the inevitable collision

The surprise victory of the 1972 season was achieved by Beltoise on a streaming wet Monte Carlo circuit. In a virtuoso performance he led every lap

## Race 212 — 1972 MONACO GP Monte Carlo

**Round 4/12** — **14 May 1972**

## JEAN-PIERRE BELTOISE

**BRM P160B** 102.756kph, 63.849mph

From row two in the teeming rain, Jean-Pierre Beltoise aimed his BRM down the inside at Ste Devote to lead up the hill in a ball of spray. The advantage of a clear track ahead enabled him to pull away from the rest, but it was more than that – he was driving brilliantly. By half-distance, as he adroitly gained time passing backmarkers, even the sceptics had stopped waiting for the Frenchman's inevitable collision with the barriers. After 2½ hours in unrelenting weather, he finished more than 30s ahead of an acknowledged rainmaster, Ickx in the Ferrari, the only two cars to complete the full distance. Beltoise's one and only Grand Prix victory was a virtuoso performance, the exceptional conditions he coped with borne out by his race average of under 64mph.

| Pos | Driver | Car | Time/gap | Grid | Stops | Tyres |
|---|---|---|---|---|---|---|
| 1 | Jean-Pierre Beltoise | BRM | 2h 26m 54.7s | 4 | 0 | F |
| 2 | Jacky Ickx | Ferrari | –38.2s | 2 | 0 | F |
| 3 | Emerson Fittipaldi | Lotus-Ford | –1 lap | 1 | 0 | F |
| 4 | Jackie Stewart | Tyrrell-Ford | –2 laps | 8 | 0 | G |
| 5 | Brian Redman | McLaren-Ford | –3 laps | 10 | 0 | G |
| 6 | Chris Amon | Matra | –3 laps | 6 | 4 | G |

**POLE POSITION** Fittipaldi, Lotus-Ford, 1m 21.4s (0.2s), 139.091kph, 86.427mph
**LAPS** 80 x 3.145km, 1.954 miles
**DISTANCE** 251.600 km, 156.337 miles
**STARTERS/FINISHERS** 25/17
**WEATHER** Overcast, rain
**LAP LEADERS** Beltoise 1-80 (80)
**WINNER'S LAPS** 1-80 P1
**FASTEST LAP** Beltoise, BRM, 1m 40.0s (lap 9), 113.220kph, 70.352mph
**CHAMPIONSHIP** Fittipaldi 19, Ickx 16, Hulme 15, Stewart 12, Regazzoni 7

*RACE POD*

**4** REGENMEISTERS

# Clark's extraordinary winning margin was very nearly five minutes

The original 8.8-mile Spa was a fearsome racetrack of gruesome disasters that Clark loathed, making his astonishing 1963 display all the more courageous

## Race 113 | 1963 BELGIAN GP Spa-Francorchamps | JIM CLARK

**Round 2/10** | **9 June 1963** | **Lotus-Climax 25** 183.175kph, 113.819mph

After a troubled practice, Clark made a scintillating start from the third row to lead by Eau Rouge. In damp to wet conditions he pulled away at an astonishing rate from the rest of the field led by pole-sitter Graham Hill, the Lotus more then 30s to the good by half-distance. The gearbox on Hill's BRM didn't last much longer and it was also around this time that a thunderstorm hit the circuit, the track awash, visibility minimal. Times increased from around four minutes per lap to more than six as the drivers tiptoed their way around. The storm reached its peak on lap 28, by which time Clark had lapped all but Bruce McLaren, who crossed the line to start his final lap just as Clark finished the race. Thus, Clark's extraordinary winning margin was very nearly five minutes.

| Pos | Driver | Car | Time/gap | Grid | Stops | Tyres |
|---|---|---|---|---|---|---|
| 1 | Jim Clark | Lotus-Climax | 2h 27m 47.6s | 8 | 0 | D |
| 2 | Bruce McLaren | Cooper-Climax | –4m 54.0s | 5 | 0 | D |
| 3 | Dan Gurney | Brabham-Climax | –1 lap | 2 | 0 | D |
| 4 | Richie Ginther | BRM | –1 lap | 9 | 0 | D |
| 5 | Jo Bonnier | Cooper-Climax | –2 laps | 13 | NA | D |
| 6 | Carel Godin de Beaufort | Porsche | –2 laps | 18 | NA | D |

**POLE POSITION** G Hill, BRM, 3m 54.1s (0.9s), 216.830kph, 134.732mph
**LAPS** 32 x 14.100 km, 8.761 miles
**DISTANCE** 451.200 km, 280.363 miles
**STARTERS/FINISHERS** 20/8
**WEATHER** Overcast, wet mid-race and very wet over closing laps
**LAP LEADERS** Clark 1-32 (32)
**WINNER'S LAPS** 1-32 P1
**FASTEST LAP** Clark, Lotus-Climax, 3m 58.1s (lap 16), 213.188kph, 132.469mph
**CHAMPIONSHIP** McLaren 10, G Hill 9, Clark 9, Ginther 9, Gurney 4

**RACE POD**

Schumacher dives past Villeneuve on his way to a 45s victory, his first for Ferrari

3

REGENMEISTERS

# Schumacher's first Ferrari win was one of the great wet-weather drives

Michael Schumacher's first triumph for the Scuderia at a rain-soaked Barcelona was a masterclass. Despite lacking dry-weather pace – Schumacher's F310 was nearly a second off Damon Hill's pole-sitting Williams – Ferrari gambled on a full-wet setup, maximising downforce and softening the suspension.

From his P3 grid slot, Schumacher endured a disastrous start – "I went for the clutch and there was nothing," he later explained. "I nearly stalled, then tried it again – I just had an on/off clutch for some reason," after which he produced a pace utterly beyond any of his rivals as he began to slice through the field. Once in the lead, he held it through two pit stops – even when his V10 engine intermittently dropped cylinders – preventing anyone from challenging his dominance. Meanwhile, more than half the field spun out or retired in the treacherous conditions.

Schumacher's knack for finding grip, experimenting with unconventional lines, and pushing the limits of the drenched circuit stood out. This victory is widely acknowledged as one of Formula 1's legendary wet-weather drives, earning comparison with Ayrton Senna's masterclass at Estoril in 1985.

Even rival Williams engineer James Robinson told *Autosport* magazine: "Watching the Ferrari, I don't think the car was that brilliant. It looked like it was on ice. But the guy is just something else. He was pretty amazing."

**Race 588** **1996 SPANISH GP** Cataluña
**Round 7/16** **2 June 1996**

**MICHAEL SCHUMACHER**
**Ferrari F310** 153.785kph, 95.558mph

Two weeks after his Monaco *faux pas*, the reigning champion claimed his first Ferrari victory with one of the great wet-weather drives. He almost stalled on the grid, dropping way behind, but recovered to P6 after one lap. On lap nine he overtook Alesi for P2, then overcame leader Villeneuve on lap 12. "He left me standing," Jacques shrugged afterwards, the Ferrari going away at a rate of 4s a lap, Schumacher's lead over a minute at its maximum. On lap 37 Alesi got ahead of Villeneuve during the pit stops, both drivers doing well to remain on the same lap as the mesmeric Michael. On the other hand, the German's V10 sometimes sounded more like a V8 or V9… Only six cars completed the two-hour ordeal, while pole-sitter Damon Hill got his wet race set-up badly wrong, going off for a third and final time on lap 11.

| Pos | Driver | Car | Time/gap | Grid | Stops | Tyres |
|---|---|---|---|---|---|---|
| 1 | Michael Schumacher | Ferrari | 1h 59m 49.307s | 3 | 2 | G |
| 2 | Jean Alesi | Benetton-Renault | –45.302s | 4 | 1 | G |
| 3 | Jacques Villeneuve | Williams-Renault | –48.388s | 2 | 1 | G |
| 4 | Heinz-Harald Frentzen | Sauber-Ford | –1 lap | 11 | 1 | G |
| 5 | Mika Häkkinen | McLaren-Mercedes | –1 lap | 10 | 1 | G |
| 6 | Pedro Diniz | Ligier-Mugen Honda | –2 laps | 17 | 1 | G |

**POLE POSITION** D Hill, Williams-Renault, 1m 20.650s (0.434s), 211.000kph, 131.110mph
**LAPS** 65 x 4.727 km, 2.937 miles
**DISTANCE** 307.114 km, 190.832 miles
**STARTERS/FINISHERS** 20/6
**WEATHER** Overcast, warm, torrential rain
**LAP LEADERS** Villeneuve 1-11 (11); Schumacher 12-65 (54)
**WINNER'S LAPS** 1 P6, 2-3 P5, 4 P4, 5-8 P3, 9-11 P2, 12-65 P1
**FASTEST LAP** Schumacher, Ferrari, 1m 45.517s (lap 14), 161.274kph, 100.211mph
**CHAMPIONSHIP** Hill 43, Schumacher 26, Villeneuve 26, Alesi 17, Panis 11

***RACE POD***

**2** REGENMEISTERS

# From only his 16th Grand Prix start, Senna took a stupendous win to signal his intent

The 1993 European Grand Prix at Donington may be celebrated as Senna's wet-weather masterpiece, but the man himself held his first Formula 1 world championship victory in even higher regard. Considering his relative inexperience and the challenging nature of the turbocharged 1985 Lotus-Renault, it's easy to see why.

Senna had already shown his brilliance in the rain coming from behind during the 1984 Monaco GP. But at Estoril, he started from pole position for the first time in his career – an advantage he immediately capitalised on, leading from the outset in treacherous conditions. By the end of the first lap, he had pulled 2.7 seconds clear of teammate Elio de Angelis.

Senna continued to stretch his lead as de Angelis fended off Alain Prost's advancing McLaren. The rain intensified just before the halfway mark, prompting Senna – 37 seconds ahead at the time – to signal for the race to be stopped. "The big danger was that conditions changed all the time," Senna said later. "It was difficult even to keep the car in a straight line sometimes and for sure the race should have been stopped. It was *much* worse than Monaco last year. Once I nearly spun in front of the pits, like Prost, and I was lucky to stay on the road."

Senna's performance at Estoril stands as one of Formula 1's most iconic wet-weather drives, his spellbinding performance solidifying his reputation as a true rainmaster.

**In only his second race for Lotus, Senna took the first of his 41 championship race victories. It was a virtuoso performance by the 25-year-old**

## Race 406 — 1985 PORTUGUESE GP Estoril — AYRTON SENNA

**Round 2/16** — **21 April 1985** — **Lotus-Renault 97T** 145.160kph, 90.198mph

From only his 16th Grand Prix start, Senna made his presence known with a stunning pole in the dry and a stupendous win in the wet. Never headed over the two-hour duration, it was a mesmeric error-free performance when many others, including Alain Prost (McLaren-TAG) and Keke Rosberg (Williams-Honda), were bested by the atrocious conditions. For over half the race teammate de Angelis held P2, albeit an ever-widening gap, finishing up fourth with a deflating tyre. Alboreto took another well-driven second and an early championship lead, but finished a minute behind Senna, the remainder lapped. Near half-distance an incident emphasised the magnitude of Senna's feat. Chasing de Angelis, Prost's McLaren fishtailed, spun, then crashed… and that was on the straight!

| Pos | Driver | Car | Time/gap | Grid | Stops | Tyres |
|---|---|---|---|---|---|---|
| 1 | Ayrton Senna | Lotus-Renault | 2h 0m 28.006s | 1 | 0 | G |
| 2 | Michele Alboreto | Ferrari | –1m 2.978s | 5 | 0 | G |
| 3 | Patrick Tambay | Renault | –1 lap | 12 | 0 | G |
| 4 | Elio de Angelis | Lotus-Renault | –1 lap | 4 | 0 | G |
| 5 | Nigel Mansell | Williams-Honda | –2 laps | 9 | 0 | G |
| 6 | Stefan Bellof | Tyrrell-Ford | –2 laps | 21 | 0 | G |

**POLE POSITION** Senna, Lotus-Renault, 1m 21.007s (0.413s), 193.317kph, 120.121mph
**LAPS** 67 x 4.350 km, 2.703 miles (Scheduled for 69 laps but stopped after two hours)
**DISTANCE** 291.450 km, 181.099 miles
**STARTERS/FINISHERS** 26/9
**WEATHER** Overcast, cold, rain
**LAP LEADERS** Senna 1-67 (67)
**WINNER'S LAPS** 1-67 P1
**FASTEST LAP** Senna, Lotus-Renault, 1m 44.121s (lap 15), 150.402kph, 93.455mph
**CHAMPIONSHIP** Alboreto 12, Prost 9, Senna 9, de Angelis 7, Tambay 6

RACE POD

1 **REGENMEISTERS**

# Winning by four minutes around the Nordschleife with an injured wrist did seem Herculean

It was Stewart himself who gave the sinuous, undulating, 14.2-mile Nürburgring winding through the forested Eifel mountains the nickname 'Green Hell', and his own words explain why. "An F1 car round the 'Ring was a monster – you were travelling so fast and you took off (and landed) something like 13 times, and it was narrower than today," recalled Stewart. "It was definitely the daddy of them all, there was no racetrack in the world that was even close."

Starting from the third row after a chaotic practice affected by rain, fog, and electrical issues with his blue Tyrrell Matra, Stewart made an exceptional getaway by finding better grip along the pit lane's concrete surface. By the end of the first lap, he had surged past Chris Amon's Ferrari and Graham Hill's Lotus to lead by eight seconds.

Stewart's pace was relentless, extending his lead lap after lap. On lap eight, he recorded the fastest lap of the race, a 9m36s effort that was a staggering 15 seconds quicker than anyone else could manage. *Autosport*'s report described the conditions as "unbelievably bad," calling them "probably the worst at the 'Ring since pre-war days".

By the race's end, Stewart's advantage had grown to over four minutes, a colossal margin underscoring the magnitude of his dominance. This performance, described as "mesmeric" even by Stewart's high standards, stands out as Formula 1's finest display of skill, courage, and mastery in adverse conditions.

Stewart won by more than four minutes around the fearsome Nordschleife, equivalent to winning by over two laps at most circuits!

## Race 169 — 1968 GERMAN GP Nürburgring — JACKIE STEWART

**Round 8/12** — **4 August 1968** — **Matra-Ford MS10** 137.943kph, 85.714mph

Stewart's tame British Grand Prix showing, inhibited by his painful wrist injury, made his Nürburgring drive two weeks later even more extraordinary, winning by over four minutes from Graham Hill. Maybe the atrocious weather made it easier on the injury, but even equipped with Dunlop 'super-wets', two hours 19 minutes around the Nordschleife wearing a wrist support did seem Herculean. Starting from only the third row, Stewart took the lead halfway around the first lap and pulled steadily away in the rain and mist. Despite the challenging conditions, Stewart's performance was near flawless, his only near slip-up when he hit an ever-shifting river of water shortly after the Karussell, but unlike so many others, he neither spun nor crashed.

| Pos | Driver | Car | Time/gap | Grid | Stops | Tyres |
|---|---|---|---|---|---|---|
| 1 | Jackie Stewart | Matra-Ford | 2h 19m 3.2s | 6 | 0 | D |
| 2 | Graham Hill | Lotus-Ford | –4m 3.2s | 4 | 0 | F |
| 3 | Jochen Rindt | Brabham-Repco | –4m 9.4s | 3 | 0 | G |
| 4 | Jacky Ickx | Ferrari | –5m 55.2s | 1 | 2 | F |
| 5 | Jack Brabham | Brabham-Repco | –6m 21.1s | 15 | 0 | G |
| 6 | Pedro Rodríguez | BRM | –6m 25.0s | 14 | 0 | G |

**POLE POSITION** Ickx, Ferrari, 9m 4.0s (10.9s), 151.114kph, 93.898mph
**LAPS** 14 x 22.835km, 14.189 miles
**DISTANCE** 319.690 km, 198.646 miles
**STARTERS/FINISHERS** 20/14
**WEATHER** Murky, very wet
**LAP LEADERS** Stewart 1-14 (14)
**WINNER'S LAPS** 1-14 P1
**FASTEST LAP** Stewart, Matra-Ford, 9m 36.0s (lap 8), 142.719kph, 88.681mph
**CHAMPIONSHIP** G Hill 30, Stewart 26, Ickx 23, Hulme 15, Rodríguez 11

*RACE POD*

CHAPTER 7

# SURPRISES

## SHOCK VICTORIES

Many talented drivers and proficient teams spend years chasing glory, their potential unfulfilled by the cruel realities of racing. Yet Formula 1 occasionally delivers the unpredictable surprise winner defying all expectations. Often born out of circumstance, for many it's a singular, fleeting victory. But even if their day of days was just that once, these upsets and underdog triumphs bring hope to every Formula 1 driver and team owner.

Shock race victories are rare. Across 75 years and 1120 Grands Prix, only 25 drivers and 11 teams have won just the once, a testament to how difficult it is to break through against the sport's dominant forces.

This collection of races includes five drivers who mounted the top step of the podium despite rarely showing race-winning form before, or indeed after, their day of days. Prevailing circumstances, such as weather, served them well, though that takes nothing from their achievement. Two other drivers, after their surprise maiden victory, went on to win again and prove they were not merely 'one hit wonders'. And a further two claimed unexpected victories for unfancied teams, yet the manner of their triumph offered an early glimpse of their latent promise. Both went on to become World Champions.

In this top ten, 'shock wins' as they apply to winning cars and teams include two that etched their name into the sport's history by securing their one and only Formula 1 victory, whereas another 'minnow' team appears twice, yet in two distinct guises and separated by 12 years, proving that lightning can indeed strike twice.

One particular victory marked the arrival of a constructor that would go on to transform Formula 1. To the shocked astonishment of its Italian rival, its innovative rear-engined design not only revolutionised car performance in general but, in this instance, demonstrated one of its numerous benefits, reduced tyre wear, changing the course of the sport forever. Even if it did require the help of a true legend.

From privateer teams defying the might of manufacturers to midfield drivers seizing their moment of destiny, these victories remain some of the most celebrated in the sport's history and, as such, deservedly take their place among the greatest races. Almost without exception they were highly deserved victories, as, on that particular day, the best man or machine triumphed… even if, in many cases, it was just that once.

**EVEN IF THEIR DAY OF DAYS WAS JUST THE ONCE, THESE SHOCK VICTORIES AND SURPRISE TRIUMPHS BRING HOPE TO EVERY FORMULA 1 DRIVER AND TEAM OWNER**

10 SURPRISES

# Superb Pérez wins for midfield team from plumb last

A 1-3 finish for the 'pink Mercs' brought a maiden victory to Sergio Pérez and to Racing Point. He was Mexico's first victor since Pedro Rodríguez 50 years back

## Race 1034 2020 SAKHIR GP BIC, Outer Track

**Round 16/17** **6 December 2020**

From a record 190 starts, Sergio Pérez took his first GP win. Punted down to P18 in a first-lap mêlée that eliminated Max Verstappen and culprit Charles Leclerc, Checo bolted on fresh 'mediums' under the SC and began a stunning one-stop fight back. The Mercedes pair led initially, George Russell, subbing for Covid-hit Lewis Hamilton, leading from a perfect start alongside pole-sitter Bottas to build a 4.9s lead by the end of lap 60. But the following lap, a SC forced Mercedes into a second stop. Recognising its 26s lead over the pack would be negated and make its cars susceptible to the undercut, Mercedes double-stacked its cars, but a disastrous tyre mix-up badly delayed both drivers, Pérez taking the lead. In his extraordinary drive from last place, Sergio had crucially passed the other one-stoppers, Ocon and Stroll, these three making up the final podium.

| Pos | Driver | Car | Time/gap | Grid (pen) | Stops | Tyres (c2/c3/c4) |
|---|---|---|---|---|---|---|
| 1 | Sergio Pérez | Racing Point-Mercedes | 1h 31m 15.114s | 5 | 2 | smh |
| 2 | Esteban Ocon | Renault | –10.518s | 11 | 1 | mh |
| 3 | Lance Stroll | Racing Point-Mercedes | –11.869s | 10 | 1 | sm |
| 4 | Carlos Sainz | McLaren-Renault | –12.580s | 8 | 2 | smm |
| 5 | Daniel Ricciardo | Renault | –13.330s | 7 | 2 | smh |
| 6 | Alex Albon | Red Bull-Honda | –13.842s | 12 | 2 | mhs |

## SERGIO PÉREZ

**Racing Point-Mercedes RP20** 202.513kph, 125.835mph

**POLE POSITION** Bottas, Mercedes, 53.377s (0.026s), 238.956kph, 148.480mph
**LAPS** 87 x 3.543 km, 2.201 miles
**DISTANCE** 307.995 km, 191.379 miles
**STARTERS/FINISHERS** 20/17
**WEATHER** Night race, overcast, warm but cooling, dry but initially sandy surface, gusty wind
**LAP LEADERS** Russell 1-45, 50-63 (59); Bottas 46-49 (4); Pérez 64-87 (24); SC 1-6, 61-68 (14); VSC 55-56 (2)
**WINNER'S LAPS** 1-6 P18, 7 P16, 8 P14, 9 P13, 10 P12, 11-19 P11, 20 P10, 21-27 P9, 28 P8, 29 P6, 30-40 P5, 41-42 P4, 43-47 P3, 48-51 P9, 52-53 P8, 54-55 P7, 56 P4, 57-62 P3, 63 P2, 64-87 P1
**FASTEST LAP** Russell, Mercedes, 55.404s (lap 80), 230.214kph, 143.048mph
**CHAMPIONSHIP** Hamilton 332, Bottas 205, Verstappen 189, Pérez 125, Ricciardo 112

*RACE POD*

9 SURPRISES

# Monza miracle as Gasly wins for AlphaTauri (née Minardi)

Little more than 12 months since his Spa nadir, being dropped by RBR and the death of close friend Anthoine Hubert, Gasly spent a few personal moments on the podium coming to terms with his maiden Grand Prix victory

## Race 1026 2020 ITALIAN GP Monza

**Round 8/17** **6 September 2020**

Until a lap 20 Safety Car, Sainz was on course to finish a brilliant P2 behind Lewis Hamilton. Gasly, holding P10, fortuitously pitted the lap before the SC, rocketing him to P3 behind Hamilton and non-stopping Stroll. On lap 24 an accident red flagged the race and, after a delay, the grid formed up for a standing restart, the order Hamilton, Stroll, Gasly with Sainz P6. Stroll was quickly out of contention, so when Hamilton served his stop/go penalty, for pitting when the pit lane was closed, on lap 28, Gasly led. On lap 34 Sainz passed Kimi Räikkönen for P2, now 4.3s behind Gasly with 19 to go. With a maiden GP victory the prize, both drivers were really on it. Sainz closed to 1.6s by the end of lap 47 but could not reach DRS range until the penultimate lap. Gasly resisted to win by 0.4s and emulate Sebastian Vettel's 2008 victory for Toro Rosso (née Minardi) [See page 101].

| Pos | Driver | Car | Time/gap | Grid (pen) | Stops† | Tyres (c2/c3/c4) |
|---|---|---|---|---|---|---|
| 1 | Pierre Gasly | AlphaTauri-Honda | 1h 47m 6.056s | 10 | 2 | shm |
| 2 | Carlos Sainz | McLaren-Renault | −0.415s | 3 | 2 | smm |
| 3 | Lance Stroll | Racing Point-Mercedes | −3.358s | 8 | 1 | sm |
| 4 | Lando Norris | McLaren-Renault | −6.000s | 6 | 2 | smm |
| 5 | Valtteri Bottas | Mercedes | −7.108s | 2 | 2 | smm |
| 6 | Daniel Ricciardo | Renault | −8.391s | 7 | 2 | smm |

† Including red flag stop

## PIERRE GASLY

**AlphaTauri-Honda AT01** 171.830kph, 106.770mph

**POLE POSITION** Hamilton, Mercedes, 1m 18.887s (0.069s), 264.362kph, 164.266mph
**LAPS** 53 x 5.793 km, 3.600 miles (Race red flagged on lap 26 for accident; suspended for approximately 26 minutes)
**DISTANCE** 306.720 km, 190.586 miles
**STARTERS/FINISHERS** 20/16
**WEATHER** Sunny, hot, dry
**LAP LEADERS** Hamilton 1-20, 22-27 (26); Sainz 21 (1); Gasly 28-53 (26); SC 20-23, 26-27 (6)
**WINNER'S LAPS** 1-18 P10, 19 P11, 20 P15, 21 P14, 22 P9, 23-27 P3, 28-53 P1
**FASTEST LAP** Hamilton, Mercedes, 1m 22.746 (lap 34), 252.033kph, 156.606mph
**CHAMPIONSHIP** Hamilton 164, Bottas 117, Verstappen 110, Stroll 57, Norris 57

RACE POD

## 8 SURPRISES

# Fisichella's Jordan-Ford declared winner after U-turn!

**With Alonso hospitalised following his hefty crash, only winner Räikkönen and second-placed Fisichella mounted the São Paulo podium. Two weeks later at the San Marino GP, the result now reversed, they good naturedly exchanged trophies, as did Ron Dennis and Eddie Jordan**

## Race 700 — 2003 BRAZILIAN GP Interlagos

**Round 3/16** — **6 April 2003**

## GIANCARLO FISICHELLA

**Jordan-Ford EJ13** 152.902kph, 95.009mph

With the track awash and unsuitable 'one-choice' rain tyres, the race was chaotic but thankfully not catastrophic. Starting under the SC, a series of accidents caused three more deployments, the 'river' flowing across turn three collecting six aquaplaning victims. Rubens Barrichello, from his first home GP pole, was denied a fairy tale ending when fuel-feed halted his Ferrari after 46 laps. Coulthard also came close to victory, pitting for tyres while in the lead just one lap before the race was terminated 17 laps early. This was when Mark Webber's Jaguar crashed and Alonso violently smashed into the wreckage. Räikkönen was declared the winner on countback but when the results were re-examined some days later, it confirmed that Fisichella's Jordan had passed Räikkönen when Kimi ran wide on lap 54, the final official lap of the race.

| Pos | Driver | Car | Time/gap | Grid | Stops | Tyres |
|---|---|---|---|---|---|---|
| 1 | Giancarlo Fisichella | Jordan-Ford | 1h 31m 17.748s | 8 | 1 | B |
| 2 | Kimi Räikkönen | McLaren-Mercedes | −0.945s | 4 | 1 | M |
| 3 | Fernando Alonso | Renault | −6.348s | 10 | 4 | M |
| 4 | David Coulthard | McLaren-Mercedes | −8.096s | 2 | 2 | M |
| 5 | Heinz-Harald Frentzen | Sauber-Petronas | −8.642s | 14 | 1 | B |
| 6 | Jacques Villeneuve | BAR-Honda | −16.054s | 13 | 1 | B |

**POLE POSITION** R Barrichello, Ferrari, 1m 13.807s (0.011s), 210.175kph, 130.597mph
**LAPS** 54 x 4.309 km, 2.677 miles (Race scheduledfor 71 laps but stopped due to accident)
**DISTANCE** 232.656 km, 144.566 miles
**STARTERS/FINISHERS** 20/10
**WEATHER** Overcast, hot, heavy rain drying later
**LAP LEADERS** Barrichello 1-8, 45-46 (10); Coulthard 9-10, 27-44, 47-52 (26); Räikkönen 11-26, 53 (17); Fisichella 54 (1); SC 1-8, 20-22, 28-29; 34-36 (16)
**WINNER'S LAPS** 1-6 P8, 7 P10, 8 P19, 9-15 P18, 16-17 P17, 18-19 P16, 20 P14, 21-22 P13, 23-24 P12, 25 P10, 26 P11, 27 P10, 28-29 P8, 30 P9, 31-32 P8, 33 P7, 34-41 P6, 42-46 P5, 47 P4, 48-52 P3, 53 P2, 54 P1
**FASTEST LAP** R Barrichello, Ferrari, 1m 22.032s (lap 46), 189.101kph, 117.502mph
**CHAMPIONSHIP** Räikkönen 24, Coulthard 15, Alonso 14, Fisichella 10, Trulli 9

*RACE POD*

SURPRISES

# Jones was there to claim his and Shadow's maiden victory

**As surprise victories go, at the time this was a big one. Alan Jones! Who's he? Alan was soon to straighten out that misconception, claiming the world title with Williams just three seasons later**

## Race 292 — 1977 AUSTRIAN GP Österreichring — ALAN JONES

**Round 12/17** — **14 August 1977** — **Shadow-Ford DN8** 197.914kph, 122.978mph

Championship leader Lauda stuck it on pole for his home GP, Hunt alongside. With the track drenched from recent rain, most teams opted for wets. Mario Andretti led until yet another engine failure presented James Hunt with the lead on lap 12. Meanwhile, the Shadow of Jones was working exceptionally well in the conditions, and from P14 on the grid came through the field, including passing Lauda, to reach P6 by the end of lap 10. On lap 16 he took P2, where he remained for almost 30 laps, Hunt edging away on the drying surface. But when Hunt's engine let go after 43 laps, Jones was there to reel off the final 11 laps and claim his and Shadow's maiden victory. Behind the shock winner, Lauda finished P2 by a massive 20s. It was all about those opening 10 laps, the track at its wettest, Lauda his most cautious, and Jones simply flying.

| Pos | Driver | Car | Time/gap | Grid | Stops | Tyres |
|---|---|---|---|---|---|---|
| 1 | Alan Jones | Shadow-Ford | 1h 37m 16.49s | 14 | 0 | G |
| 2 | Niki Lauda | Ferrari | –20.13s | 1 | 0 | G |
| 3 | Hans-Joachim Stuck | Brabham-Alfa | –34.50s | 4 | 0 | G |
| 4 | Carlos Reutemann | Ferrari | –34.75s | 5 | 0 | G |
| 5 | Ronnie Peterson | Tyrrell-Ford | –1m 2.09s | 15 | 0 | G |
| 6 | Jochen Mass | McLaren-Ford | –1 lap | 9 | 1 | G |

**POLE POSITION** Lauda, Ferrari, 1m 39.32s (0.13s), 215.377kph, 133.829mph
**LAPS** 54 x 5.942 km, 3.692 miles
**DISTANCE** 320.868 km, 199.378 miles
**STARTERS/FINISHERS** 26/17
**WEATHER** Damp track, drying
**LAP LEADERS** M Andretti, Lotus-Ford 1-11 (11); J Hunt, McLaren-Ford 12-43 (32); Jones 44-54 (11)
**WINNER'S LAPS** 1 P13, 2-4 P12, 5 P11, 6-7 P10, 8 P9, 9 P8, 10 P6, 11 P5, 12-14 P4, 15 P3, 16-43 P2, 44-54 P1
**FASTEST LAP** J Watson, Brabham-Alfa, 1m 40.96s (lap 52), 211.878kph, 131.655mph
**CHAMPIONSHIP** Lauda 54, Scheckter 38, Reutemann 34, Andretti 32, Hunt 22

**RACE POD**

# Astonished winner Brambilla crashes after receiving the chequer

Some say that Vittorio crossed the finish line backwards, but it was 'only' sideways. Reports also have it that he lost control by raising both arms in celebration, his astonished reaction to being given the chequered flag soon after half distance

## Race 262 — 1975 AUSTRIAN GP Österreichring

**Round 12/14** — **17 August 1975**

A tragicomedy. During race-day warm-up Mark Donohue and a track marshal lost their lives when the Penske March left the circuit due to tyre failure. The comedy was to come at the chequered flag. Extreme wet weather stopped the race prematurely after 29 of 54 laps, half-points awarded. After a brilliant wet-weather drive from P8, winner Vittorio Brambilla lost control on being shown the chequer, crossed the finish line sideways, then struck the barrier to complete his jubilant *tour d'honneur* in a very battered March 751. Lauda had started his home GP from pole, resisting Hunt until lap 15, the Ferrari set-up wrong. But Brambilla, up to P3 on lap six, had also slipped by Lauda, and within four laps was leading once the Hesketh lost a cylinder. Vittorio then pulled out 27s in 11 laps before his spectacular sideways victory.

| Pos | Driver | Car | Time/gap | Grid | Stops | Tyres |
|---|---|---|---|---|---|---|
| 1 | Vittorio Brambilla | March-Ford | 57m 56.69s | 8 | 0 | G |
| 2 | James Hunt | Hesketh-Ford | −27.03s | 2 | 0 | G |
| 3 | Tom Pryce | Shadow-Ford | −34.85s | 15 | 0 | F |
| 4 | Jochen Mass | McLaren-Ford | −1m 12.66s | 9 | 0 | F |
| 5 | Ronnie Peterson | Lotus-Ford | −1m 23.33s | 13 | 1 | G |
| 6 | Niki Lauda | Ferrari | −1m 30.28s | 1 | 0 | G |

## VITTORIO BRAMBILLA

**March-Ford 751** 177.499kph, 110.293mph

**POLE POSITION** Lauda, Ferrari, 1m 34.85s (0.12s), 224.350kph, 139.405mph

**LAPS** 29 x 5.911 km, 3.673 miles (Scheduled for 54 laps but stopped due to rain)

**DISTANCE** 171.419 km, 106.515 miles (Minimum distance incomplete; half points awarded)

**STARTERS/FINISHERS** 26/17

**WEATHER** Very wet thoughout

**LAP LEADERS** Lauda 1-14 (14); Hunt 15-18 (4); Brambilla 19-29 (11)

**WINNER'S LAPS** 1 P6, 2-4 P5, 5 P4, 6-14 P3, 15-18 P2, 19-29 P1

**FASTEST LAP** Brambilla, March-Ford, 1m 53.90s (lap 11), 186.827kph, 116.089mph

**CHAMPIONSHIP** Lauda 51.5, Reutemann 34, Fittipaldi 33, Hunt 28, Pace 24

*RACE POD*

5 SURPRISES

# Panis, final leader of this bizarre race, drove magnificently

**Shock but highly deserving winner Olivier Panis holds the French tricolour aloft on his *tour d'honneur*. It was the Frenchman's one and only GP victory**

## Race 587 1996 MONACO GP Monte Carlo

**Round 6/16** **19 May 1996**

## OLIVIER PANIS

**Ligier-Mugen Honda JS43** 124.014kph, 77.059mph

On a wet surface Michael Schumacher was beaten away from pole by Damon Hill and within a minute had sensationally crashed out. Hill drew away from Jean Alesi, then a long gap to a throng headed by Irvine, but with a 26s lead, Hill's Renault blew on lap 41. It was now Alesi's race, but on lap 60 he too retired, a broken rear spring. The third and final leader of this bizarre race, from a P14 grid slot, was Olivier Panis and his Ligier-Mugen. Crucial to his ultimate success were laps 28-30 when the field switched to slicks on the drying surface, Olivier gaining three places to P4. Of 21 starters, just four were running at the finish, 14 retirements due to accidents. In difficult conditions, the race ending three laps early at the two-hour mark, Panis drove magnificently, and to his eternal credit the other finishers all started ahead of him.

| Pos | Driver | Car | Time/gap | Grid | Stops | Tyres |
|---|---|---|---|---|---|---|
| 1 | Olivier Panis | Ligier-Mugen Honda | 2h 0m 45.629s | 14 | 1 | G |
| 2 | David Coulthard | McLaren-Mercedes | –4.828s | 5 | 1 | G |
| 3 | Johnny Herbert | Sauber-Ford | –37.503s | 13 | 1 | G |
| 4 | Heinz-Harald Frentzen | Sauber-Ford | –1 lap | 9 | 3 | G |
| 5r | Mika Salo | Tyrrell-Yamaha | –5 laps | 11 | 1 | G |
| 6r | Mika Häkkinen | McLaren-Mercedes | –5 laps | 8 | 1 | G |

**POLE POSITION** M Schumacher, Ferrari, 1m 20.356s (0.510s), 149.096kph, 92.644mph
**LAPS** 75 x 3.328 km, 2.068 miles (Scheduled for 78 laps but stopped after two hours)
**DISTANCE** 249.600 km, 155.094 miles
**STARTERS/FINISHERS** 21/7
**WEATHER** Overcast, warm, rain, drying later
**LAP LEADERS** D Hill, Williams-Renault 1-27, 30-40 (38); Alesi 28-29, 41-59 (21); Panis 60-75 (16)
**WINNER'S LAPS** 1-6 P12, 7-9 P11, 10-15 P10, 16-17 P9, 18-24 P8, 25-27 P7, 28 P9, 29 P6, 30-35 P4, 36-40 P3, 41-59 P2, 60-75 P1
**FASTEST LAP** J Alesi, Benetton-Renault, 1m 25.205s (lap 59), 140.611kph, 87.372mph
**CHAMPIONSHIP** Hill 43, Villeneuve 22, Schumacher 16, Panis 11, Alesi 11

**RACE POD**

**4** SURPRISES

# Vettel brought Toro Rosso (née Minardi) victory in treacherous conditions

Left, Red Bull chief Dietrich Mateschitz has just won his first GP three years into F1 team ownership (ironically, his senior team didn't win until the following season). Centre, 21-year-old Seb Vettel, youngest ever GP winner, raises a glass to Helmut Marko, his career developed under his wing from the age of 12

## Race 799 2008 ITALIAN GP Monza

**Round 14/18** **14 September 2008**

A rainy Saturday disrupted the Monza grid, a Toro Rosso on pole, the four championship contenders P6, P11, P14, P15. But it would all sort itself out on race day. Wouldn't it? But the unrelenting weather provided conditions ideal for Sebastian Vettel to confound the establishment and convert his first pole into a maiden victory, also inheriting the mantle of youngest GP winner. The low-drag Toro Rosso plus a strong Ferrari engine was perfect for Monza, but it was a masterly drive in treacherous conditions, beating Kovalainen's McLaren, that had started alongside but was never able to get on terms, by 12.5s. Seb's greater challenge might have come from the McLaren starting P15. Lewis Hamilton's one-stop strategy on extreme wets required the rain to intensify as forecast, but the threatened storm passed the circuit by.

| Pos | Driver | Car | Time/gap | Grid (pen) | Stops | Tyres (m/s) |
|---|---|---|---|---|---|---|
| 1 | Sebastian Vettel | Toro Rosso-Ferrari | 1h 26m 47.494s | 1 | 2 | xxw |
| 2 | Heikki Kovalainen | McLaren-Mercedes | -12.512s | 2 | 2 | xxw |
| 3 | Robert Kubica | BMW | -20.471s | 11 | 1 | xw |
| 4 | Fernando Alonso | Renault | -23.903s | 8 | 1 | xw |
| 5 | Nick Heidfeld | BMW | -27.748s | 10 | 1 | xw |
| 6 | Felipe Massa | Ferrari | -28.816s | 6 | 2 | xxw |

## SEBASTIAN VETTEL

**Toro Rosso-Ferrari STR03** 212.039kph, 131.755mph

**POLE POSITION** Vettel, Toro Rosso-Ferrari, 1m 37.555s (0.076s), 213.774kph, 132.833mph
**LAPS** 53 x 5.793 km, 3.600 miles
**DISTANCE** 306.719 km, 190.586 miles
**STARTERS/FINISHERS** 20/19
**WEATHER** Overcast, cold, rain, drying later
**LAP LEADERS** Vettel 1-18, 23-53 (49); Kovalainen 19-22 (4); SC 1-2 (2)
**WINNER'S LAPS** 1-18 P1, 19-22 P4, 23-53 P1
**FASTEST LAP** K Räikkönen, Ferrari, 1m 28.047 (lap 53), 236.859kph, 147.178mph
**CHAMPIONSHIP** Hamilton 78, Massa 77, Kubica 64, Räikkönen 57, Heidfeld 53

*RACE POD*

Up against heavier Italian front-engined opposition, Stirling Moss exhibited one of the numerous benefits of the lightweight rear-engined F1 Cooper – better tyre wear. His surprise victory sounded the death knell for the front-engined dinosaurs, extinct within two years

# 3 SURPRISES

## Against all expectations, Moss's Cooper took the first championship victory for a rear-engined car

In his book, *Stirling Moss: My Cars, My Career*, written with Doug Nye, Moss said:

"Rob's team had found the latest Continental racing tyres to be very good, so we were using them on the Cooper. We were told our tyres would not last more than 30-40 laps, while the race was over 80. The Cooper wheels were retained by four studs instead of centre-lock knock-offs, so any tyre change would have been a fatal handicap, possibly taking two minutes or more.

"I was going as fast as I could along the straights, then easing the car into corners to preserve my precious tyres. I accelerated very gently, trying to find optimum traction and avoid wheelspin.

"With about 14 laps to go a little white spot began flicking around the left-rear tyre. It showed where the tread had worn through, and the white breaker strip between tread and carcass had been exposed. The other tyres were soon going, too. These spots became longer and longer, they became a continuous line and then began to broaden into an undulating band which now darkened as the casing proper was exposed. I was actively seeking oily, slippery bits of road to molly-coddle my tyres. I got it just about right. This was quite staggering. I could scarcely believe it."

**Race 65** **1958 ARGENTINEAN GP** Buenos Aires No 2 **STIRLING MOSS**

**Round 1/11** **19 January 1958** **Cooper-Climax T43** 134.547kph, 83.604mph

Stirling Moss driving Rob Walker's Cooper-Climax recorded the first championship race victory for a rear-engined car, a configuration that would soon revolutionise Formula 1. Up against the very best from Italy, three Ferraris and six Maseratis, only ten cars participated as Vanwall and BRM were absent. Fangio annexed his customary Buenos Aires pole, his quasi-works Maserati taking the lead from Hawthorn's Ferrari on lap 10. But a stop for tyres on lap 34 allowed Moss' Cooper to assume the lead, a lead he never lost because he unexpectedly didn't stop. This was much to the annoyance of his rivals feeling misled by the pre-race insistence by the Walker team that a tyre stop was essential! It was a narrow victory, 2.7s from Musso's charging Ferrari, and a finely judged one, Moss's tyres showing the canvas.

| Pos | Driver | Car | Time/gap | Grid | Stops | Tyres |
|---|---|---|---|---|---|---|
| 1 | Stirling Moss | Cooper-Climax | 2h 19m 33.7s | 7 | 0 | C |
| 2 | Luigi Musso | Ferrari | –2.7s | 5 | 1 | E |
| 3 | Mike Hawthorn | Ferrari | –12.6s | 2 | 1 | E |
| 4 | Juan Manuel Fangio | Maserati | –53.0s | 1 | 1 | P |
| 5 | Jean Behra | Maserati | –2 laps | 4 | 2 | P |
| 6 | Harry Schell | Maserati | –3 laps | 8 | NA | P |

**POLE POSITION** Fangio, Maserati, 1m 42.0s (0.6s), 138.071kph, 85.793mph
**LAPS** 80 x 3.912 km, 2.431 miles
**DISTANCE** 312.960 km, 194.464 miles
**STARTERS/FINISHERS** 10/9
**WEATHER** Sunny, warm, dry
**LAP LEADERS** Behra 1 (1); Hawthorn 2-9 (8); Fangio 10-34 (25); Moss 35-80 (46)
**WINNER'S LAPS** 1-2 P3, 3 P4, 4-9 P5, 10-17 P4, 18-20 P3, 21-34 P2, 35-80 P1
**FASTEST LAP** Fangio, Maserati, 1m 41.8s (lap 30), 138.382kph, 85.962mph
**CHAMPIONSHIP** Moss 8, Musso 6, Hawthorn 4, Fangio 4, Behra 2

**RACE POD**

2 SURPRISES

# Baghetti wins his first championship race to spare Ferrari's blushes

*Autosport* founding editor Gregor Grant described Baghetti's success like this:

"It was a complete upset for the book. Baghetti displayed the cool-headedness of a veteran, and not sheer desperation. His older-type Ferrari was challenged by Gurney and Bonnier in their Porsches, and then followed a battle reminiscent of the unforgettable Hawthorn v Fangio duel in 1953 (See page 30). All round the circuit the three cars chopped and changed places. The more experienced Gurney and Bonnier really went to work, but nothing seemed to shake the Italian. No one could possibly have blamed Baghetti for making an error, but he drove an inspired race, countering every move of the Porsche pilots.

"That last lap was packed full of drama. At Thillois, Gurney had the lead, but about 300 yards from the finishing line, Baghetti suddenly pulled out of the Porsche's slipstream and darted in front, to the cheers of the madly excited crowd. It was truly a magnificent finish, one which will go down in motor racing history."

Remarkable as winning on your GP debut is, Baghetti wasn't the first or the last to win on their *Ferrari* debut. There have been a surprising number: Juan Manuel Fangio and Luigi Musso (1956 Argentinian GP); Giancarlo Baghetti (1961 French GP); Mario Andretti (1971 South African GP); Nigel Mansell (1989 Brazilian GP); Kimi Raikkonen (2007 Australian GP); Fernando Alonso (2010 Bahrain GP), but not Lewis Hamilton!

## Race 98 — 1961 FRENCH GP Reims

**Round 4/8** — **2 July 1961**

## GIANCARLO BAGHETTI

**Ferrari 156** 192.880kph, 119.850mph

At Reims, Ferrari's utter command of the season almost derailed. Dominant in qualifying as usual, the race was a different matter. Wolfgang von Trips' was the first Ferrari to yield on lap 18 with a holed radiator, but pole-sitter Phil Hill was right behind to regain his early lead. Then on lap 37, when Hill spun it away at Thillois, Richie Ginther's Ferrari took over for three laps until, with 12 still to go, his engine failed. But a fourth Ferrari, a non-works car driven by Baghetti in his first championship race, was there to save the day. Starting P12, Giancarlo had climbed through the steadily depleting field to P3, only seven cars completing the distance. Under immense pressure from Jo Bonnier and Gurney in Porches, all three holding the lead over those closing laps, the final excruciating lap went to rookie Baghetti by a mere one-tenth!

| Pos | Driver | Car | Time/gap | Grid | Stops | Tyres |
|---|---|---|---|---|---|---|
| 1 | Giancarlo Baghetti | Ferrari | 2h 14m 17.5s | 12 | 0 | D |
| 2 | Dan Gurney | Porsche | –0.1s | 9 | 0 | D |
| 3 | Jim Clark | Lotus-Climax | –1m 1.1s | 5 | 0 | D |
| 4 | Innes Ireland | Lotus-Climax | –1m 10.3s | 10 | 0 | D |
| 5 | Bruce McLaren | Cooper-Climax | –1m 41.8s | 8 | 0 | D |
| 6 | Graham Hill | BRM-Climax | –1m 41.9s | 6 | 0 | D |

**POLE POSITION** P Hill, Ferrari, 2m 24.9s (1.5s), 206.261kph, 128.165mph
**LAPS** 52 x 8.302 km, 5.159 miles
**DISTANCE** 431.704 km, 268.248 miles
**STARTERS/FINISHERS** 26/15
**WEATHER** Sunny, very hot, dry
**LAP LEADERS** P Hill, Ferrari 1-12, 18-37 (32); W von Trips, Ferrari 13-17 (5); R Ginther, Ferrari 38-40 (3); Baghetti 41-43, 45, 47, 50, 52 (7); J Bonnier, Porsche 44 (1); Gurney 46, 48-49, 51 (4)
**WINNER'S LAPS** 1 P13, 2 P11, 3 P10, 4 P9, 5 P8, 6-7 P9, 8 P7, 9 P8, 10-13 P5, 14 P4, 15 P6, 16-18 P4, 19-22 P3, 23 P4, 24-32 P3, 33 P4, 34-38 P3, 39-40 P2, 41-43 P1, 44 P2, 45 P1, 46 P3, 47 P1, 48-49 P2, 50 P1, 51 P2, 52 P1
**FASTEST LAP** P Hill, Ferrari, 2m 29.9s (lap 44), 199.333kph, 123.860mph
**CHAMPIONSHIP** P Hill 19, von Trips 18, Moss 12, Ginther 12, Baghetti 9

**RACE POD**

**Bonnier's Porsche (10), rookie winner Baghetti's Ferrari (50), and Gurney's Porsche (12), play out the closing laps of one of the most astounding results in Championship history**

1 SURPRISES

# Pastor Maldonado's victory was a shock to all at many levels

Maldonado told *Autosport* and the Independent newspaper:

"We made big changes in the factory, have new staff and we have completely changed the approach to building the car. This year's car has great performance and great potential. I am driving well, I have a good feeling with the team and the car so everything is possible.

"It wasn't the best start ever [in Spain]. The clutch slipped quite a lot. I tried to defend the position but Fernando was already on the better part of the track, so I decided to back off and follow him. I thought, 'OK, the race is long. Just stay with him.' We changed our strategy to attack Ferrari. From the second stop we did pretty good and I think we surprised them because we did it [pitted] so early.

"Fernando was so close but we were looking to manage the tyre degradation so I wasn't pushing too hard, to keep the tyres alive to the end of the race. We had a small mistake in our last pit stop but that didn't affect our performance. We had an extremely good strategy today, with everything under control. I had better traction than him, was using my KERS well, so I was managing the race, the gaps and the pace."

"This is exactly what we needed, and I don't believe that Pastor put a wheel wrong all race," said team boss Frank Williams.

## Race 863 — 2012 SPANISH GP Cataluña

**Round 5/20** — **13 May 2012**

## PASTOR MALDONADO

**Williams-Renault FW34** 185.837kph, 115.474mph

Lewis Hamiton's relegation to the back for a fuelling error promoted Maldonado's Williams to pole position (Shock 1). Alonso's revamped Ferrari was alongside, the Lotus pair filling row two. Inevitably, turn 1 belonged to the local hero, the Ferrari leading the first two stints. But Pastor, dropping Kimi, kept Fernando's advantage to a couple of seconds (Shock 2) and on lap 24 made a crucial early second tyre-stop to fit new primes. With help from a backmarker, it propelled him 6s ahead of Alonso (Shock 3). But his three-stop strategy required a final stint appreciably longer than his pursuers. Yet despite the Ferrari closing to 0.7s on lap 57, and Kimi homing in fast from 23s back, Pastor soaked up all the pressure in an enthralling race to the flag (Shock 4). Pastor's multi-shock win also brought success to Williams after eight long seasons.

| Pos | Driver | Car | Time/gap | Grid | Stops | Tyres |
|---|---|---|---|---|---|---|
| 1 | Pastor Maldonado | Williams-Renault | 1h 39m 9.145s | 1 | 3 | oppp |
| 2 | Fernando Alonso | Ferrari | -3.195s | 2 | 3 | oppp |
| 3 | Kimi Räikkönen | Lotus-Renault | -3.884s | 4 | 3 | oopp |
| 4 | Romain Grosjean | Lotus-Renault | -14.799s | 3 | 3 | oopp |
| 5 | Kamui Kobayashi | Sauber-Ferrari | -1m 4.641s | 9 | 3 | oppp |
| 6 | Sebastian Vettel | Red Bull-Renault | -1m 7.576s | 7 | 3 | oppp |

**POLE POSITION** Maldonado, Williams-Renault, 1m 22.285s (0.017s), 203.658kph, 126.587mph (L Hamilton, McLaren-Mercedes, took pole in 1m 21.707s but was relegated to the back for a fuelling irregularity)
**LAPS** 66 x 4.655 km, 2.892 miles
**DISTANCE** 307.104 km, 190.826 miles
**STARTERS/FINISHERS** 24/19
**WEATHER** Sunny, hot, dry
**LAP LEADERS** Alonso 1-9, 12-26, 42-44 (27); Maldonado 10-11, 27-41, 47-66 (37); Räikkönen 45-46 (2)
**WINNER'S LAPS** 1-9 P2, 10-11 P1, 12-24 P2, 25-26 P3, 27-41 P1, 42-44 P3, 45-46 P2, 47-66 P1
**FASTEST LAP** Grosjean, Lotus-Renault, 1m 26.250s (lap 53), 194.295kph, 120.729mph
**CHAMPIONSHIP** Vettel 61, Alonso 61, Hamilton 53, Räikkönen 49, Webber 48

RACE POD

How Pastor Maldonado, nicknamed 'Crashtor' due to his propensity for collisions with his rivals, won a Grand Prix still remains an enigma. In 95 GP starts he never took another podium and only scored points on 13 other occasions. Truly the stars aligned

## CHAPTER 8

# PASS MASTERS

## DRAMATIC OVERTAKES

Few moments in Formula 1 embody the essence of racing quite like the visceral thrill of a decisive wheel-to-wheel overtake. For many, overtaking is what motor RACING is all about.

In this collection of dramatic overtakes, the focus is on those moments when a brilliant pass, or series of moves, executed with immense skill, led directly to victory. But more than that, it's the manner by which it was achieved that makes it exceptional as there are numerous ways to overtake in Formula 1.

Opportunism is one, when a fleeting chance opens up and the driver instinctively pounces, 'goes for the gap'. Anticipation is another, reading how backmarkers might create a passing chance. Some passes are about deception, lulling a rival into a false sense of security before catching them napping by making a daring lunge from a long way back. Others require patience and calculation, probing to work out where will be the best place. And if still you cannot find a way by, harrying a driver into an error or even pushing their car to the limits of reliability.

Overtaking a closely matched car, its driver equally intent on victory, isn't easy. So it's not just about executing the pass, it's also about who you're passing. Certain drivers are as aggressive in defence as they are in attack. When a driver attempts to overtake by out-braking a rival on the inside of a corner, the defending car may block the move by 'closing the door', taking the racing line to shut off the gap. For the more uncompromising defender, 'slamming the door' might be a better description. The infamous Schumacher 'chop' took this a step further even when the corner was lost, forcing the attacker into a stark choice: back off or crash.

An outside pass is always a high-risk move, leaving the attacker vulnerable unless the defender respects the space. When it works, it can be sheer poetry, an exquisite demonstration of skill and bravery. Yet, more often than not, there's an element of 'eyes wide open' desperation attached to it.

Which brings us to another overlooked factor in overtaking: anger. Sometimes, a driver's fury fuels a moment equivalent to road rage. One particularly unbelievable outside pass in this collection was undoubtedly the result of the old 'red mist', and astonishingly, it wasn't even for the win, but for P2!

**FEW MOMENTS IN FORMULA 1 EMBODY THE ESSENCE OF RACING QUITE LIKE THE VISCERAL THRILL OF A DECISIVE WHEEL-TO-WHEEL OVERTAKE. FOR MANY, OVERTAKING IS WHAT MOTOR RACING IS ALL ABOUT**

10 PASS MASTERS

# Brooks' pass of Hawthorn wrapped up the constructors' title for Vanwall

Industrialist Tony Vandervell put Britain on the F1 map by winning the inaugural Constructors' Championship in 1958. Tony Brooks is seen here at Monza, one of six Vanwall victories that year

## Race 74 — 1958 ITALIAN GP Monza

**Round 10/11** — **7 September 1958**

Following his brake troubles in Portugal, Hawthorn's Ferrari was sporting disc brakes for the first time, qualifying on the front row with three Vanwalls. After an incursion by Phil Hill's Ferrari in the opening laps, the Hawthorn/Moss battle quickly resumed at the head of the field until Stirling retired with gearbox trouble on lap 17. The Ferraris took command, but once again Brooks played the perfect role for Vanwall. Dropping to P9 on lap 14 to check an oil leak, Brooks was now making relentless progress. When the Ferraris made tyre stops mid-race he was suddenly in contention, reaching P2 on lap 46 before dramatically sweeping past Hawthorn with ten laps to go. His superb victory wrapped up the constructors' championship for Vanwall and kept open Moss' title chances at the upcoming Casablanca finale.

| Pos | Driver | Car | Time/gap | Grid | Stops | Tyres |
|---|---|---|---|---|---|---|
| 1 | Tony Brooks | Vanwall | 2h 3m 47.8s | 2 | 1 | D |
| 2 | Mike Hawthorn | Ferrari | –24.2s | 3 | 1 | E |
| 3 | Phil Hill | Ferrari | –28.3s | 7 | 2 | E |
| 4 | Masten Gregory/Carroll Shelby | Maserati | –1 lap | 11 | 1P | |
| 5 | Roy Salvadori | Cooper-Climax | –8 laps | 14 | NA | D |
| 6 | Graham Hill | Lotus-Climax | –8 laps | 12 | NA | D |

## TONY BROOKS

**Vanwall VW (57)** 195.078kph, 121.216mph

**POLE POSITION** S Moss, Vanwall, 1m 40.5s (0.7s), 205.970kph, 127.984mph
**LAPS** 70 x 5.750 km, 3.573 miles
**DISTANCE** 402.500 km, 250.102 miles
**STARTERS/FINISHERS** 21/7
**WEATHER** Sunny, hot, dry
**LAP LEADERS** P Hill 1-4, 35-37 (7); Hawthorn 5-6, 9, 15-34, 38-60 (46); Moss 7-8,10-14 (7); Brooks 61-70 (10)
**WINNER'S LAPS** 1-6 P5, 7-11 P4, 12-13 P5, 14 P9, 15-17 P8, 18-24 P7, 25-29 P6, 30 P5, 31-37 P4, 38-45 P3, 46-60 P2, 61-70 P1
**FASTEST LAP** P Hill, Ferrari, 1m 42.9s (lap 26), 201.166kph, 124.999mph
**CHAMPIONSHIP** Hawthorn 40, Moss 32, Brooks 24, Salvadori 15, Collins 14

RACE POD

## 9 PASS MASTERS

# Ricciardo overtook Hamilton and Alonso to clinch victory with two laps to spare

An elated Daniel Ricciardo, adrenaline still pumping, raises the winner's trophy after passing Hamilton and Alonso in successive laps to secure victory on lap 68 of 70

## Race 908 — 2014 HUNGARIAN GP Hungaroring — DANIEL RICCIARDO

**Round 11/19** — **27 July 2014** — **Red Bull-Renault RB10** 162.691kph, 101.091mph

Drenched by pre-start rain, Rosberg led on the treacherous surface until a lap eight SC changed everything. The leaders had to complete the lap whereas P5 Ricciardo and the rest could pit instantly for fresh rubber. Then crucially, a second SC on lap 23 saw new leader Ricciardo switch to a three-stop strategy. When the five ahead made their second stops, Daniel resumed the lead for 15 laps before making his own third and final stop. On lap 55 he rejoined behind an inspired Alonso, on worn-out options, Hamilton, charging from dead last on fading primes, and Rosberg, about to pit. It set up a thrilling finish as for eight laps Ricciardo on fresh tyres harried Hamilton before dramatically passing him around the outside of turn 2, then, next lap with just two remaining, passing Alonso equally decisively for a brilliant victory.

| Pos | Driver | Car | Time/gap | Grid (pen) | Stops | Tyres (h/m) |
|---|---|---|---|---|---|---|
| 1 | Daniel Ricciardo | Red Bull-Renault | 1h 53m 5.058s | 4 | 3 | iooo |
| 2 | Fernando Alonso | Ferrari | –5.225s | 5 | 2 | ioo |
| 3 | Lewis Hamilton | Mercedes | –5.857s | 21(PL) | 2 | iop |
| 4 | Nico Rosberg | Mercedes | –6.361s | 1 | 3 | iooo |
| 5 | Filipe Massa | Williams-Mercedes | –29.841s | 6 | 3 | iopp |
| 6 | Kimi Räikkönen | Ferrari | –31.491s | 16 | 2 | ioo |

**POLE POSITION** Rosberg, Mercedes, 1m 22.715s (0.486s), 190.674kph, 118.479mph
**LAPS** 70 x 4.381 km, 2.722 miles
**DISTANCE** 306.630 km, 190.531 miles
**STARTERS/FINISHERS** 22/16
**WEATHER** Cloudy, hot, wet first then drying
**LAP LEADERS** Rosberg 1-9 (9); Ricciardo 10-13, 15-23, 39-54, 68-70 (32); Button 14 (1); Alonso 24-37, 55-67 (27); Hamilton 38 (1); SC 9-13, 23-26 (9)
**WINNER'S LAPS** 1-8 P6, 9 P5, 10-13 P1, 14 P2, 15-23 P1, 24-31 P6, 32-33 P4, 34-38 P3, 39-54 P1, 55 P4, 56-66 P3, 67 P2, 68-70 P1
**FASTEST LAP** Rosberg, Mercedes, 1m 25.724s (lap 64), 183.981kph, 114.320mph
**CHAMPIONSHIP** Rosberg 202, Hamilton 191, Ricciardo 131, Alonso 115, Bottas 95

RACE POD

8

PASS MASTERS

# Jones made a ballsy pass when Gilles offered a minuscule opportunity

For 50 laps Jones sat on the tail of Villeneuve's Ferrari (12) until, at the hairpin on lap 51, he made a dramatic winning pass

## Race 327 — 1979 CANADIAN GP Montréal

**Round 14/15** — **30 September 1979**

Villeneuve beat pole-man Jones off the grid to then keep him at bay on this hard-to-pass-at circuit for the next 50 laps. The Williams was clearly the quicker car as Jones was within a couple of lengths of the Ferrari throughout their duel, patiently awaiting the mistake that was his only way past. It came on lap 51 when Gilles offered a minuscule opportunity due to a fractionally slower exit from the tight turn 9. It was enough, but only by virtue of Jones sending a daring pass down the inside at the hairpin, Villeneuve's squeeze giving only just enough room as they brushed wheels at the apex. Once past, instead of Jones sailing away over the final 21 laps, Villeneuve put on an unforgettable display for his home crowd to finish just 1s behind at the flag. It was a titanic contest between two drivers at their absolute peak.

| Pos | Driver | Car | Time/gap | Grid | Stops | Tyres |
|---|---|---|---|---|---|---|
| 1 | Alan Jones | Williams-Ford | 1h 52m 6.892s | 1 | 0 | G |
| 2 | Gilles Villeneuve | Ferrari | –1.080s | 2 | 0 | M |
| 3 | Clay Regazzoni | Williams-Ford | –1m 13.656s | 3 | 0 | G |
| 4 | Jody Scheckter | Ferrari | –1 lap | 9 | 1 | M |
| 5 | Didier Pironi | Tyrrell-Ford | –1 lap | 6 | 0 | G |
| 6 | John Watson | McLaren-Ford | –2 laps | 17 | 1 | G |

## ALAN JONES

**Williams-Ford FW07** 169.926kph, 105.587mph

**POLE POSITION** Jones, Williams-Ford, 1m 29.892s (0.662s), 176.612kph, 109.742mph
**LAPS** 72 x 4.410 km, 2.740 miles
**DISTANCE** 317.520 km, 197.298 miles
**STARTERS/FINISHERS** 24/10
**WEATHER** Sunny, warm, dry
**LAP LEADERS** Villeneuve 1-50 (50); Jones 51-72 (22)
**WINNER'S LAPS** 1-50 P2, 51-72 P1
**FASTEST LAP** Jones, Williams-Ford, 1m 31.272s (lap 65), 173.942kph, 108.082mph
**CHAMPIONSHIP** Scheckter 51, Villeneuve 44, Jones 40, Laffite 36, Regazzoni 29

*RACE POD*

**7** PASS MASTERS

# Pass master Ricciardo wins humdinger to leave Mercedes and Ferrari gasping

Ricciardo (3) shortly before overtaking leader Valtteri Bottas (77) to complete a stunning sequence of passes to win that included the Mercedes pair, both Ferraris, and his teammate

## Race 979 — 2018 CHINESE GP Shanghai

**Round 3/21** — **15 April 2018**

## DANIEL RICCIARDO

**Red Bull-TAG Heuer RB14** 191.451kph, 118.962mph

Smart Red Bull tactics and passing poetry by Ricciardo produced a surprise winner in China, victory also hinging on a herculean engine change to get Dan into qualifying. For half the race pole-sitter Sebastian Vettel's Ferrari vied for victory with the Mercedes of Bottas until a game-changing SC on lap 31. Red Bull smartly 'stacked' its pit-stops to switch both Verstappen and Ricciardo to quicker soft tyres. Max quickly blew his chances, ending up P5, whereas Dan's progress was utterly spellbinding. From the SC restart he scythed from P6 to P1 in just 10 laps with a succession of scintillating passes: Räikkönen on lap 37 for P5; Verstappen lap 39 for P4; Hamilton lap 40 for P3; Vettel lap 42 for P2 and finally squeezing inside Bottas on lap 45 for victory by 9s.

| Pos | Driver | Car | Time/gap | Grid (pen) | Stops | Tyres (m/s/us) |
|---|---|---|---|---|---|---|
| 1 | Daniel Ricciardo | Red Bull-TAG Heuer | 1h 35m 36.380s | 6 | 2 | ums |
| 2 | Valtteri Bottas | Mercedes | –8.894s | 3 | 1 | su |
| 3 | Kimi Räikkönen | Ferrari | –9.637s | 2 | 1 | su |
| 4 | Lewis Hamilton | Mercedes | –16.985s | 4 | 1 | su |
| 5 | Max Verstappen | Red Bull-TAG Heuer | –20.436s * | 5 | 2 | ums |
| 6 | Nico Hülkenberg | Renault | –21.052s | 7 | 2 | ums |

*Including 10s penalty

**POLE POSITION** Vettel, Ferrari, 1m 31.095s (0.087s), 215.419kph, 133.855mph
**LAPS** 56 x 5.451 km, 3.387 miles
**DISTANCE** 305.066 km, 189.559 miles
**STARTERS/FINISHERS** 20/20
**WEATHER** Sunny, warm, dry
**LAP LEADERS** Vettel 1-20 (20); Räikkönen 21-26 (6); Bottas 27-44 (18); Ricciardo 45-56 (12); SC 31-35 (5)
**WINNER'S LAPS** 1-17 P6, 18 P7, 19-27 P6, 28-31 P5, 32-36 P6, 37-38 P5, 39 P4, 40-41 P3, 42-44 P2, 45-56 P1
**FASTEST LAP** Ricciardo, Red Bull-TAG Heuer, 1m 35.785s (lap 55), 204.871kph, 127.300mph
**CHAMPIONSHIP** Vettel 54, Hamilton 45, Bottas 40, Ricciardo 37, Räikkönen 30

*RACE POD*

6 PASS MASTERS

# Coulthard made an exquisite three-abreast pass on the soaking track

Remarkably, Schumacher lost the lead twice, first, seen here, when rookie Montoya sensationally blasted past at turn 1 on lap three, and again when Coulthard, top right in this shot, made a stunning three abreast pass on lap 50

## Race 666 — 2001 BRAZILIAN GP Interlagos

**Round 3/17** — **1 April 2001**

Following a brief first lap SC, and despite the heavier fuel load for his intended one-stop strategy, rookie Juan Pablo Montoya sensationally blasted past the more lightly fuelled Schumacher at turn 1. For 25 laps these two plus Coulthard's one-stopping McLaren raced closely until the two-stopping Michael peeled off on lap 25. But Montoya's fairy tale ended on lap 39 when, with a 5.7s lead, he was punted off by a lapped Jos Verstappen at turn 4. Coulthard now led but when the light rain that had been falling for some minutes intensified on lap 45, he lost out to Schumacher in the switch to wet tyres. But it was only for two laps as on lap 50 he regained the lead with an epic three-abreast turn 1 pass on the soaking track, Michael around the outside of the backmarker, DC diving down the inside to take them both.

| Pos | Driver | Car | Time/gap | Grid | Stops | Tyres |
|---|---|---|---|---|---|---|
| 1 | David Coulthard | McLaren-Mercedes | 1h 39m 0.834s | 5 | 2 | B |
| 2 | Michael Schumacher | Ferrari | –16.164s | 1 | 2 | B |
| 3 | Nick Heidfeld | Sauber-Petronas | –1 lap | 9 | 1 | B |
| 4 | Olivier Panis | BAR-Honda | –1 lap | 11 | 2 | B |
| 5 | Jarno Trulli | Jordan-Honda | –1 lap | 7 | 1 | B |
| 6 | Giancarlo Fisichella | Benetton-Renault | –1 lap | 18 | 2 | M |

## DAVID COULTHARD

**McLaren-Mercedes MP4-16** 185.373kph, 115.186mph

**POLE POSITION** M Schumacher, Ferrari, 1m 13.780s (0.310s), 210.252kph, 130.645mph
**LAPS** 71 x 4.309 km, 2.677 miles
**DISTANCE** 305.909 km, 190.083 miles
**STARTERS/FINISHERS** 22/11
**WEATHER** Cloudy, hot, dry at first, heavy shower then drying
**LAP LEADERS** M Schumacher 1-2, 48-49 (4); J P Montoya, Williams-BMW 3-38 (36); Coulthard 39-47, 50-71 (31); SC 1-2 (2)
**WINNER'S LAPS** 1-24 P3, 25-38 P2, 39-47 P1, 48-49 P2, 50-71 P1
**FASTEST LAP** R Schumacher, Williams-BMW, 1m 15.693s (lap 38), 204.938kph, 127.343mph
**CHAMPIONSHIP** M Schumacher 26, Coulthard 20, Barrichello 10, Heidfeld 7, Frentzen 5

RACE POD

# 5 PASS MASTERS

# At the 180° *Parabolica Ayrton Senna*, JV audaciously drove around the Ferrari

Here, Jacques Villeneuve leads Williams-Renault teammate Damon Hill having kept his title hopes alive by virtue of his dramatic pass of Schumacher

## Race 596 — 1996 PORTUGUESE GP Estoril

**Round 15/16** — **22 September 1996**

In their internecine battle for the title, Damon Hill beat teammate Jacques Villeneuve to pole by 0.009s and pulled away at the start. With Villeneuve pinned behind Alesi and Schumacher it looked to be game over. Villeneuve's superb victory drive began on lap 16 with a heart-stopping passing move. At the long 180° *Parabolica Ayrton Senna*, he audaciously drove around the outside of Schumacher's Ferrari to set off after Alesi. Passing him left 48 laps to make up 10s on Hill and find a way past, and by lap 40 the two were together. But passing was another thing, so JV bided his time until their third stop, stunning Hill and his pit crew by rejoining just ahead on lap 51. That day Villeneuve was irresistible and, by beating teammate Hill, guaranteed a Suzuka showdown between them.

| Pos | Driver | Car | Time/gap | Grid | Stops | Tyres |
|---|---|---|---|---|---|---|
| 1 | Jacques Villeneuve | Williams-Renault | 1h 40m 22.915s | 2 | 3 | G |
| 2 | Damon Hill | Williams-Renault | −19.966s | 1 | 3 | G |
| 3 | Michael Schumacher | Ferrari | −53.765s | 4 | 3 | G |
| 4 | Jean Alesi | Benetton-Renault | −55.109s | 3 | 2 | G |
| 5 | Eddie Irvine | Ferrari | −1m 27.389s | 6 | 2 | G |
| 6 | Gerhard Berger | Benetton-Renault | −1m 33.141s | 5 | 2 | G |

## JACQUES VILLENEUVE

**Williams-Renault FW18** 182.423kph, 113.353mph

**POLE POSITION** Hill, Williams-Renault, 1m 20.330s (0.009s), 195.393kph, 121.412mph
**LAPS** 70 x 4.360 km, 2.709 miles
**DISTANCE** 305.200 km, 189.642 miles
**STARTERS/FINISHERS** 20/16
**WEATHER** Cloudy with sunny intervals, warm, dry
**LAP LEADERS** Hill 1-17, 22-33, 36-48 (42); Alesi 18-21 (4); Villeneuve 34-35, 49-70 (24)
**WINNER'S LAPS** 1-15 P4, 16-17 P3, 18 P2, 19 P7, 20 P4, 21-22 P3, 23-33 P2, 34-35 P1, 36-48 P2, 49-70 P1
**FASTEST LAP** Villeneuve, Williams-Renault, 1m 22.873s (lap 37), 189.398kph, 117.687mph
**CHAMPIONSHIP** Hill 87, Villeneuve 78, Schumacher 53, Alesi 47, Häkkinen 27

*RACE POD*

4

PASS MASTERS

# In a flash Häkkinen dived to the right beneath them, three abreast

Post race, Mika Häkkinen (left) is either explaining to an enrapt Michael Schumacher his fleeting opportunity to overtake and win, or expressing his displeasure at Schuey's earlier defensive chop!

## Race 659 | 2000 BELGIAN GP Spa-Francorchamps | MIKA HÄKKINEN

**Round 13/17** | **27 August 2000** | **McLaren-Mercedes MP4-15** 208.467kph, 129.536mph

Starting behind the SC on a wet track, Häkkinen led from pole but, after switching to slicks, a spin at Stavelot on lap 13 cost him 9s and gifted Schumacher the lead. Rejoining from his pit stop on five-lap fresher tyres, he took 10 laps to close the 5.85s gap but, by the ferocity of the chop dealt to Mika on lap 40, Michael was disinclined to surrender the lead. The following lap, still closely chasing with three to go, Häkkinen got the better run out of Eau Rouge. Approaching Les Combes, Schumacher flicked left to pass backmarker Ricardo Zonta. In a flash, in one of the great overtakes, Häkkinen in an awe-inspiring move dived to the right beneath the pair of them, three abreast. In their three-season rivalry for supremacy, this stands as the most iconic encounter between the two Champions.

| Pos | Driver | Car | Time/gap | Grid | Stops | Tyres |
|---|---|---|---|---|---|---|
| 1 | Mika Häkkinen | McLaren-Mercedes | 1h 28m 14.494s | 1 | 2 | B |
| 2 | Michael Schumacher | Ferrari | -1.104s | 4 | 2 | B |
| 3 | Ralf Schumacher | Williams-BMW | -38.096s | 6 | 2 | B |
| 4 | David Coulthard | McLaren-Mercedes | -43.281s | 5 | 2 | B |
| 5 | Jenson Button | Williams-BMW | -49.914s | 3 | 2 | B |
| 6 | Heinz-Harald Frentzen | Jordan-Mugen Honda | -55.984s | 8 | 2 | B |

**POLE POSITION** Häkkinen, McLaren-Mercedes, 1m 50.646s (0.773s), 226.712kph, 140.872mph
**LAPS** 44 x 6.968 km, 4.330 miles
**DISTANCE** 306.592 km, 190.507 miles
**STARTERS/FINISHERS** 22/17
**WEATHER** Cloudy, warm, wet then drying
**LAP LEADERS** Häkkinen 1-12, 23-27, 41-44 (21); M Schumacher 13-22, 28-40 (23); SC 1 (1)
**WINNER'S LAPS** 1-12 P1, 13-22 P2, 23-27 P1, 28-40 P2, 41-44 P1
**FASTEST LAP** R Barrichello, Ferrari, 1m 53.803s (lap 30), 220.423kph, 136.965mph
**CHAMPIONSHIP** Häkkinen 74, M Schumacher 68, Coulthard 61, Barrichello 49, R Schumacher 20

RACE POD

3

PASS MASTERS

# A Safety Car triggered two storming drives by the title rivals

Years later, Räikkönen told *Autosport* his Japanese GP win was a career highlight: "Suzuka in 2005 was in many ways a special race.

"I think that was one of my best races ever with a lot of hard work, and I really enjoyed myself. Considering all the problems we had, to come away with a win was just fantastic.

"There was a lot happening on the first lap and both Juan Pablo [Montoya] and myself got involved, which is often inevitable when you are starting so far down. I was pushing as hard as I could and the car just got better and better.

"After the second stop I had gained enough on Fisichella to go for it, and I did. I got past him on the last lap coming into the first corner, and it was one of those opportunities you have to take."

Fisichella said: "The team told me Kimi was close after the last stop, and he caught me up quite quickly – especially when I got chopped by a backmarker into 130R, which cost me a lot of time.

"He was very fast in the final part of the lap, and I did my best to hold him off, but he held the line into the first corner, and that was that."

Paddy Lowe, part of the McLaren engineering team that year, agreed it was the Finn at his zenith: "That was a fantastic win – probably Kimi's best ever race. I'd say that was Kimi at his peak in 2005."

## Race 749 — 2005 JAPANESE GP Suzuka

**Round 18/19** — **9 October 2005**

## KIMI RÄIKKÖNEN

**McLaren-Mercedes MP4-20** 207.266kph, 128.790mph

Wet qualifying produced a mixed-up grid, title rivals Fernando Alonso and Kimi Räikkönen starting P16 and P17. A lengthy SC at the start bunched the field but triggered storming drives from each of them. First Räikkönen, slicing through the field to reach P2 by half distance before his lap 26 first stop, rejoining P6. On lap 30 he passed Schumacher for P4, taking the lead on lap 41 as others pitted. His second stop came on lap 45, rejoining 5s behind leader Fisichella with eight laps to go, then miraculously passing him on the final lap to take the win. Now Alonso. Some say that but for an unwarranted penalty, his recovery from P16 even eclipsed Räikkönen's, being just as potent and committed, and splendidly illustrated by his lap 20 pass of Michael Schumacher around the outside of the fearsome 130R.

| Pos | Driver | Car | Time/gap | Grid (pen) | Stops | Tyres |
|---|---|---|---|---|---|---|
| 1 | Kimi Räikkönen | McLaren-Mercedes | 1h 29m 2.212s | 17 (-10) | 2 | M |
| 2 | Giancarlo Fisichella | Renault | –1.633s | 3 | 2 | M |
| 3 | Fernando Alonso | Renault | –17.456s | 16 | 2 | M |
| 4 | Mark Webber | Williams-BMW | –22.274s | 7 | 2 | M |
| 5 | Jenson Button | BAR-Honda | –29.507s | 2 | 2 | M |
| 6 | David Coulthard | Red Bull-Cosworth | –31.601s | 6 | 2 | M |

**POLE POSITION** R Schumacher, Toyota, 1m 46.106s (0.035s), 197.021kph, 122.424mph
**LAPS** 53 x 5.807 km, 3.608 miles
**DISTANCE** 307.573 km, 191.117 miles
**STARTERS/FINISHERS** 20/17
**WEATHER** Cloudy with sunny intervals, warm, dry, breezy
**LAP LEADERS** R Schumacher 1-12 (12); Fisichella 13-20, 27-38, 46-52 (27); Button 21-22, 39-40 (4); Coulthard 23 (1); M Schumacher, Ferrari 24-26 (3); Räikkönen 41-45, 53 (6); SC 2-7 (6)
**WINNER'S LAPS** 1-7 P12, 8 P11, 9 P10, 10-13 P9, 14-20 P7, 21-22 P6, 23 P4, 24-26 P2, 27-28 P6, 29 P5, 30-38 P4, 39-40 P4, 41-45 P1, 46-52 P2, 53 P1
**FASTEST LAP** Räikkönen, McLaren-Mercedes, 1m 31.540s (lap 44), 228.372kph, 141.904mph
**CHAMPIONSHIP** Alonso 123, Räikkönen 104, M Schumacher 62, Montoya 60, Fisichella 53

**RACE POD**

**As they exit the chicane and enter the final lap, leader Fisichella is hounded by Räikkönen shortly before Kimi's stunning pass of the Renault for a miraculous win**

# Mansell daringly repassed Berger around the outside of the banked Curva Peraltada

In a later interview with *Autosport* Mansell said:

"I was so incensed with the way Gerhard passed me down the straight, I thought, 'There was no way you are going to take second place from me!'

"It was one of the greatest overtaking manoeuvres of my career probably. It was a complete on the spur manoeuvre. I had to try it because if you think it, you are already too late. In that day, if it went wrong you were going to get seriously hurt. You had to be a bit mental to take it on. I executed it on the entry as we were really close, and I thought if he touches me now, I am history big time.

"It's not the place to go off, because it's a very dangerous corner. But it was fantastic. As a driver you are not suicidal, you don't want to go and lose your life, but you had to fight with your right foot and your brain because your head is saying, 'Back off a little bit', but you want to be quicker and you want to do it and it to come off.

"You cannot stop your foot coming off. Your brain has a self-preservation chip which we all have. You know when you are right on the edge, that it is going to do that. So when you can overcome that, and just change it like the rev limiter on an engine, you can up it to a different level and it is pretty neat."

Lap 61, eight to go, Prost now leads Senna and Mansell would pass him next lap. But Nigel's half-spin would give Berger the chance to barge by, only for Mansell to seize second back with a heroic outside overtake

## Race 490 — 1990 MEXICAN GP Mexico City — ALAIN PROST

**Round 6/16** — **24 June 1990** — **Ferrari 641/2** 197.664kph, 122.823mph

By lap 42, pole-sitter Ayrton Senna's 18s lead suggested the Ferraris of Mansell and Prost posed little threat. Mansell had reached P2 after a poor start, but ten on-track passes had also brought Prost into play, making startling progress from his lowly P13 grid slot. But Senna was beginning to slow, mistakenly believing a slow puncture to be tyre wear, his tyre finally letting go on lap 63. On lap 55 the charging Prost overtook teammate Mansell, and by the end of lap 60 the three leading cars were just 0.6s apart. Next time round Prost passed Senna for a sensational victory, but the defining moment of the race was still to come: on lap 64 Mansell half-spun and was then barged off line by Berger for P2, but on lap 68, the penultimate, Nigel heroically retook Berger around the outside of the formidable Curva Peraltada for a Ferrari 1-2.

| Pos | Driver | Car | Time/gap | Grid | Stops | Tyres |
|---|---|---|---|---|---|---|
| 1 | Alain Prost | Ferrari | 1h 32m 35.783s | 13 | 0 | G |
| 2 | Nigel Mansell | Ferrari | –25.351s | 4 | 0 | G |
| 3 | Gerhard Berger | McLaren-Honda | –25.530s | 1 | 1 | G |
| 4 | Alessandro Nannini | Benetton-Ford | –41.099s | 14 | 0 | G |
| 5 | Thierry Boutsen | Williams-Renault | –46.669s | 5 | 0 | G |
| 6 | Nelson Piquet | Benetton-Ford | –46.943s | 8 | 1 | G |

**POLE POSITION** Berger, McLaren-Honda, 1m 17.227s (0.271s), 206.089kph, 128.057mph
**LAPS** 69 x 4.421 km, 2.747 miles
**DISTANCE** 305.049 km, 189.549 miles
**STARTERS/FINISHERS** 26/20
**WEATHER** Cloudy, warm, dry
**LAP LEADERS** Senna 1-60 (60), Prost 61-69 (9)
**WINNER'S LAPS** 1 P13, 2 P12, 3 P11, 4-6 P10, 7-8 P9, 9-11 P8, 12 P7, 13-25 P6, 26-30 P5, 31-41 P4, 42-54 P3, 55-60 P2, 61-69 P1
**FASTEST LAP** Prost, Ferrari, 1m 17.958s (lap 58), 204.156kph, 126.857mph
**CHAMPIONSHIP** Senna 31, Prost 23, Berger 23, Alesi 13, Mansell 13

*RACE POD*

## 1 PASS MASTERS

# Piquet made a spectacular if chancy outside pass of Senna at turn 1 to clinch it

Afterwards, Piquet said: "Everything went perfectly. Above all, this was going to be a race to finish. It was long and hot and the Williams and Honda mechanics did a great job preparing the car. The engine and the chassis were everything I needed. I made one stop for new Goodyears, and my pit crew again did a super-quick job.

"The grip of the track changed as the afternoon went on, and I was able to have a very close race with Senna. Our cars were pretty even, but overall I think we had the edge. I passed him on the outside of turn 1 and from then on it was a matter of making it to the finish.

"I would like to say that the Hungarians did a great job with their first Grand Prix – and I would particularly like to thank the marshal who waved a blue flag at Senna when I was catching him!"

Senna felt the Williams-Honda's power made a counter-attack difficult: "I could close up, but there is only one place to pass here – at the end of the pit straight. He was faster than me in the straight, so overtaking him there was almost impossible."

## Race 431 — 1986 HUNGARIAN GP Hungaroring — NELSON PIQUET

**Round 11/16** — **10 August 1986** — **Williams-Honda FW11** 151.804kph, 94.327mph

Piquet won the first ever Championship race held in the Soviet bloc, although compatriot Senna made him work extremely hard for it, the two Brazilians engaging in a dramatic two-hour battle in the sweltering heat. Senna led from pole but once Piquet had muscled past teammate Mansell, he quickly caught the leader and on lap 12, overtook him down the inside of turn 1, rapidly pulling out a gap of around 5s. On lap 35 Piquet made his tyre stop, Senna then upping his pace to ensure that, when he rejoined from his own stop, he kept the lead. Until lap 50 the Lotus was looking good for the win, but then Nelson came on strong, making up 9s in five laps. But Senna defended robustly until, on lap 57, Piquet settled it with a perilous tyre-smoking, sideways, opposite-lock, outside pass into turn 1.

| Pos | Driver | Car | Time/gap | Grid | Stops | Tyres |
|---|---|---|---|---|---|---|
| 1 | Nelson Piquet | Williams-Honda | 2h 0m 34.508s | 2 | 1 | G |
| 2 | Ayrton Senna | Lotus-Renault | –17.673s | 1 | 1 | G |
| 3 | Nigel Mansell | Williams-Honda | –1 lap | 4 | 2 | G |
| 4 | Stefan Johansson | Ferrari | –1 lap | 7 | 2 | G |
| 5 | Johnny Dumfries | Lotus-Renault | –2 laps | 8 | 1 | G |
| 6 | Martin Brundle | Tyrrell-Renault | –2 laps | 16 | 1 | G |

**POLE POSITION** Senna, Lotus-Renault, 1m 29.450s (0.335s), 161.547kph, 100.381mph
**LAPS** 76 x 4.014 km, 2.494 miles (Scheduled for 77 laps but stopped after two hours)
**DISTANCE** 305.064 km, 189.558 miles
**STARTERS/FINISHERS** 26/10
**WEATHER** Sunny, hot, dry
**LAP LEADERS** Senna 1-11, 36-56 (32); Piquet 12-35, 57-76 (44)
**WINNER'S LAPS** 1-2 P3, 3-11 P2, 12-35 P1, 36-56 P2, 57-76 P1
**FASTEST LAP** Piquet, Williams-Honda, 1m 31.001s (lap 73), 158.794kph, 98.670mph
**CHAMPIONSHIP** Mansell 55, Senna 48, Piquet 47, Prost 44, Rosberg 19

RACE POD

Four drivers dominated 1986, Senna, Piquet, Prost (McLaren-TAG) and Mansell, the first three seen here. Piquet won this one with a simply monumental pass of Senna

CHAPTER 9

# FOLKLORE

## UNFORGETTABLE CONTESTS

The preceding eight chapters have explored Formula 1's greatest races through recurring themes – thrilling finishes, dramatic overtakes, storming comebacks, and epic victories against the odds. We've celebrated masters in the rain and shock winners who defied expectations.

Yet some races stand apart, defying classification. Folklore is where nostalgia overlays the storyline, so this is a chapter less defined by statistics or strict criteria, and more by the stories we tell and retell, passed down through generations and featured frequently in F1 journals. These races are part of the sport's shared mythology, the ones that provoke fond recollection and animated debate. They are the races we remember not just for what happened, but for how they made us feel at the time.

They include moments of pure racing brilliance or historical significance, unforgettable for reasons beyond any single theme. Some unfold in a 'don't blink or you'll miss it' flash of magic, while others linger in the memory as the start of something monumental. Whether through game-changing innovation, such as the Brabham fan-car; a career-defining performance, like young Max Verstappen's maiden victory; or the sheer spectacle of Nigel Mansell's fruitless attempts to pass Ayrton Senna at Monaco, these races transcend the norm, their legends woven deep into the fabric of Formula 1 folklore.

Some may be those expected all along, finally making their appearance and reassuring readers that they haven't been overlooked. Others stand out as unique, defying easy categorisation but nonetheless earning their place in this penultimate list. After which, we savour one final collection of ten – the classic season finales listed in Chapter 10 – to round out the process of identifying Formula 1's 100 Greatest Races.

**WHETHER THROUGH GAME-CHANGING INNOVATION, CAREER-DEFINING PERFORMANCES, OR SHEER SPECTACLE, THESE RACES TRANSCEND THE NORM, THEIR LEGENDS WOVEN DEEP INTO THE FABRIC OF FORMULA 1 FOLKLORE**

10 FOLKLORE

# Trapped in the wreckage, 25 minutes passed before Stewart's release

Jochen Rindt leading John Surtees in the rain, this photo clearly illustrating the woefully inadequate safety measures for the original 8.8 mile Spa circuit

## Race 143 — 1966 BELGIAN GP Spa-Francorchamps — JOHN SURTEES

**Round 2/9** **12 June 1966**

**Ferrari 312** 183.360kph, 113.935mph

A ferocious squall decimated the already small field, eight cars failing to complete the first lap. One was Jackie Stewart, his BRM leaving the track and crashing heavily. Jackie was trapped in the wreckage for 25 minutes, a bent steering column pinning his leg, split tanks spilling fuel into the cockpit, the fire risk extremely high. Assistance came only from BRM colleagues Graham Hill and Bob Bondurant, fellow victims of the deluge, who bravely worked to extricate him with tools borrowed from a spectator. These events inspired Stewart to campaign for greater safety, an existential initiative for F1's future. Meanwhile, Rindt led superbly in his Cooper-Maserati on the streaming track, but as it dried out towards the end, the handling deteriorated enabling Surtees' pole-sitting Ferrari to retake the lead and pull away.

| Pos | Driver | Car | Time/gap | Grid | Stops | Tyres |
|---|---|---|---|---|---|---|
| 1 | John Surtees | Ferrari | 2h 9m 11.3s | 1 | 0 | D |
| 2 | Jochen Rindt | Cooper-Maserati | –42.1s | 2 | 0 | D |
| 3 | Lorenzo Bandini | Ferrari | –1 lap | 5 | 0 | F |
| 4 | Jack Brabham | Brabham-Repco | –2 laps | 4 | 0 | G |
| 5 | Richie Ginther | Cooper-Maserati | –3 laps | 8 | 0 | D |
| - | Only five classified finishers | | - | - | - | - |

**POLE POSITION** J Surtees, Ferrari, 3m 38.0s (3.2s), 232.844kph, 144.683mph
**LAPS** 28 x 14.100 km, 8.761 miles
**DISTANCE** 394.800 km, 245.317 miles
**STARTERS/FINISHERS** 15/5
**WEATHER** Overcast, rain squalls, drying later
**LAP LEADERS** Surtees 1, 3, 24-28 (7); Bandini 2 (1); Rindt 4-23 (20)
**WINNER'S LAPS** 1 P1, 2 P2, 3 P1, 4-23 P2, 24-28 P1
**FASTEST LAP** J Surtees, Ferrari, 4m 18.7s (lap 18), 196.212kph, 121.920mph
**CHAMPIONSHIP** Bandini 10, Stewart 9, Surtees 9, Rindt 6, G Hill 4

*RACE POD*

9 FOLKLORE

# Schumacher/Brawn bounced back with a sensational 'How did they do that?' win

Schumacher raises his arm in exultation as he with Race Engineer Ross Brawn conjure a victory from seemingly nowhere with a brilliant three-stop winning strategy

## Race 626 | 1998 HUNGARIAN GP Hungaroring | MICHAEL SCHUMACHER

**Round 12/16** **16 August 1998** **Ferrari F300** 174.062kph, 108.157mph

Following back-to-back victories by McLaren, the Scuderia bounced back in its intense title battle with one of those 'How did they do that?' Schumacher/Brawn wins. The first stint had Michael in close chase of the McLaren pair, but at their first fuel stop, any undercut chance was hindered by Villeneuve. The second stint saw Schumacher unable to pass Coulthard let alone leader Häkkinen. So Brawn opted for a radical three-stop, advising his driver at their second stop that he had "19 laps to pick up 25s". Despite a brief off on lap 52, Schumacher obliged brilliantly, his third stop a comparative formality, rejoining 5s ahead. McLaren was totally wrong footed, a tactical blunder curtailing Coulthard's response and Mika developing a handling problem, his one-point finish revitalising the championship chase.

| Pos | Driver | Car | Time/gap | Grid | Stops | Tyres |
|---|---|---|---|---|---|---|
| 1 | Michael Schumacher | Ferrari | 1h 45m 25.550s | 3 | 3 | G |
| 2 | David Coulthard | McLaren-Mercedes | –9.433s | 2 | 2 | B |
| 3 | Jacques Villeneuve | Williams-Mecachrome | –44.444s | 6 | 2 | G |
| 4 | Damon Hill | Jordan-Mugen Honda | –55.076s | 4 | 2 | G |
| 5 | Heinz-Harald Frentzen | Williams-Mecachrome | –56.510s | 7 | 2 | G |
| 6 | Mika Häkkinen | McLaren-Mercedes | –1 lap | 1 | 2 | B |

**POLE POSITION** Häkkinen, McLaren-Mercedes, 1m 16.973s (0.158s), 185.769kph, 115.432mph
**LAPS** 77 x 3.972 km, 2.468 miles
**DISTANCE** 305.844 km, 190.043 miles
**STARTERS/FINISHERS** 21/16
**WEATHER** Cloudy with sunny intervals, hot, dry
**LAP LEADERS** Häkkinen 1-46 (46); M Schumacher 47-77 (31)
**WINNER'S LAPS** 1-25 P3, 26-30 P4, 31-44 P3, 45-46 P2, 47-77 P1
**FASTEST LAP** M Schumacher, Ferrari, 1m 19.286s (lap 60), 180.349kph, 112.064mph
**CHAMPIONSHIP** Häkkinen 77, M Schumacher 70, Coulthard 48, Irvine 32, Villeneuve 20

RACE POD

## 8 FOLKLORE

# Button carved through the field from P14, for his maiden win

In Honda's first season back in 38 years as a fully fledged F1 team, Jenson Button won his first and Honda's third-ever race victory, here making one of three pit stops

**Race 763** **2006 HUNGARIAN GP** Hungaroring **JENSON BUTTON**

**Round 13/18** **6 August 2006** **Honda RA106** 163.773kph, 101.764mph

The first wet race in the 21 years of the Hungarian GP was special. At the start, Button, a P14 grid slot due to an engine-change penalty, and Alonso, P15 for an infringement, carved through the field on their Michelin intermediates. By the end of lap seven they were running fourth and third respectively behind the McLarens of pole-sitter Kimi Räikkönen and Pedro del a Rosa. Kimi built a 20s lead during this first stint but on lap 25 was forced to retire after tripping over a backmarker. So from lap 18 Alonso led, chased by Button, Jenson attacking on lap 45 before peeling off for his fuel stop. On lap 51, a switch to dries went disastrously wrong for Alonso, the championship leader on three wheels soon after the stop. This left Button to reel off the final 18 laps, including a third stop, and take his maiden GP victory.

| Pos | Driver | Car | Time/gap | Grid (pen) | Stops | Tyres |
|---|---|---|---|---|---|---|
| 1 | Jenson Button | Honda | 1h 52m 20.941s | 14 (-10) | 3 | M |
| 2 | Pedro de la Rosa | McLaren-Mercedes | -30.837s | 4 | 3 | M |
| 3 | Nick Heidfeld | BMW | -43.822s | 10 | 2 | M |
| 4 | Rubens Barrichello | Honda | -45.205s | 3 | 3 | M |
| 5 | David Coulthard | Red Bull-Ferrari | -1 lap | 12 | 2 | M |
| 6 | Ralf Schumacher | Toyota | -1 lap | 6 | 2 | B |

**POLE POSITION** K Räikkönen, McLaren-Mercedes, 1m 19.599s (0.287s), 198.138kph, 123.117mph
**LAPS** 70 x 4.381 km, 2.722 miles
**DISTANCE** 306.663 km, 190.552 miles
**STARTERS/FINISHERS** 20/14
**WEATHER** Cloudy, cool, intermittent heavy rain
**LAP LEADERS** K Räikkönen, McLaren-Mercedes 1-17 (17); F Alonso, Renault 18-51 (34); J Button, 52-70 (19); SC 27-31 (5)
**WINNER'S LAPS** 1 P11, 2 P9, 3 P8, 4-5 P7, 6 P5, 7-16 P4, 17 P3, 18-25 P4, 26 P3, 27-51 P2, 52-70 P1
**FASTEST LAP** Massa, Ferrari, 1m 23.516s (lap 65), 188.845kph, 117.343mph
**CHAMPIONSHIP** Alonso 100, M Schumacher 90, Massa 52, Fisichella 49, Räikkönen 49

*RACE POD*

7

FOLKLORE

# In his efforts to overtake, Mansell almost drove over the top of Senna

Ayrton Senna absorbs intense pressure on his way to his fifth Monaco victory, Nigel Mansell climbing all over him for the closing four laps

## Race 522 — 1992 MONACO GP Monte Carlo

**Round 6/16** — **31 May 1992**

Round six, Monaco, the tale of the 1992 season so far being that Mansell and his Williams-Renault had won every race from pole. And here again, at the Monte Carlo street circuit, it was exactly the same story… until lap 71 of 78. Leading Senna by almost 30s, a sideways moment in the tunnel signified a suspected left rear puncture that necessitated Nigel to drive slowly to the pits for a tyre change. The stop wasn't that quick either, Mansell rejoining 7s behind new leader Senna. In the faster car and with fresh tyres, Mansell was quickly on his tail, darting left then right to outmanoeuvre or force an error, almost driving over the top of the McLaren in his efforts to overtake. But Senna knew Monaco far too well, holding his line to become five-time winner, equalling Graham Hill's record set in 1969.

| Pos | Driver | Car | Time/gap | Grid | Stops | Tyres |
|---|---|---|---|---|---|---|
| 1 | Ayrton Senna | McLaren-Honda | 1h 50m 59.372s | 3 | 0 | G |
| 2 | Nigel Mansell | Williams-Renault | –0.215s | 1 | 1 | G |
| 3 | Riccardo Patrese | Williams-Renault | –31.843s | 2 | 0 | G |
| 4 | Michael Schumacher | Benetton-Ford | –39.294s | 6 | 0 | G |
| 5 | Martin Brundle | Benetton-Ford | –1m 21.347s | 7 | 1 | G |
| 6 | Bertrand Gachot | Larrousse-Lamborghini | –1 lap | 15 | 0 | G |

## AYRTON SENNA

**McLaren-Honda MP4/7A** 140.329kph, 87.196mph

**POLE POSITION** Mansell, Williams-Renault, 1m 19.495s (0.873s), 150.711kph, 93.648mph
**LAPS** 78 x 3.328 km, 2.068 miles
**DISTANCE** 259.584 km, 161.298 miles
**STARTERS/FINISHERS** 26/12
**WEATHER** Cloudy with sunny intervals, warm, dry
**LAP LEADERS** Mansell 1-70 (70), Senna 71-78 (8)
**WINNER'S LAPS** 1-70 P2, 71-78 P1
**FASTEST LAP** Mansell, Williams-Renault, 1m 21.598s (lap 74), 146.827kph, 91.234mph
**CHAMPIONSHIP** Mansell 56, Patrese 28, Schumacher 20, Senna 18, Berger 8

RACE POD

6 FOLKLORE

# Eyes turned to the charge through the field by rookie Senna in the Toleman

Here, Senna is about to overtake Rosberg (Williams) for P5 on lap 12, to be followed by Arnoux (Ferrari) for P4 on lap 14 and, after Mansell's crash, Lauda (McLaren) for P2 on lap 19

## Race 394 1984 MONACO GP Monte Carlo

**Round 6/16** **3 June 1984**

In streaming wet conditions, Prost led from pole chased by Nigel Mansell from P2. On lap 11 the Lotus got by, and for five glorious laps Nigel led a GP for the first time, only to lose it on the slick road markings going up the hill. Other casualties were the Renault pair, both out within a few hundred metres of the start, and Lauda who spun away third at Casino Square on lap 24. But increasingly all eyes turned to the charge through the field by rookies Senna and Stefan Bellof (later dsq from P3), the Toleman displacing Niki Lauda from second on lap 19 and now reeling in the leader. Prost meanwhile was gesticulating for the rain-hit race to be stopped, and controversially, well before half-distance, race director Jacky Ickx obliged, leaving Prost with a half-points victory, Senna a brilliant first podium, but many unanswered questions.

| Pos | Driver | Car | Time/gap | Grid | Stops | Tyres |
|---|---|---|---|---|---|---|
| 1 | Alain Prost | McLaren-TAG | 1h 1m 7.740s | 1 | 0 | M |
| 2 | Ayrton Senna | Toleman-Hart | -7.446s | 13 | 0 | P |
| 3 | René Arnoux | Ferrari | -29.077s | 20 | 0 | G |
| 4 | Keke Rosberg | Williams-Honda | -35.246s | 3 | 0 | G |
| 5 | Elio de Angelis | Lotus-Renault | -44.439s | 10 | 0 | G |
| 6 | Michele Alboreto | Ferrari | -1 lap | 11 | 0 | G |

## ALAIN PROST

**McLaren-TAG Porsche MP4/2** 100.776kph, 62.618mph

**POLE POSITION** Prost, McLaren-TAG, 1m 22.661s (0.091s), 144.242kph, 89.628mph
**LAPS** 31 x 3.312 km, 2.058 miles (Race scheduled for 77 laps but stopped due to rain)
**DISTANCE** 102.672 km, 63.797 miles (Minimum distance incomplete; half points awarded)
**STARTERS/FINISHERS** 20/8
**WEATHER** Overcast, cold, very wet
**LAP LEADERS** Prost 1-10, 16-31 (26); N Mansell, Lotus-Renault 11-15 (5)
**WINNER'S LAPS** 1-10 P1, 11-15 P2, 16-31 P1
**FASTEST LAP** Senna, Toleman-Hart, 1m 54.334s (lap 24), 104.284kph, 64.799mph
**CHAMPIONSHIP** Prost 28.5, Lauda 18, Arnoux 15, Warwick 13, de Angelis 13

RACE POD

5 FOLKLORE

# Soon after the death of Enzo Ferrari, the Scuderia was gifted an emotional 1-2

**In the hands of Senna and Prost, the superiority of the McLaren-Hondas in 1988 was devastating. Had Senna not tripped over Schlesser here at Monza, it would have been a clean sweep**

## Race 464 — 1988 ITALIAN GP Monza

**Round 12/16** — **11 September 1988**

## GERHARD BERGER

**Ferrari F1-87/88C** 228.528kph, 142.000mph

In the 16-round 1988 season, Monza was the only race McLaren failed to win. At two-thirds distance, McLaren posted their first and only mechanical retirement, Prost, close behind Senna, out with engine trouble. So Senna then eased up, his fuel marginal, the chasing Ferraris closing in from 25s to just five. With two laps remaining, the charging Ferraris bearing down, Senna saw a backmarker ahead, the Williams-Judd of Jean-Louis Schlesser in his one and only GP appearance, subbing for the ill Nigel Mansell. At the Rettifilo chicane they collided, a mixture of Schlesser's desperation to steer clear and Senna's impetuosity. With both McLarens out, Ferrari was gifted an unexpected and emotional 1-2 *doppietta* at Monza, just four weeks after the death of *il Commendatore*, Enzo Ferrari.

| Pos | Driver | Car | Time/gap | Grid | Stops | Tyres |
|---|---|---|---|---|---|---|
| 1 | Gerhard Berger | Ferrari | 1h 17m 39.744s | 3 | 0 | G |
| 2 | Michele Alboreto | Ferrari | –0.502s | 4 | 0 | G |
| 3 | Eddie Cheever | Arrows-Megatron | –35.532s | 5 | 0 | G |
| 4 | Derek Warwick | Arrows-Megatron | –36.114s | 6 | 0 | G |
| 5 | Ivan Capelli | March-Judd | –52.522s | 11 | 0 | G |
| 6 | Thierry Boutsen | Benetton-Ford | –59.878s | 8 | 0 | G |

**POLE POSITION** A Senna, McLaren-Honda, 1m 25.974s (0.303s), 242.864kph, 150.909mph
**LAPS** 51 x 5.800 km, 3.604 miles
**DISTANCE** 295.800 km, 183.802 miles
**STARTERS/FINISHERS** 26/13
**WEATHER** Cloudy with sunny intervals, hot, dry
**LAP LEADERS** Senna 1-49 (49); Berger 50-51 (2)
**WINNER'S LAPS** 1-34 P3, 35-49 P2, 50-51 P1
**FASTEST LAP** Alboreto, Ferrari, 1m 29.070 (lap 44), 234.422kph, 145.663mph
**CHAMPIONSHIP** Senna 75, Prost 72, Berger 37, Alboreto 22, Boutsen 21

RACE POD

**FOLKLORE**

# Gurney was closing in the Eagle and took the lead with eight laps remaining

Dan Gurney's triumphant Eagle-Weslake plunges down the hill towards Eau Rouge on its way to making history as the first American car to win an F1 Championship race

## Race 154 · 1967 BELGIAN GP Spa-Francorchamps · DAN GURNEY

**Round 4/11** · **18 June 1967** · **Eagle-Weslake T1G** 234.946kph, 145.988mph

Just as it had in practice, Clark's Lotus 49 dominated the race, but shortly before half-distance made a couple of pit stops with spark-plug trouble, finishing P6. Stewart now led, for once enjoying a fine drive in the H16 BRM, but Dan Gurney's V12 Eagle-Weslake had closed in to within 1s. But around the time Clark made his stop for attention, so too did the Eagle, Gurney complaining of fluctuating fuel pressure. He quickly rejoined, still in second place, and began to narrow the now 15s gap to the BRM, in part because Stewart was driving one-handed, the other holding his car in gear. With eight laps left the Eagle took the lead and, despite some alarms over fuel pressure, held on to the finish. It was a popular and famous victory, the first for a US-built car and the second for a driver/constructor.

| Pos | Driver | Car | Time/gap | Grid | Stops | Tyres |
|---|---|---|---|---|---|---|
| 1 | Dan Gurney | Eagle-Weslake | 2h 40m 49.4s | 2 | 1 | G |
| 2 | Jackie Stewart | BRM | –1m 3.0s | 6 | 0 | G |
| 3 | Chris Amon | Ferrari | –1m 40.0s | 5 | 0 | F |
| 4 | Jochen Rindt | Cooper-Maserati | –2m 13.9s | 4 | 0 | F |
| 5 | Mike Spence | BRM | –1 lap | 11 | 0 | G |
| 6 | Jim Clark | Lotus-Ford | –1 lap | 1 | 2 | F |

**POLE POSITION** Clark, Lotus-Ford, 3m 28.1s (3.1s), 243.921kph, 151.566mph
**LAPS** 28 x 14.100 km, 8.761 miles
**DISTANCE** 394.800 km, 245.317 miles
**STARTERS/FINISHERS** 18/10
**WEATHER** Sunny, warm, dry
**LAP LEADERS** Clark 1-12 (12); Stewart 13-20 (8); Gurney 21-28 (8)
**WINNER'S LAPS** 1 P5, 2-12 P3, 13-20 P2, 21-28 P1
**FASTEST LAP** Gurney, Eagle-Weslake, 3m 31.9s (lap 19), 239.547kph, 148.848mph
**CHAMPIONSHIP** Hulme 16, Rodríguez 11, Amon 11, Clark 10, Gurney 9

RACE POD

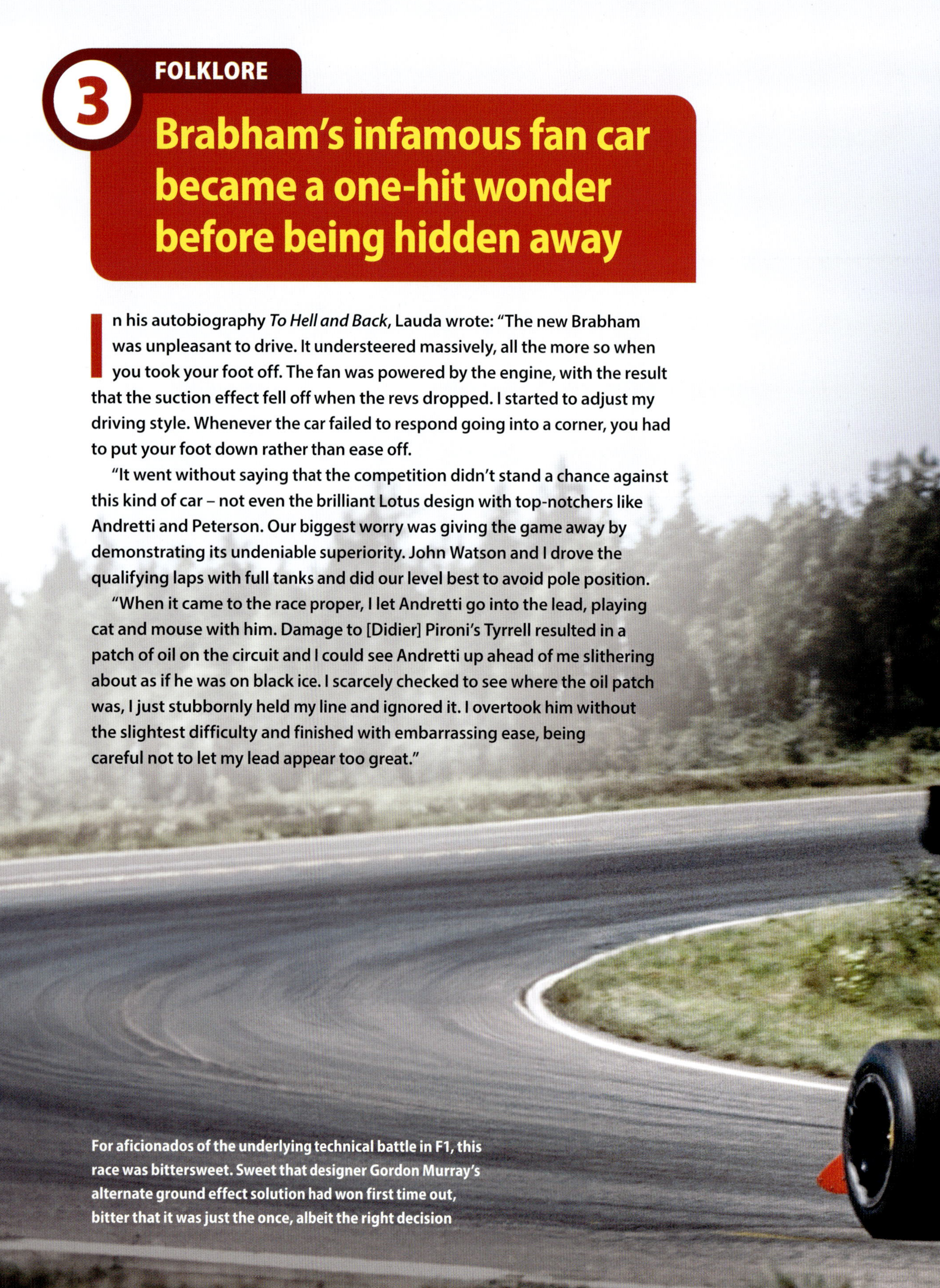

3 FOLKLORE

# Brabham's infamous fan car became a one-hit wonder before being hidden away

In his autobiography *To Hell and Back*, Lauda wrote: "The new Brabham was unpleasant to drive. It understeered massively, all the more so when you took your foot off. The fan was powered by the engine, with the result that the suction effect fell off when the revs dropped. I started to adjust my driving style. Whenever the car failed to respond going into a corner, you had to put your foot down rather than ease off.

"It went without saying that the competition didn't stand a chance against this kind of car – not even the brilliant Lotus design with top-notchers like Andretti and Peterson. Our biggest worry was giving the game away by demonstrating its undeniable superiority. John Watson and I drove the qualifying laps with full tanks and did our level best to avoid pole position.

"When it came to the race proper, I let Andretti go into the lead, playing cat and mouse with him. Damage to [Didier] Pironi's Tyrrell resulted in a patch of oil on the circuit and I could see Andretti up ahead of me slithering about as if he was on black ice. I scarcely checked to see where the oil patch was, I just stubbornly held my line and ignored it. I overtook him without the slightest difficulty and finished with embarrassing ease, being careful not to let my lead appear too great."

**For aficionados of the underlying technical battle in F1, this race was bittersweet. Sweet that designer Gordon Murray's alternate ground effect solution had won first time out, bitter that it was just the once, albeit the right decision**

## Race 305 — 1978 SWEDISH GP Anderstorp — NIKI LAUDA

**Round 8/16** — **17 June 1978** — **Brabham-Alfa Romeo BT46B** 167.609kph, 104.147mph

Brabham's 'fan car' won the battle, yet lost the war. After this single victory it was never raced again in anticipation of a ban the following season, the fan was deemed a movable aero device that also vented 'dangerous' debris. In their only head-to-head, Brabham's alternative 'ground effect' car beat the Lotus solution: unacceptable 'fan-suck' outperforming acceptable 'venturi-suck'. Andretti's 'venturi' won pole from Watson's 'fan', and in the race led the first 38 laps from Lauda's 'fan'. But on the 39th tour Mario Andretti made that tiny slip Lauda needed and once by, the Brabham pulled easily ahead on the oily track surface. John Watson's 'fan' Brabham went out after 19 laps, and after an early puncture Peterson's 'venturi' Lotus just failed to chase down Patrese for second after Andretti's engine blew up on lap 47.

| Pos | Driver | Car | Time/gap | Grid | Stops | Tyres |
|---|---|---|---|---|---|---|
| 1 | Niki Lauda | Brabham-Alfa | 1h 41m 0.606s | 3 | 0 | G |
| 2 | Riccardo Patrese | Arrows-Ford | –34.019s | 5 | 0 | G |
| 3 | Ronnie Peterson | Lotus-Ford | –34.105s | 4 | 1 | G |
| 4 | Patrick Tambay | McLaren-Ford | –1 lap | 15 | 0 | G |
| 5 | Clay Regazzoni | Shadow-Ford | –1 lap | 16 | 0 | G |
| 6 | Emerson Fittipaldi | Fittipaldi-Ford | –1 lap | 13 | 0 | G |

**POLE POSITION** M Andretti, Lotus-Ford, 1m 22.058s (0.679s), 176.846kph, 109.887mph
**LAPS** 70 x 4.031 km, 2.505 miles
**DISTANCE** 282.170 km, 175.332 miles
**STARTERS/FINISHERS** 24/15
**WEATHER** Sunny, warm, dry
**LAP LEADERS** Andretti 1-38 (38); Lauda 39-70 (32)
**WINNER'S LAPS** 1-38 P2, 39-70 P1
**FASTEST LAP** Lauda, Brabham-Alfa, 1m 24.836s (lap 33), 171.055kph, 106.288mph
**CHAMPIONSHIP** Andretti 36, Peterson 30, Lauda 25, Depailler 23, Reutemann 22

**RACE POD**

## 2 FOLKLORE

# After all the pain since the 2021 finale, Lewis ended his drought with a record ninth Silverstone victory

"This is my last race here at the British Grand Prix with this team," said Hamilton afterwards, "so I wanted to win this so much for them, because I love them, I appreciate them so much, all the hard work they've been putting in all over these years. We've had so many amazing times here and today was the most emotional end to a win I've ever had.

"The changeable conditions made it a real challenge. We kept our cool and made the right call at the right time to switch back to slicks. That helped us take back the lead and, from there, we were able to bring it home.

"That's the longest stint I've not had a win and the emotion has accumulated over that time. So, this one feels like it could be one of the most special ones for me, I think, if not *the* most special.

"It's so tough, I think for anyone. The important thing is just how you continue to get up, and you've got to continue to dig deep even when you feel like you're at the bottom of the barrel. There's definitely been days between 2021 and here where I didn't feel like I was good enough, or whether I was going to get back to where I am today, but the important thing is I had great people around me, continuing to support me. My team, every time I turn up and see them putting in the effort, that really encouraged me to do the same thing."

**Race 1113** **2024 BRITISH GP** Silverstone
**Round 12/24** **7 July 2024**

**LEWIS HAMILTON**
**Mercedes F1 W15** 222.821kph, 138.454mph

Home drivers filled the top three grid slots, expectation of British success by the record crowd palpable. All three Brits led the race, George Russell initially from pole until showers caused him to lose P1 to Hamilton on lap 18. Then Norris overtook both Mercedes to lead lap 20, teammate Piastri swiftly following. But as the rain intensified, the switch to inters dropped Oscar out of contention while Russell retired with overheating. This left Lando leading Lewis by 3s, Verstappen 10s further back, but the July sun drying out the track. In the switch back to slicks, a slow stop by leader Norris allowed Hamilton to retake the lead with 12 laps to go. Verstappen, on a charge, also passed Lando, but Lewis had Max covered, the crowd erupting as he crossed the line for his 104th victory, 56 races and 945 days since his last!

| Pos | Driver | Car | Time/gap | Grid | Stops | Tyres |
|---|---|---|---|---|---|---|
| 1 | Lewis Hamilton | Mercedes | 1h 22m 27.059s | 2 | 2 | mis |
| 2 | Max Verstappen | Red Bull-Honda RBPT | –1.465s | 4 | 2 | mih |
| 3 | Lando Norris | McLaren-Mercedes | –7.547s | 3 | 2 | mis |
| 4 | Oscar Piastri | McLaren-Mercedes | –12.429s | 5 | 2 | mim |
| 5 | Carlos Sainz | Ferrari | –47.318s | 7 | 3 | mihs |
| 6 | Nico Hülkenberg | Haas-Ferrari | –55.722s | 6 | 2 | mis |

**POLE POSITION** G Russell, Mercedes, 1m 25.819s (0.171s), 247.120kph, 153.553mph
**LAPS** 52 x 5.891 km, 3.660 miles
**DISTANCE** 306.198 km, 190.262 miles
**STARTERS/FINISHERS** 20/18
**WEATHER** Overcast, cool, mid-race showers
**LAP LEADERS** Russell 1-17 (17); Hamilton 18-19, 40-52 (15); Norris 20-27, 29-39 (19); Piastri 28 (1)
**WINNER'S LAPS** 1-17 P2, 18-19 P1, 20-26 P3, 27 P2, 28 P3, 29-38 P2, 39 P3, 40-52 P1
**FASTEST LAP** Sainz, Ferrari, 1m 28.293s (lap 52), 240.195kph, 149.250mph
**CHAMPIONSHIP** Verstappen 255, Norris 171, Leclerc 150, Sainz 146, Piastri 124

RACE POD

The inaugural F1 championship race was at Silverstone. So winning at Silverstone for a record ninth time is really something. And winning your 104th, yes 104th, race after a 30-month win-drought is something else. Little wonder there was emotion

When a youthful Max Verstappen took his first GP win aged 18, no one was surprised. But who might have anticipated four World Championships, and counting, inside ten years? Max and Jos for sure!

1 FOLKLORE

# Teenager Verstappen took a fairy tale maiden victory on his Red Bull début

Winner's words:

"It's a very special feeling. Of course I didn't expect to win; after the Mercedes pair crashed then you're targeting a podium, but in the end to come out on top, it's incredible. To hear the Dutch national anthem for the first time in F1, I have to think about my dad for sure and I heard he was crying, so yeah it's unbelievable. He invested a lot of time in me and this achievement is also because of him.

"I wasn't nervous during the race, I was just trying to focus and drive the best I could. We focused a lot on keeping the tyres alive because at my last stop I still had to do 32 laps until the end, but it worked out well! With five laps to the end I saw Kimi was dropping off a bit, he tried a few times and of course it kills your tyres and from there I was just like, 'OK, focus on the tyres now and bring it home'.

"I will for sure remember this and at the moment it's just a great feeling. It's amazing, I have no words for it. It was very good company on the podium, I mean Kimi even raced against my dad, so it's very funny! I was celebrating a lot on the in-lap and I got a bit of cramp, but that's part of it!"

## Race 940 — 2016 SPANISH GP Cataluña

**Round 5/21** — **15 May 2016**

Within 30s of the start the Mercedes pair had wiped each other out, their exit presaging a tense struggle between Red Bull and Ferrari. Once the Ferraris got past local hero Carlos Sainz in P3, they began to close in on the two Bulls. So Red Bull decided to split strategies by pitting leader Ricciardo to cover Vettel for two stops or three. Vettel followed suit then made an early third stop that successfully undercut Daniel for P3. Meanwhile Max led from Kimi, both two-stopping. Could the youngest (18) and oldest (36) drivers reach the finish to foil Seb and Dan closing in on faster rubber? Despite his worn tyres, the teenager made no mistake, keeping Räikkönen at bay in style. With a fairy tale maiden victory on his Red Bull début, Max Verstappen became the youngest-ever GP winner and first Dutchman to mount the podium top step.

| Pos | Driver | Car | Time/gap | Grid | Stops | Tyres |
|---|---|---|---|---|---|---|
| 1 | Max Verstappen | Red Bull-TAG Heuer | 1h 41m 40.017s | 4 | 2 | smm |
| 2 | Kimi Räikkönen | Ferrari | -0.616s | 5 | 2 | smm |
| 3 | Sebastian Vettel | Ferrari | -5.581s | 6 | 3 | smsm |
| 4 | Daniel Ricciardo | Red Bull-TAG Heuer | -43.950s | 3 | 4 | smsms |
| 5 | Valtteri Bottas | Williams-Mercedes | -45.271s | 7 | 2 | smm |
| 6 | Carlos Sainz | Toro Rosso-Ferrari | -1m 1.395s | 8 | 2 | smm |

## MAX VERSTAPPEN

**Red Bull-TAG Heuer RB12** 181.241kph, 112.617mph

**POLE POSITION** L Hamilton, Mercedes, 1m 22.000s (0.280s), 204.365kph, 126.986mph
**LAPS** 66 x 4.655 km, 2.892 miles
**DISTANCE** 307.104 km, 190.826 miles
**STARTERS/FINISHERS** 22/17
**WEATHER** Sunny, warm, dry
**LAP LEADERS** Ricciardo 1-10, 16-27, 36-43 (30); Verstappen 11, 28-33, 44-66 (30); Vettel 12-15 (4); Räikkönen 34-35 (1); SC 1-3 (3)
**WINNER'S LAPS** 1-10 P2, 11 P1, 12 P2, 13-14 P4, 15 P3, 16-27 P2, 28-33 P1, 34 P2, 35 P4, 36-37 P3, 38-43 P2, 44-66 P1
**FASTEST LAP** Kvyat, Toro Rosso-Ferrari, 1m 26.948s (lap 53), 192.735kph, 119.759mph
**CHAMPIONSHIP** Rosberg 100, Räikkönen 61, Hamilton 57, Vettel 48, Ricciardo 48

RACE POD

## CHAPTER 10

# DECIDERS

## DOWN TO THE WIRE

The FIA Formula 1 World Championship is the glue that binds a season of up to 24 races together. While each Grand Prix is a prestigious event in its own right, the ultimate goal for drivers and teams is to accumulate enough points to secure the most coveted prize in motorsport: the World Championship.

When the season finale also decides the title, that last race can become an electrifying winner-takes-all shootout. The culmination of a gruelling season condenses into one, single, down-to-the-wire endgame. The tension is palpable, the psychological strain immense, the drivers and their teams aware that every corner, each pit stop could determine their place in history. It's Formula 1 at its most awe-inspiring.

Over Formula 1's 75-year history, the Drivers' title has been decided in the final race of the season on 30 occasions. These high-stakes finales have produced unforgettable moments – titles won or lost by a half-point, the Championship lead changing multiple times during the race, and even instances where the outcome wasn't clear until after the chequered flag had fallen. Some saw drivers deliver brilliance under immense pressure, securing glory in style; others were heartbreakingly lost in the cruellest fashion at the final hurdle.

It is in these all-or-nothing finales that Formula 1 delivers some of its most defining and dramatic moments. A single race can encapsulate an entire season's worth of effort, heartbreak, and triumph. This collection revisits the greatest of those rare and electrifying occasions when the World Championship hung in the balance until the final race – when one last showdown determined who would be immortalised as Formula 1 World Champion.

**WHEN THE SEASON FINALE ALSO DECIDES THE TITLE, THAT LAST RACE BECOMES AN ELECTRIFYING WINNER-TAKES-ALL SHOOTOUT. THE CULMINATION OF A GRUELLING SEASON CONDENSES INTO ONE, SINGLE, DOWN-TO-THE-WIRE ENDGAME**

10

DECIDERS

# *They think it's all over!* It is now: Schumacher punctures on lap one

Fernando Alonso celebrates with the Renault team having supplanted Michael Schumacher as the youngest-ever back-to-back champion

## Race 768 — 2006 BRAZILIAN GP Interlagos

**Round 18/18** — **22 October 2006**

*They think it's all over*: Schumacher needed victory, Alonso a point. Alonso qualifies P4, Schumacher P10. It is now: Schumacher punctures on lap one. That's the downbeat yet poignant way the 2006 title showdown played out. Many feel the display that followed was Michael at his classic best, a farewell virtuoso performance, a sequence of scintillating lappery culminating in the symbolic pass of his Ferrari successor Kimi Räikkönen on lap 69. Why was this man retiring? Maybe part of the answer finished P2, stripping Schumacher of one of his numerous titles, youngest double champion. Maybe another factor was the driver who finished first, winning his home GP on his first visit with Ferrari. Ferrari/Bridgestone had won another battle but, with both titles, Renault/Michelin had won the war.

| Pos | Driver | Car | Time/gap | Grid (pen) | Stops | Tyres |
|---|---|---|---|---|---|---|
| 1 | Felipe Massa | Ferrari | 1h 31m 53.751s | 1 | 2 | B |
| 2 | Fernando Alonso | Renault | –18.658s | 4 | 2 | M |
| 3 | Jenson Button | Honda | –19.394s | 14 | 2 | M |
| 4 | Michael Schumacher | Ferrari | –24.094s | 10 | 2 | B |
| 5 | Kimi Räikkönen | McLaren-Mercedes | –28.503s | 2 | 2 | M |
| 6 | Giancarlo Fisichella | Renault | –30.287s | 6 | 2 | M |

## FELIPE MASSA

**Ferrari 248 F1** 199.731kph, 124.107mph

**POLE POSITION** Massa, Ferrari, 1m 10.680s (0.619s), 219.473kph, 136.374mph
**LAPS** 71 x 4.309 km, 2.677 miles
**DISTANCE** 305.909 km, 190.083 miles
**STARTERS/FINISHERS** 22/17
**WEATHER** Cloudy with sunny intervals, warm, dry
**LAP LEADERS** Massa 1-24, 27-71 (69); Alonso 25-26 (2); SC 2-6 (5)
**WINNER'S LAPS** 1-24 P1, 25 P3, 26 P2, 27-71 P1
**FASTEST LAP** M Schumacher, Ferrari, 1m 12.162s (lap 70), 214.966kph, 133.574mph
**CHAMPIONSHIP** Alonso 134, M Schumacher 121, Massa 80, Fisichella 72, Räikkönen 65

RACE POD

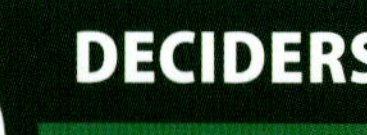

DECIDERS

# Collins handed over his Lancia Ferrari to teammate Fangio to secure title

The early stages with Fangio (22) leading Moss (36) and teammate Collins (26). Fangio would finish just 5.7s behind winner Moss… but driving Collins' car!

## Race 56 — 1956 ITALIAN GP Monza

**Round 8/8** — **2 September 1956**

## STIRLING MOSS

**Maserati 250F** 208.785kph, 129.733mph

From the all-Lancia Ferrari front row, Luigi Musso and Eugenio Castellotti put on a dazzling if foolhardy display. It only lasted four laps, the concrete Monza banking playing havoc with their tyres. Now Moss duelled for the lead with Harry Schell's Vanwall until a rain shower helped Stirling pull away to win. Fangio meanwhile, only requiring two points to secure his fourth title, had pulled over on lap 19 with a broken steering arm, Italian teammate Musso bluntly refusing to car-share here at Monza. However, holding third place and still with a chance to win both race and title, Collins made a routine pit stop on lap 32. In perhaps the most sporting gesture ever seen, having spotted his team-leader on the pit-wall, Collins handed over his car to Fangio, later saying, "I would not have been proud of beating him thanks to bad luck."

| Pos | Driver | Car | Time/gap | Grid | Stops | Tyres |
|---|---|---|---|---|---|---|
| 1 | Stirling Moss | Maserati | 2h 23m 41.3s | 6 | 1 | P |
| 2 | Peter Collins /Juan Manuel Fangio | Lancia Ferrari | –5.7s | 7 | 1 | E |
| 3 | Ron Flockhart | Connaught-Alta | –1 lap | 23 | NA | P/A |
| 4 | Paco Godia | Maserati | –1 lap | 17 | NA | P |
| 5 | Jack Fairman | Connaught-Alta | –3 laps | 15 | 1 | P/A |
| 6 | Luigi Piotti | Maserati | –3 laps | 14 | NA | P |

**POLE POSITION** Fangio, Lancia Ferrari, 2m 42.6s (0.8s), 221.402kph, 137.573mph
**LAPS** 50 x 10.000 km, 6.214 miles
**DISTANCE** 500.000 km, 310.686 miles
**STARTERS/FINISHERS** 24/11
**WEATHER** Warm with showers
**LAP LEADERS** E Castellotti, Lancia Ferrari 1-4 (4); Moss 5-10, 12-45, 48-50 (43); H Schell, Vanwall 11 (1); L Musso, Lancia Ferrari 46-47 (2)
**WINNER'S LAPS** 1-4 P6, 5-10 P1, 11 P2, 12-45 P1, 46-47, P2, 48-50 P1
**FASTEST LAP** Moss, Maserati, 2m 45.5s (lap 47), 217.523kph, 135.162mph
**CHAMPIONSHIP** Fangio 30, Moss 27, Collins 25, Behra 22, Flaherty 8

RACE POD

**8** DECIDERS

# The champion didn't need to finish but elected to push his dead car a quarter-mile

**Little wonder team owner John Cooper is beaming. The Cooper Car Co. has just won its first Championship courtesy of Jack Brabham, and the first US Grand Prix thanks to Bruce McLaren (left)**

## Race 84 — 1959 UNITED STATES GP Sebring

**Round 9/9** — **12 December 1959**

## BRUCE MCLAREN

**Cooper-Climax T51** 159.047kph, 98.827mph

Because of the 'best five scores count' system, the three contenders each needed victory to clinch the title. Chased by Brabham, Stirling Moss roared into a growing lead from pole, but tension didn't last long. After a mere five laps Stirling was out with yet another broken gearbox while Brooks' Ferrari was never in the hunt for victory after an early stop. So Brabham became the new champion and looked about to lift his title in style with a third race victory of the season. But on the very final lap his Cooper ran dry, triggering an exciting finish. Teammate McLaren shot past Brabham to defy a fast-closing Trintignant by 0.6s as well as becoming the youngest-ever Grand Prix winner. As for the new champion, Jack didn't need to finish but elected to push his dead car a quarter-mile uphill to finish fourth in a virtual state of collapse!

| Pos | Driver | Car | Time/gap | Grid | Stops | Tyres |
|---|---|---|---|---|---|---|
| 1 | Bruce McLaren | Cooper-Climax | 2h 12m 35.7s | 10 | 0 | D |
| 2 | Maurice Trintignant | Cooper-Climax | –0.6s | 5 | 0 | D |
| 3 | Tony Brooks | Ferrari | –3m 0.9s | 4 | 0 | D |
| 4 | Jack Brabham | Cooper-Climax | –4m 57.3s | 2 | 0 | D |
| 5 | Innes Ireland | Lotus-Climax | –3 laps | 9 | NA | D |
| 6 | Wolfgang von Trips | Ferrari | –4 laps | 6 | NA | D |

**POLE POSITION** S Moss, Cooper-Climax, 3m 0.0s (3.0s), 167.372kph, 104.000mph
**LAPS** 42 x 8.369 km, 5.200 miles
**DISTANCE** 351.481 km, 218.400 miles
**STARTERS/FINISHERS** 18/7
**WEATHER** Sunny, warm, dry
**LAP LEADERS** Moss 1-5 (5); Brabham 6-41 (36); McLaren 42 (1)
**WINNER'S LAPS** 1-5 P3, 6-41 P2, 42 P1
**FASTEST LAP** Trintignant, Cooper-Climax, 3m 5.0s (lap 39), 162.848kph, 101.189mph
**CHAMPIONSHIP** Brabham 31, Brooks 27, Moss 25.5, P Hill 20, Trintignant 19

**RACE POD**

7 DECIDERS

# Brabham-BMW's resolute strategy showed immense self-belief

Nelson Piquet, flat out at Kyalami as he pulls a 30s lead in the opening 27 laps in Brabham-BMW's audacious strategy to defeat Prost's McLaren

## Race 388 — 1983 SOUTH AFRICAN GP Kyalami

**Round 15/15** — **15 October 1983**

## RICCARDO PATRESE

**Brabham-BMW BT52B** 202.941kph, 126.102mph

Alain Prost versus Piquet for the 1983 Drivers' title. Nelson on a roll of two consecutive wins had closed Prost's 14-point lead to just two. A Piquet hat-trick would settle it regardless of Prost's result, so he set a blistering pace out front on an exceptionally light fuel load in the hope that the Renault turbo might not stand the pace. But when he rejoined from his lap 28 fuel stop, Prost was still there albeit 10s in arrears. Then, around half-distance, with Prost holding a 'losing' P3 behind the Brabham pair, the Renault turbo duly expired. As Piquet no longer needed to win, just score three points, he turned down the wick and stroked home to third place and the Championship, teammate Patrese winning the race. In winning both race and Drivers' title, Brabham-BMW's resolute strategy had shown immense self-belief.

| Pos | Driver | Car | Time/gap | Grid | Stops | Tyres |
|---|---|---|---|---|---|---|
| 1 | Riccardo Patrese | Brabham-BMW | 1h 33m 25.708s | 3 | 1 | M |
| 2 | Andrea de Cesaris | Alfa Romeo | –9.319s | 9 | 1 | M |
| 3 | Nelson Piquet | Brabham-BMW | –21.969s | 2 | 1 | M |
| 4 | Derek Warwick | Toleman-Hart | –1 lap | 13 | 1 | P |
| 5 | Keke Rosberg | Williams-Honda | –1 lap | 6 | 1 | G |
| 6 | Eddie Cheever | Renault | –1 lap | 14 | 1 | M |

**POLE POSITION** P Tambay, Ferrari, 1m 06.554s (0.238s), 221.991kph, 137.939mph
**LAPS** 77 x 4.104 km, 2.550 miles
**DISTANCE** 316.008 km, 196.358 miles
**STARTERS/FINISHERS** 26/12
**WEATHER** Sunny, hot, dry
**LAP LEADERS** Piquet 1-59 (59); Patrese 60-77 (18)
**WINNER'S LAPS** 1-59 P2, 60-77 P1
**FASTEST LAP** Piquet, Brabham-BMW, 1m 09.948s (lap 6), 211.220kph, 131.246mph
**CHAMPIONSHIP** Piquet 59, Prost 57, Arnoux 49, Tambay 40, Rosberg 27

RACE POD

# On lap 31 Bandini got it wrong, punting title favourite Hill off

Garlanded race winner Dan Gurney and new World Champion John Surtees congratulate one another, each a beneficiary of the retirement of Clark's Lotus on the penultimate lap

## Race 131 — 1964 MEXICAN GP Mexico City

**Round 10/10** — **25 October 1964**

So the title would be decided between Hill, Surtees and Clark. From pole Clark eased out a lead over Gurney, these two in turn pulling away from the rest. Surtees had done his prospects no good by losing nine places at the start with an early misfire that cleared. By the end of lap 11 Graham Hill had moved into the crucial P3 that would deliver the title even if Clark was victorious. But Bandini in the flat-12 Ferrari was constantly harrying him, and on lap 31 got it wrong, controversially punting the BRM off. The title was now Clark's, Gurney's Brabham occupying the P2 required by Surtees to snatch the title. But on the last lap a split oil line dropped Clark back and for a few incredible moments it was Hill's title again – until Bandini waved Ferrari team leader Surtees through into second place, and with it the championship by a single point.

| Pos | Driver | Car | Time/gap | Grid | Stops | Tyres |
|---|---|---|---|---|---|---|
| 1 | Dan Gurney | Brabham-Climax | 2h 9m 5.32s | 2 | 0 | D |
| 2 | John Surtees | Ferrari | –1m 8.94s | 4 | 0 | D |
| 3 | Lorenzo Bandini | Ferrari | –1m 9.63s | 3 | 0 | D |
| 4 | Mike Spence | Lotus-Climax | –1m 21.86s | 5 | 0 | D |
| 5r | Jim Clark | Lotus-Climax | –1 lap | 1 | 0 | D |
| 6 | Pedro Rodríguez | Ferrari | –1 lap | 9 | 0 | D |

## DAN GURNEY

**Brabham-Climax BT7** 150.186kph, 93.321mph

**POLE POSITION** Clark, Lotus-Climax, 1m 57.24s (1.7s), 153.531ph, 95.400mph
**LAPS** 65 x 5.000 km, 3.107 miles
**DISTANCE** 325.000 km, 201.946 miles
**STARTERS/FINISHERS** 19/13
**WEATHER** Sunny, warm, dry
**LAP LEADERS** Clark 1-63 (63); Gurney 64-65 (2)
**WINNER'S LAPS** 1-63 P2, 64-65 P1
**FASTEST LAP** Clark, Lotus-Climax, 1m 58.37s (lap 46 & 56), 152.066kph, 94.489mph
**CHAMPIONSHIP** Surtees 40, G Hill 39, Clark 32, Bandini 23, Ginther 23

*RACE POD*

5 DECIDERS

# Mansell retired from the crucial P2, handing Lauda a third title

A glorious photo of Niki Lauda on his way to clinching his third World Championship

## Race 404 1984 PORTUGUESE GP Estoril

**Round 16/16** **21 October 1984**

Put simply, even if Prost won, second would still be enough to bring Lauda his third championship. Once Prost had dispensed with the fast-starting Keke Rosberg, he did everything required of him by winning comfortably, chased by Nigel Mansell. So it was all down to Lauda, who had qualified only P11. Relentlessly he made his way through the field: Lap 10 P9, lap 20 P7, lap 30 P5. He then passed first Rosberg, then Senna to reach P3 on lap 33. But there progress stalled, Mansell, driving his Lotus swansong, way ahead. *La belle France* prepared to crown their first Champion until, 18 laps from *le gloire*, Mansell retired brakeless from the crucial P2, handing Lauda his third championship. Despite his 7-5 race win superiority, another title had slipped by Prost, this time by the narrowest margin of half a point.

| Pos | Driver | Car | Time/gap | Grid | Stops | Tyres |
|---|---|---|---|---|---|---|
| 1 | Alain Prost | McLaren-TAG | 1h 41m 11.753s | 2 | 0 | M |
| 2 | Niki Lauda | McLaren-TAG | –13.425s | 11 | 0 | M |
| 3 | Ayrton Senna | Toleman-Hart | –20.042s | 3 | 0 | M |
| 4 | Michele Alboreto | Ferrari | –20.317s | 8 | 0 | G |
| 5 | Elio de Angelis | Lotus-Renault | –1m 32.169s | 5 | 0 | G |
| 6 | Nelson Piquet | Brabham-BMW | –1 lap | 1 | 1 | M |

## ALAIN PROST

**McLaren-TAG Porsche MP4/2** 180.541kph, 112.183mph

**POLE POSITION** Piquet, Brabham-BMW, 1m 21.703s (0.071s), 191.670kph, 119.098mph
**LAPS** 70 x 4.350 km, 2.703 miles
**DISTANCE** 304.500 km, 189.208 miles
**STARTERS/FINISHERS** 27/17
**WEATHER** Sunny, hot, dry
**LAP LEADERS** K Rosberg, Williams-Honda 1-8 (8); Prost 9-70 (62)
**WINNER'S LAPS** 1 P3, 2-8 P2, 9-70 P1
**FASTEST LAP** Lauda, McLaren-TAG, 1m 22.996s (lap 51), 188.684kph, 117.243mph
**CHAMPIONSHIP** Lauda 72, Prost 71.5, de Angelis 34, Alboreto 30.5, Piquet 29

*RACE POD*

## 4 DECIDERS

# Title favourite Vettel ended up dead last, spun around in a hefty collision

The photo captures the moment Vettel fell to last place on the first lap, yet Seb recovered to replace his hero Ayrton Senna as the youngest-ever triple title winner

## Race 878 — 2012 BRAZILIAN GP Interlagos

**Round 20/20** — **25 November 2012**

Changeable weather brought Ferrari its chance, an Alonso podium with Seb out of the points being the miracle it craved. It almost happened at the start. Swamped in midfield after a cautious start, Vettel ended up dead last, spun around in a hefty collision with Bruno Senna. Alonso snatched two places off the grid then began lap two by blasting past Webber and Massa at turn one to claim his crucial podium. As things stood, Fernando would do it. But incredibly, despite damage, Vettel was P6 by the end of lap eight and now Alonso needed victory. Tension ebbed and flowed with the rain as cars switched between slicks and inters, Red Bull almost giving Ferrari a reprieve when Sebastian briefly dropped out of the points by pitting twice due to radio failure. But ultimately, Alonso's P2 behind winner Button was simply not enough.

| Pos | Driver | Car | Time/gap | Grid (pen) | Stops | Tyres (h/m) |
|---|---|---|---|---|---|---|
| 1 | Jenson Button | McLaren-Mercedes | 1h 45m 22.656s | 2 | 2 | opi |
| 2 | Fernando Alonso | Ferrari | -2.754s | 7 | 3 | oioi |
| 3 | Felipe Massa | Ferrari | -3.615s | 5 | 3 | oioi |
| 4 | Mark Webber | Red Bull-Renault | -4.936s | 3 | 3 | oipi |
| 5 | Nico Hülkenberg | Force India-Mercedes | -5.708s | 6 | 2 | opi |
| 6 | Sebastian Vettel | Red Bull-Renault | -9.453s | 4 | 4 | oipoi |

## JENSON BUTTON

**McLaren-Mercedes MP4-27** 174.178kph, 108.229mph

**POLE POSITION** L Hamilton, McLaren-Mercedes, 1m 12.458s (0.055s), 214.088kph, 133.028mph
**LAPS** 71 x 4.309 km, 2.677 miles
**DISTANCE** 305.909 km, 190.083 miles
**STARTERS/FINISHERS** 24/19
**WEATHER** Warm but overcast with misting drizzle, worsening towards the end
**LAP LEADERS** Hamilton 1-5, 7, 48-54 (13); Button 6, 8-17, 55-71 (28); Hülkenberg 18-47 (30); SC 23-29, 70-71 (9)
**WINNER'S LAPS** 1-5 P2, 6 P1, 7 P2, 8-17 P1, 18-30 P2, 31-54 P3, 55-71 P1
**FASTEST LAP** Hamilton, McLaren-Mercedes, 1m 18.069s (lap 38), 198.701kph, 123.467mph
**CHAMPIONSHIP** Vettel 281, Alonso 278, Räikkönen 207, Hamilton 190, Webber 179

*RACE POD*

## 3 DECIDERS

# The title was decided on the final corner of the final lap of the final race

Hamilton said:

"I knew I had at least to finish fifth, so I was focusing on that. I was in fourth; I was comfortable there. I was just trying to bring the car home, trying to look after the gearshifts, the tyres and manage everything.

"Towards the end it got quite tough because I went out with a huge fuel load and we used our tyres more than most in certain places.

"I was keeping Vettel at bay, but then the weather got bad. We'd changed tyres but I had less downforce than other people, which hurt us in the rain. The last two laps were the toughest two laps of my entire career. After I lost the position there was nothing I could do. I was pushing and pushing to get close to him, so I was taking more risks. Not unnecessary risks, but I knew I was in P6 and was one point away from the Championship."

Massa said: "I had completely mixed emotions because, by the time I had crossed the line, I was still the Champion, and then suddenly my engineer was telling me everything on the radio, and then he told me when I was already in turn 3 that Lewis had passed Glock."

**Timo Glock, pictured here behind Hamilton, never won a GP but forever his name will be preserved in pub quizzes as the driver Lewis passed on that final corner to win his first World Championship**

## Race 803 — 2008 BRAZILIAN GP Interlagos — FELIPE MASSA

**Round 18/18** — **2 November 2008** — **Ferrari F2008** 194.865kph, 121.083mph

The final showdown, Massa needing a home victory, points leader and favourite Hamilton P5 or better. Massa duly won the race superbly whereas McLaren chose an ultra-conservative strategy that appeared to backfire badly when rain caused a late-race switch to wets for all but the Toyotas. With three laps to go Vettel overtook Hamilton, demoting him to a championship-losing P6. Unable to retake Vettel McLaren had blown it, but on the final corner of the last breathtaking lap Lewis overtook Timo Glock for P5, the Toyotas now scrabbling on their dry-tyres gamble, to deny Massa and win the title by a single point. Television provided unforgettable human images: Felipe's father, euphoric one moment, frozen in disbelief the next, and his son's podium dignity in disappointed defeat, Champion for 39 seconds.

| Pos | Driver | Car | Time/gap | Grid (pen) | Stops | Tyres (m/s) |
|---|---|---|---|---|---|---|
| 1 | Felipe Massa | Ferrari | 1h 34m 11.435s | 1 | 3 | wppw |
| 2 | Fernando Alonso | Renault | –13.298s | 6 | 3 | wppw |
| 3 | Kimi Räikkönen | Ferrari | –16.235s | 3 | 3 | wppw |
| 4 | Sebastian Vettel | Toro Rosso-Ferrari | –38.011s | 7 | 4 | wpppw |
| 5 | Lewis Hamilton | McLaren-Mercedes | –38.907s | 4 | 3 | wppw |
| 6 | Timo Glock | Toyota | –44.368s | 10 | 2 | wpp |

**POLE POSITION** Massa, Ferrari, 1m 12.368s (0.369s), 214.354kph, 133.193mph
**LAPS** 71 x 4.309 km, 2.677 miles
**DISTANCE** 305.909 km, 190.083 miles
**STARTERS/FINISHERS** 20/18
**WEATHER** Cloudy, hot, showers at start and finish
**LAP LEADERS** Massa 1-9, 12-38, 44-71 (64); J Trulli, Toyota 10-11 (2); Alonso 39-40 (2); Räikkönen 41-43 (3); SC 1-4 (4)
**WINNER'S LAPS** 1-9 P1, 10-11 P4, 12-38 P1, 39-40 P4, 41-43 P2, 44-71 P1
**FASTEST LAP** Massa, Ferrari, 1m 13.736s (lap 36), 210.377kph, 130.723mph
**CHAMPIONSHIP** Hamilton 98, Massa 97, Räikkönen 75, Kubica 75, Alonso 61

RACE POD

## 2 DECIDERS

# Hunt charged back, regaining P3 and with it this Championship epic by a single point

Talking to *Autosport*'s Eoin Young shortly after the finale, Hunt said: "I wasn't racing hard from the 15th lap. I was anxious to protect the tyres with the track drying out.

"I wasn't even defending my lead at that stage [when a puncture forced his late stop]. I was just trying to finish without a pit stop.

"I thought [McLaren team manager] Teddy Mayer must be mistaken. I didn't want to let myself think I'd won the Championship if I hadn't. The disappointment would have been terrible. Then everyone started shouting that I'd won the Championship and I realised that I really had."

In the 'Hunt-Lauda *Autosport* Legends' special magazine, Lauda said: "Since my accident at the Nürburgring, I just didn't have the reserves to take any crazy chances. I decided to do just one lap and go home. The mechanics accepted my decision – they had to. Even Mr Ferrari accepted it. I rang him afterwards and told him. Anyway, I didn't lose the Championship in Japan – I lost it at the Nürburgring.

"I was driven back to the airport with the race still going on. I told the driver to keep the radio on, but we drove through a tunnel and lost the signal. It was only when we finally stopped at the terminal and I saw the Japanese Ferrari importer's face that I immediately knew I'd lost the Championship. I was happy that James had won it. He was my mate."

## Race 280 — 1976 JAPANESE GP Fuji

**Round 16/16** — **24 October 1976**

## MARIO ANDRETTI

**Lotus-Ford 77** 183.615kph, 114.093mph

The finale of the epic 1976 Hunt versus Lauda Championship battle. If Hunt won the race the title was his regardless. If he didn't, Niki Lauda needed to finish close enough to the McLaren to retain it. These scenarios were valid for a mere two laps, Lauda and three others withdrawing their cars, deciding the atrociously wet and misty weather to be unsuitable for racing. Meanwhile Hunt had taken the lead, holding it for 61 laps of the 73-lap race. But as the track dried he was forced to pit for new tyres, dropping him to fifth with five laps to go, the championship now Lauda's. But on the penultimate lap Hunt charged back on his fresh rubber and overtook non-stopping cars struggling on worn tyres, regaining the crucial P4, then P3 and with it the championship by a single point. Pole-man Andretti won the race for Lotus.

| Pos | Driver | Car | Time/gap | Grid | Stops | Tyres |
|---|---|---|---|---|---|---|
| 1 | Mario Andretti | Lotus-Ford | 1h 43m 58.86s | 1 | 0 | G |
| 2 | Patrick Depailler | Tyrrell-Ford | –1 lap | 13 | 1 | G |
| 3 | James Hunt | McLaren-Ford | –1 lap | 2 | 1 | G |
| 4 | Alan Jones | Surtees-Ford | –1 lap | 20 | 0 | G |
| 5 | Clay Regazzoni | Ferrari | –1 lap | 7 | 0 | G |
| 6 | Gunnar Nilsson | Lotus-Ford | –1 lap | 16 | 0 | G |

**POLE POSITION** Andretti, Lotus-Ford, 1m 12.77s (0.03s), 215.644kph, 133.995mph
**LAPS** 73 x 4.359 km, 2.709 miles
**DISTANCE** 318.207 km, 197.725 miles
**STARTERS/FINISHERS** 25/11
**WEATHER** Overcast, rain, misty
**LAP LEADERS** Hunt 1-61 (61); Depailler 62-63 (2); Andretti 64-73 (10)
**WINNER'S LAPS** 1 P3, 2 P2, 3-5 P3, 6-15 P2, 16-20 P3, 21 P4, 22-32 P5, 33-35 P6, 36-38 P5, 39-46 P4, 47-61 P3, 62-63 P2, 64-73 P1
**FASTEST LAP** J Laffite, Ligier-Matra, 1m 19.97s (lap NA), 196.229kph, 121.931mph
**CHAMPIONSHIP** Hunt 69, Lauda 68, Scheckter 49, Depailler 39, Regazzoni 31

**RACE POD**

James Hunt, here leading teammate Jochen Mass, splashes his way to the 1976 title to bring to a close possibly the most anguished Championship battle ever

1

DECIDERS

# Title favourite Mansell, at 180mph, wrestled his swerving, bucking steed to a stop

Drivers' words from Nigel Roebuck's report in the October 30 1986 issue of *Autosport* magazine.

*Winner Prost:* "Even when I came in for tyres it [the fuel readout] was reading minus five, and in an ordinary race I would have backed off until it had come back on the right side again – maybe settled for a safe third place or something like that. But on a day like this there was no way to back off, no point. I thought, 'OK, maybe I finish, maybe I don't – but if I don't win the race, I don't win the championship', so there was no point in backing off. A good finish was no good to me. I kept pushing. This championship means more to me than last year's, because I truly did not believe we could beat the Williams-Hondas this year. And also this year I can't remember making a serious mistake.

"Please, let me say something about Nigel. I have lost two world championships at the last race, and I know how he feels. I like Nigel very much, and I truly believe he deserved the title this year. All I can say is that he can win the title next year, and I hope he does. But I must also say that I will be fighting as hard as ever in 1987."

*Loser Mansell:* "To be honest, I'm glad simply to be in one piece. There was no warning of it, no sign that anything was wrong. In fact, I was just cruising along, knowing that I was in the right position to take the title. It just wasn't meant to be, was it?"

**Nigel Mansell in 'Red 5': This astonishing photo captures the instant the left-rear tyre of his Williams-Honda delaminated, the Championship snatched from his grasp**

## Race 436 — 1986 AUSTRALIAN GP Adelaide — ALAIN PROST

**Round 16/16** — **26 October 1986** — **McLaren-TAG Porsche MP4/2C** 162.609kph, 101.041mph

The 1986 title was between Prost, Piquet and favourite Mansell. On lap 63, comfortable leader Rosberg heard his engine blow. Actually, a rear Goodyear had unaccountably delaminated, the death-rattle Keke misheard being stripped tread flailing the McLaren's bodywork. Next lap, holding P3 and so perfectly poised for the title, Nigel Mansell spectacularly suffered the same fate at 180mph, needing 14s to wrestle his swerving, bucking steed to a standstill. Piquet, now leading Prost and the race, would become champion, until, that is, Goodyear advised a precautionary tyre stop. Prost, on fresher tyres due to a lap 32 puncture, now led but, uneasy about a negative cockpit readout, gave up most of his 20s lead to conserve fuel. But despite Piquet closing in fast, Alain went on to win the race and back-to-back titles.

| Pos | Driver | Car | Time/gap | Grid | Stops | Tyres |
|---|---|---|---|---|---|---|
| 1 | Alain Prost | McLaren-TAG | 1h 54m 20.388s | 4 | 1 | G |
| 2 | Nelson Piquet | Williams-Honda | –4.205s | 2 | 1 | G |
| 3 | Stefan Johansson | Ferrari | –1 lap | 12 | 1 | G |
| 4 | Martin Brundle | Tyrrell-Renault | –1 lap | 16 | 0 | G |
| 5r | Philippe Streiff | Tyrrell-Renault | –2 laps | 10 | 0 | G |
| 6 | Johnny Dumfries | Lotus-Renault | –2 laps | 14 | 1 | G |

**POLE POSITION** N Mansell, Williams-Honda, 1m 18.403s (0.311s), 173.519kph, 107.820mph
**LAPS** 82 x 3.779 km, 2.348 miles
**DISTANCE** 309.878 km, 192.549 miles
**STARTERS/FINISHERS** 26/10
**WEATHER** Cloudy with sunny intervals, warm, dry
**LAP LEADERS** Piquet 1-6,63-64 (8); K Rosberg, McLaren-TAG 7-62 (56); Prost 65-82 (18)
**WINNER'S LAPS** 1-6 P5, 7-10 P4, 11-22 P3, 23-31 P2, 32-62 P4, 63-64 P2, 65-82 P1
**FASTEST LAP** Piquet, Williams-Honda, 1m 20.787s (lap 82), 168.398kph, 104.638mph
**CHAMPIONSHIP** Prost 72, Mansell 70, Piquet 69, Senna 55, Johansson 23

**RACE POD**

## CHAPTER 11

# THE GOAT

## THE GREATEST OF ALL TIME

So there you have it — the 100 greatest races in Formula 1 World Championship history. There are ones you already know and love, and others you'll simply love knowing better.

We hope this book leaves you smiling and nodding, rather than seething and frothing! If there's any frustration, it probably won't lie with the selection of the 100 itself - most Formula1 aficionados would probably agree with 80 to 90% of the choices made. The real sparks of debate are more likely to fly from how the races have been grouped into ten themed top-tens, and how each of those has been ranked. Each chapter ended with its own number one – the standout race for that theme – and they're summarised below.

Now comes the tricky bit. The authors have already stuck their necks out by selecting ten races as the best for each category but we can't stop there. And let's be honest, you wouldn't want us to either.

So in our search for the *greatest race of all time* – The GOAT – we start with a simple question: "Does this list of chapter winners truly represent the ten greatest races ever run?" The short answer is: not quite. It's a distinguished shortlist, certainly, but the themed structure of this book inevitably gave prominence to races that, while iconic in their specific category, don't quite merit consideration for the ultimate accolade.

Take Pastor Maldonado's stunning 2012 Spanish Grand Prix win – an unforgettable upset, yes, but not a GOAT contender. Or Max Verstappen's record-breaking debut victory in 2016, remarkable for its narrative but less so for its racing spectacle. Piquet's outrageous, sideways pass at the 1986 Hungarian Grand Prix? A moment for the ages, but fleeting. And the Villeneuve-Arnoux dogfight at Dijon in 1979, arguably the most thrilling scrap ever, was, after all, for second place.

By the same token, several races on our list are indisputably worthy GOAT contenders. Think of the 78-minute Monza slipstreamer in 1971 won by Peter Gethin – a breathless thrash decided by 0.01 seconds. Or Damon Hill's action-packed victory at Spa in 1998.

| CHAPTER | YEAR | GRAND PRIX | CIRCUIT | WINNER | WINNING CAR |
|---|---|---|---|---|---|
| Thrillers | 1971 | Italian | Monza | Peter Gethin | BRM |
| Duels | 1979 | French | Dijon-Prenois | Jean-Pierre Jabouille | Renault |
| Comebacks | 1957 | German | Nürburgring | Juan Manuel Fangio | Maserati |
| What the... | 1998 | Belgian | Spa-Francorchamps | Damon Hill | Jordan-Mugen Honda |
| Epics | 1993 | European | Donington Park | Ayrton Senna | McLaren-Ford |
| Regenmeisters | 1968 | German | Nürburgring | Jackie Stewart | Matra-Ford |
| Surprises | 2012 | Spanish | Cataluña | Pastor Maldonado | Williams-Renault |
| Pass masters | 1986 | Hungarian | Hungaroring | Nelson Piquet | Williams-Honda |
| Folklore | 2016 | Spanish | Cataluña | Max Verstappen | Red Bull-TAG Heuer Renault |
| Deciders | 1986 | Australian | Adelaide | Alain Prost | McLaren-TAG Porsche |

Jackie Stewart, Matra-Ford MS10, driving to victory at the 1968 German Grand Prix at the Nürburgring

Or Ayrton Senna's jaw-dropping first lap at Donington in 1993, often described as the greatest single lap ever raced. Then there are those two virtuoso performances on the old Nürburgring: Jackie Stewart in 1968 and Juan Manuel Fangio in 1957. There seems something right in the greatest F1 races being won by the championship's finest drivers.

These last two races stand out not just for brilliance, but for where they were held. Both were run on the fearsome 14-mile Nordschleife – the 'Green Hell' as Stewart labelled the fearsome original Nürburgring circuit – still the most daunting test of a Formula 1 driver in all 75 years of the World Championship.

Despite the atrocious weather, Stewart delivered a near-flawless performance. Driving with supreme control on the sodden Nordschleife at a level way beyond the rest of the field, he still recognised that one slip could lead to disaster. His relentless drive probed constantly for grip without overstepping the limit, his mindset that day necessarily risk averse.

By contrast, Fangio's approach was uncharacteristically bold. Eleven years earlier, on a dry but no less perilous Nürburgring, he pushed himself into unfamiliar territory. The man known for calculated precision later reflected that, compelled by his utter resolve to win, he took risks that day he would never normally have taken. The circuit had already claimed the life of his protégé, Onofre Marimón, three years before, yet on that August afternoon in 1957 Fangio chased down the Ferraris in a mesmerising display of pace and nerve to win by 3.6 seconds and with it, secure his fifth World Drivers' Championship.

And speaking of championships, after extensive thought, analysis, and no small amount of spirited debate, we reached a key conclusion in our quest to crown *The GOAT*.

Some races carry greater weight because they significantly influence the destiny of the World Championship. These are contests-within-a-contest: while one driver may win the race, another may emerge with the glittering prize. And because every Formula 1 season is ultimately a quest for the title, races that directly shape that outcome stand apart.

That's why one chapter in this book stands head and shoulders above the rest: Chapter 10 - *Deciders*. These ten races represent the very best of just 30 occasions across 75 seasons when the Drivers' Championship came down to the final round. As noted in that chapter's introduction, ***When the season finale also decides the title, that last race becomes an electrifying winner-takes-all shootout. The culmination of a gruelling season condenses into one, single, down-to-the-wire endgame.***

All three races that made our Chapter 10 'podium' were exceptional. But let's now revisit the thinking that shaped their final ranking.

Juan Manuel Fangio, Maserati 250F, accepts the flag to win the 1957 German Grand Prix at the Nürburgring

FULL RACE REPORT ON PAGE 144

# At No. 3...
# 2008 BRAZILIAN GP

Circuit: **Interlagos**

Race Winner: **Felipe Massa, Ferrari**

Champion: **Lewis Hamilton, McLaren-Mercedes**

The 2008 shootout between favourite Lewis Hamilton and local hero Felipe Massa produced one of the most dramatic championship conclusions in Formula 1 history. Rain in the closing laps reshuffled positions, swinging the title pendulum with every turn. For 39 unforgettable seconds, Massa was World Champion until Hamilton snatched fifth place at that final corner, reclaiming the title by a single point. But while the ending was pure theatre, the rest of the race was relatively subdued. Knowing they didn't need to beat Massa on the road, McLaren opted for a risk-averse strategy aimed squarely at banking the necessary points. Until the rain arrived with five laps remaining, Hamilton was always on course to secure the title, the outcome, both of race and championship, something of a foregone conclusion. Until, that is, it suddenly wasn't. This routine race suddenly exploded into an unforgettable finale, one of sport's most heart-stopping reversals of fortune.

← Having missed out on his first World Championship by one point in his 2007 rookie season, one year later Lewis Hamilton won the title by exactly the same margin on the last corner of the last lap of the last race

FULL RACE REPORT ON PAGE 146

# At No. 2...
# 1976 JAPANESE GP

Circuit: **Fuji**

Race Winner: **Mario Andretti, Lotus-Ford**

Champion: **James Hunt, McLaren-Ford**

The finale of the epic 1976 Hunt versus Lauda as immortalised in the 2013 movie, *Rush*. Tensions were sky-high before the race even began, with monsoon conditions delaying the start for hours and raising the real prospect of cancellation. Had the race been called off, the title was Lauda's. Eventually the cars took to the track, only for Lauda to retire after two laps judging the conditions still too dangerous. That decision changed everything. Now Hunt could win the championship by finishing fourth or better. For 61 of 73 laps, it looked like he'd do it in style by leading the race. But with the track drying, Hunt was forced to pit for fresh tyres, dropping to fifth with just five laps to go, the title back in Lauda's hands. Charging back on his new tyres and fired by desperation, Hunt reclaimed the crucial places with two laps left and with it the championship by a single point.

↑ In doubt about whether he had actually won the Championship, James Hunt reacts with glee as McLaren Team Principal Teddy Mayer holds up three fingers to signify he had finished third, so securing the title by a single point

The 1976 championship has been parodied 'The greatest story ever told' because its intensity was not just confined to the Fuji finale. Tension steadily mounted throughout its entire nine-month duration. What was it that made the 1976 championship so utterly compelling? Was it Hunt versus Lauda, McLaren versus Maranello, Ford versus Ferrari? Probably all of these and more. It seemed to have every facet which transforms a good script into great theatre: the unexpected, disqualifications, reinstatements, intrigue, dirty tricks, last rites, courage, bravery, all culminating in this showdown at the Fuji finale. They don't get much better than that…

…apart from one, that is.

# At No. 1...

# 1986 AUSTRALIAN GP

Circuit: **Adelaide**

Race Winner: **Alain Prost, McLaren-TAG Porsche**

Champion: **Alain Prost, McLaren-TAG Porsche**

The 1986 title was a three-way battle between Prost, Piquet and points leader Mansell, the strong favourite. Piquet and Prost effectively needed to win to beat Mansell, so it suited Nigel very well when Prost's McLaren teammate Keke Rosberg took an early lead and pulled away from the rest. This allowed Mansell to stay out of trouble and make sure he not only finished, but took the third place or better he needed to make certain of the title. Mansell stayed on course until lap 63 of 82. First Rosberg retired with a puncture, and one lap later, Mansell's left-rear tyre exploded spectacularly at over 180mph, eliminating him from contention. That left Piquet leading and Prost just three seconds adrift. Then came another twist: Goodyear advised a precautionary tyre stop for Piquet that didn't apply to Prost who had already changed his tyres due to an earlier puncture. When Piquet rejoined on fresh tyres with 18 laps to go he was 20s behind Prost. At the line it was four seconds, Prost driving to conserve fuel due to a negative cockpit readout and haemorrhaging 12 seconds over the final two laps for a nail-biting end to an utterly spine-tingling race.

What makes Australia 1986 the greatest Grand Prix in Formula 1 history? Two qualities elevate it even beyond the high theatre of Fuji 1976: First, the sheer calibre of the championship battle that framed the final race. Second, the pure improbability of the outcome that unfolded on the streets of Adelaide.

The 1986 season was among the most fiercely contested in history, featuring four legendary champions who would ultimately share 11 world titles: Senna, Prost, Piquet, and Mansell. Senna, in his turbocharged Lotus-Renault, led the standings deep into the campaign and was still mathematically in the hunt when Bernie Ecclestone famously gathered the four title contenders for a rare joint photocall (see photo insert on next page) with two rounds to go.

But it was the dominant Williams-Honda outfit, securing nine race wins between Piquet and Mansell, that seemed destined to secure both titles. Yet intra-team rivalry undermined their stranglehold. The absence of team owner Frank Williams following the road accident that left him paralysed also left a vacuum. The firm leadership needed to manage the volatile dynamic between Mansell and Piquet was missing. Still, Williams comfortably sealed the Constructors' crown and arrived in Adelaide as clear favourites for the Drivers' title.

Back in Britain, millions rose early in expectant anticipation, ready to witness the coronation of Nigel Mansell as world champion. But the astonishing drama that followed would dash those hopes and lift this race into legend. In a breathtaking sequence of events, the crown went not to Mansell, nor to Piquet, but to Alain Prost, the culmination of one of the finest campaigns in F1 history. **The man least expected to win, not the race, not the title, had seized both, and in doing so, immortalised the 1986 Australian Grand Prix as...**

**... the greatest Formula 1 Grand Prix of all time.**

A happy Alain Prost holds the trophy aloft as race winner and World Champion having, over the course of the 1986 Championship campaign, unexpectedly yet admirably come out on top against superior opposition

## EPILOGUE
# THE EYE OF THE BEHOLDER

This book is rooted in opinion. Informed opinion backed by knowledge and experience, but opinion nonetheless. And the conclusions drawn from those opinions won't resonate with everyone. So let's briefly explore why fans often differ in their views by considering some of the key factors that shape how we each perceive Formula 1's races, and why universal agreement on 'The Greatest' so often proves elusive.

First the question of what defines greatness. It's far from settled. Is it raw excitement? A singular moment of human brilliance? An extraordinary milestone?

Whichever it is, allegiance is more often the spark that ignites initial debate. A Ferrari fan might see glory in a race that a McLaren supporter would rather forget. The Lewis Hamilton supporter will never agree with the Max Verstappen fan over Abu Dhabi 2021. Jingoism and partisanship are alive and well in Formula 1 as apparent from the popularity of official F1 fan merchandise worn in support of teams and drivers alike.

So very often it's a deeply personal perspective: where we were, who we were cheering for, how the drama unfolded in our own eyes. And whether the experience came from a grandstand seat or a living room sofa. The 'I was there' syndrome is a powerful magnifier of memory. And is a great race better if it involves the sport's true legends or if it features the unusual, the 'one-off' stars?

Nostalgia plays its part too. Different generations may relish different facets of racing, and that familiar human instinct of "it's not as good as it was in my day" can gently cloud objectivity. 'Rose-tinted specs' are real, and influential as time subtly reshapes perception.

With the number of Grands Prix in a season now four times what it was in 1950, the law of diminishing returns may also be at work. When the extraordinary becomes commonplace, its impact inevitably fades. It's like chocolate: eat a box every day and what was once a treat can too easily become tepid.

Then there's jeopardy. Though Formula 1 remains a dangerous sport, thankfully it no longer carries the ever-present risk to life that once shadowed every corner of every lap. But the high peril of those early decades, particularly up to 1st May 1994, cannot be discounted.

So the concept of *greatness* is layered and complex, and those layers resonate differently with each of us. But bear in mind, the F1 knowledge, study, and lived experience of the three enthusiasts behind this book may not cover every one of the sport's 75 years, but it stretches as far back as 1957. And of the 100 races selected as the greatest, spread across each of Formula 1's three quarter-centuries, the distribution by number is fairly even: 29, 37 and 34, if not quite so proportionately.

And finally, back to 2021. As it delivered one of the fiercest World Championship battles of all time, some may ask: Where is the Abu Dhabi 2021 shootout in *The 100 Greatest Races*? The answer is that, just like Singapore 2008, and around 60 other races across the decades that were considered too tragic, too anomalous (notably the 11 Indianapolis 500 races between 1950 and 1960), or in some way made a travesty of the sport, Abu Dhabi 2021 was ultimately deemed too controversial for inclusion as one of the greatest. Feelings about it remain too raw, too polarised, for it even to feature in the 'Folklore' chapter.

But when *The 100 Greatest Races* is revisited in 2050 to mark Formula 1's first centenary… never say never.

# EXPLANATORY NOTES AND ABBREVIATIONS

**'RACE PODS'**

'Race Pods' have been designed to distil the essence of each World Championship Formula 1 race into a space no larger than an iPhone screen. Designed for quick assimilation, they offer an appreciation of each race in microcosm. Combining concise words with rich info., they deliver a clear and dynamic account of exactly what happened and why. Race Pods offer a surprisingly comprehensive and easily digestible snapshot of each race, sparing readers the need to wade through extensive reference books or web archives.

**RACE POD ABBREVIATIONS**

| | |
|---|---|
| 1-2 | Same team or marque finishing P1 and P2 |
| Box | Instruction to a driver to make a pit stop, normally to 'change tyres' |
| Cutback | Using the inside line to retake a position immediately after being overtaken |
| Deg | Tyre degradation |
| DNF | Did Not Finish race |
| DNQ | Did Not Qualify to race |
| DNS | Did Not Start race |
| DSQ | Disqualified from race |
| DRS | Drag Reduction System |
| ERS | Energy Recovery System |
| F1 | Formula 1 (also F2, F3) |
| Fastest Lap | The driver recording the fastest lap of the race (lap number in brackets) |
| FIA | Fédération Internationale de l'Automobile |
| FP1 | First Free Practice (also FP2 and FP3) |
| GP | Grand Prix |
| Grand Slam | A triple Crown plus leading every lap |
| Grid (pen) | Position on starting grid after penalties (penalties given) |
| Overcut | Overtaking by pitting later |
| P1 | First place/Position 1 in the race/ qualifying (also P2, P3, etc.) |
| Pit Stop | Stopping at your pit-box usually to 'change tyres' |
| Pits | A dedicated area in the Pits complex for mechanics to work |
| PL | Pit-Lane start |
| Pole Position | Fastest in qualifying takes P1 on grid when race starts. Figure in brackets is gap in seconds from pole to P2 |
| PU | Power Unit |
| Q1 | Qualifying session 1 (also Q2 and Q3) |
| r | Retired from race; not running at finish |
| RBPT | Red Bull Power Trains |
| RBR | Red Bull Racing |
| Red Flag | The race has been stopped |
| Rookie | A driver in his first season of Formula 1 |
| SC | Safety Car |
| Stint | The number of laps between each pitstop |
| Stops | Pitstops from which car resumed race, excluding drive-throughs |
| Tifosi | Italian Formula 1 fans |
| Triple crown | Pole, winning race and setting fastest lap |
| Time/gap | Duration of race and elapsed time gap after winner crossed the line |
| Turbo | Forced induction by turbocharging. Also Turbocharger |
| Undercut | Overtaking by pitting earlier |
| VSC | Virtual Safety Car |

**NOTES ON TYRES**

***TYRE MAKES:*** 1950-2006: A = Avon, B = Bridgestone, C = Continental, D = Dunlop, E = Engelbert, F = Firestone, G = Goodyear, M = Michelin, P = Pirelli

***CONTROL TYRES:*** 2007-2010: Bridgestone; 2011-2025: Pirelli

***TYRE COMPOUNDS:*** 2007-2025: h = hard, m = medium, s = soft, ss = super-soft, i = intermediate, w = wet, x = extreme wet

***TYRE STRATEGY:*** At least two compounds to be used at each race; 2007-2015: p = prime, the harder of the stipulated compound choice; o = option, the softer of the two; 2016-2018: h = hard, m = medium, s = soft, ss = super-soft, us = ultrasoft, i = intermediate, w = wet; 2019-2025: h = hard, m = medium, s = soft selected for each race from a range of up to seven compounds C0 (softest) to C6 (hardest). Also i = intermediate, w = wet.

## SOURCES AND BIBLIOGRAPHY

**RACE PODS**

Since 2010 'Race Pod' reports have been written in the moment to capture the essence of each Grand Prix as it plays out. They originate from live Sky Sports F1 television race coverage with the supplementary information added from Autosport.com's excellent FORIX database. As with contemporary race reports in leading publications, these reports are written immediately after the race, preserving the detail of events while they remain vivid. Adjustments are only made for accuracy or to include developments that emerged after the chequered flag.

Prior to 2010, 'Race Pod' reports drew primarily on the contemporary Grand Prix coverage published in *Autosport* magazine, and were later cross-referenced with other trusted sources such as the *Autocourse* annual to ensure accuracy and depth.

APPENDIX

# RACE WINNERS AND CHAMPIONS

From 13th May 1950 to 12th May 2025 inclusive, excluding the 11 Indy 500 races from 1950 to 1960

## WINNING DRIVERS

| | | |
|---|---|---|
| 1 | Lewis Hamilton | 105 |
| 2 | Michael Schumacher | 91 |
| 3 | Max Verstappen | 64 |
| 4 | Sebastian Vettel | 53 |
| 5 | Alain Prost | 51 |
| 6 | Ayrton Senna | 41 |
| 7 | Fernando Alonso | 32 |
| 8 | Nigel Mansell | 31 |
| 9 | Jackie Stewart | 27 |
| 10 | Jim Clark | 25 |
| 11 | Niki Lauda | 25 |
| 12 | Juan Manuel Fangio** | 24 |
| 13 | Nelson Piquet | 23 |
| 14 | Nico Rosberg | 23 |
| 15 | Damon Hill | 22 |
| 16 | Kimi Räikkönen | 21 |
| 17 | Mika Häkkinen | 20 |
| 18 | Stirling Moss* | 16 |
| 19 | Jenson Button | 15 |
| 20 | Graham Hill | 14 |
| 21 | Jack Brabham | 14 |
| 22 | Emerson Fittipaldi | 14 |
| 23 | Alberto Ascari | 13 |
| 24 | David Coulthard | 13 |
| 25 | Mario Andretti | 12 |
| 26 | Carlos Reutemann | 12 |
| 27 | Alan Jones | 12 |
| 28 | Jacques Villeneuve | 11 |
| 29 | Felipe Massa | 11 |
| 30 | Rubens Barrichello | 11 |
| 31 | James Hunt | 10 |
| 32 | Ronnie Peterson | 10 |
| 33 | Jody Scheckter | 10 |
| 34 | Gerhard Berger | 10 |
| 35 | Valtteri Bottas | 10 |
| 36 | Mark Webber | 9 |
| 37 | Jacky Ickx | 8 |
| 38 | Denny Hulme | 8 |
| 39 | Daniel Ricciardo | 8 |
| 40 | Charles Leclerc | 8 |
| 41 | René Arnoux | 7 |
| 42 | Juan Pablo Montoya | 7 |
| 43 | Tony Brooks* | 6 |
| 44 | John Surtees | 6 |
| 45 | Jochen Rindt | 6 |
| 46 | Gilles Villeneuve | 6 |
| 47 | Jacques Laffite | 6 |
| 48 | Riccardo Patrese | 6 |
| 49 | Ralf Schumacher | 6 |
| 50 | Sergio Pérez | 6 |
| 51 | Oscar Piastri | 6 |
| 52 | Nino Farina | 5 |
| 53 | Clay Regazzoni | 5 |
| 54 | John Watson | 5 |
| 55 | Michele Alboreto | 5 |
| 56 | Keke Rosberg | 5 |
| 57 | Lando Norris | 5 |
| 58 | Dan Gurney | 4 |
| 59 | Bruce McLaren | 4 |
| 60 | Eddie Irvine | 4 |
| 61 | Carlos Sainz | 4 |
| 62 | Mike Hawthorn | 3 |
| 63 | Peter Collins | 3 |
| 64 | Phil Hill | 3 |
| 65 | Didier Pironi | 3 |
| 66 | Thierry Boutsen | 3 |
| 67 | Heinz-Harald Frentzen | 3 |
| 68 | Johnny Herbert | 3 |
| 69 | Giancarlo Fisichella | 3 |
| 70 | George Russell | 3 |
| 71 | José Froilán González | 2 |
| 72 | Maurice Trintignant | 2 |
| 73 | Wolfgang von Trips | 2 |
| 74 | Pedro Rodríguez | 2 |
| 75 | Jo Siffert | 2 |
| 76 | Peter Revson | 2 |
| 77 | Patrick Depailler | 2 |
| 78 | Jean-Pierre Jabouille | 2 |
| 79 | Patrick Tambay | 2 |
| 80 | Elio de Angelis | 2 |
| 81 | Luigi Fagioli* | 1 |
| 82 | Piero Taruffi | 1 |
| 83 | Luigi Musso* | 1 |
| 84 | Jo Bonnier | 1 |
| 85 | Giancarlo Baghetti | 1 |
| 86 | Innes Ireland | 1 |
| 87 | Lorenzo Bandini | 1 |
| 88 | Richie Ginther | 1 |
| 89 | Ludovico Scarfiotti | 1 |
| 90 | Peter Gethin | 1 |
| 91 | François Cevert | 1 |
| 92 | Jean-Pierre Beltoise | 1 |
| 93 | Carlos Pace | 1 |
| 94 | Jochen Mass | 1 |
| 95 | Vittorio Brambilla | 1 |
| 96 | Gunnar Nilsson | 1 |
| 97 | Alessandro Nannini | 1 |
| 98 | Jean Alesi | 1 |
| 99 | Olivier Panis | 1 |
| 100 | Jarno Trulli | 1 |
| 101 | Robert Kubica | 1 |
| 102 | Heikki Kovalainen | 1 |
| 103 | Pastor Maldonado | 1 |
| 104 | Pierre Gasly | 1 |
| 105 | Esteban Ocon | 1 |
| | Total | 1123† |

* One shared drive
** Two shared drives
† Includes three shared drives

## WINNING CONSTRUCTORS

| | | | | | | | | |
|---|---|---|---|---|---|---|---|---|
| 1 | Ferrari | 248 | 12 | Cooper | 16 | 23 | Porsche | 1 |
| 2 | McLaren | 194 | 13 | Alfa Romeo | 10 | 24 | Eagle | 1 |
| 3 | Mercedes | 129 | 14 | Maserati | 9 | 25 | Hesketh | 1 |
| 4 | Red Bull | 123 | 15 | Vanwall | 9 | 26 | Penske | 1 |
| 5 | Williams | 114 | 16 | Matra | 9 | 27 | Shadow | 1 |
| 6 | Lotus | 81 | 17 | Ligier | 9 | 28 | Stewart | 1 |
| 7 | Brabham | 35 | 18 | Brawn | 8 | 29 | BMW Sauber | 1 |
| 8 | Renault | 35 | 19 | Jordan | 4 | 30 | Toro Rosso | 1 |
| 9 | Benetton | 27 | 20 | March | 3 | 31 | AlphaTauri | 1 |
| 10 | Tyrrell | 23 | 21 | Wolf | 3 | 32 | Racing Point | 1 |
| 11 | BRM | 17 | 22 | Honda | 3 | 33 | Alpine | 1 |
| | | | | | | | Total | 1120 |

## CHAMPION DRIVERS

| | | | | | | | | |
|---|---|---|---|---|---|---|---|---|
| 1 | Michael Schumacher | 7 | 13 | Jim Clark | 2 | 25 | Mario Andretti | 1 |
| 2 | Lewis Hamilton | 7 | 14 | Graham Hill | 2 | 26 | Jody Scheckter | 1 |
| 3 | Juan Manuel Fangio | 5 | 15 | Emerson Fittipaldi | 2 | 27 | Alan Jones | 1 |
| 4 | Alain Prost | 4 | 16 | Mika Häkkinen | 2 | 28 | Keke Rosberg | 1 |
| 5 | Sebastian Vettel | 4 | 17 | Fernando Alonso | 2 | 29 | Nigel Mansell | 1 |
| 6 | Max Verstappen | 4 | 18 | Giuseppe Farina | 1 | 30 | Damon Hill | 1 |
| 7 | Jack Brabham | 3 | 19 | Mike Hawthorn | 1 | 31 | Jacques Villeneuve | 1 |
| 8 | Jackie Stewart | 3 | 20 | Phil Hill | 1 | 32 | Kimi Räikkönen | 1 |
| 9 | Niki Lauda | 3 | 21 | John Surtees | 1 | 33 | Jenson Button | 1 |
| 10 | Nelson Piquet | 3 | 22 | Denny Hulme | 1 | 34 | Nico Rosberg | 1 |
| 11 | Ayrton Senna | 3 | 23 | Jochen Rindt | 1 | | | |
| 12 | Alberto Ascari | 2 | 24 | James Hunt | 1 | | Total | 75 |

## CHAMPION CONSTRUCTORS

| | | | | | | | | |
|---|---|---|---|---|---|---|---|---|
| 1 | Ferrari | 16 | 6 | Red Bull | 6 | 11 | BRM | 1 |
| 2 | Williams | 9 | 7 | Cooper | 2 | 12 | Matra | 1 |
| 3 | McLaren | 9 | 8 | Brabham | 2 | 13 | Tyrrell | 1 |
| 4 | Mercedes | 8 | 9 | Renault | 2 | 14 | Benetton | 1 |
| 5 | Lotus | 7 | 10 | Vanwall | 1 | 15 | Brawn | 1 |
| | | | | | | | Total | 67* |

* Began from 1958

# ABOUT THE AUTHORS

**Roger Smith**, a self-styled Formula 1 evangelist, has made it his mission through his books to both preserve the sport's rich history and turbocharge fans' passion by adding the dimension of historical perspective.

The touchstone for Roger's lifelong passion for Grand Prix racing was that heroic first Vanwall triumph by Brooks/Moss at Aintree in 1957 (see page 43). Once smitten, he became a fixture at the Formula 1 circuits of Europe in the sixties, rubbing shoulders with drivers and mechanics in the paddock, and avidly reading *Autosport*. This was the Formula 1 apprenticeship Roger served, soaking it all up like an oily rag to form a deep understanding of the sport.

Following retirement from a business life that had allowed him to indulge his passion for Formula 1 across the globe, Roger pursued his aspiration to write, blending his love for the sport with his professional background in Television Ratings. *The 100 Greatest Races* is the sixth edition in his *Formula 1: All The Races* series. First published in 2012, it was shortlisted for the British Sports Book Awards in recognition of its innovative *'Race Pods'* that have chronicled all 1,120 Grands Prix to date with comprehensive conciseness.

With his wife Rosemary, Roger divides his time between Oxford and Chichester and their three children and five grandchildren. Roger has appeared on SkySports F1 and BBC radio and is a member of The Guild of Motoring Writers.

**Kevin Turner** is *Autosport*'s Chief Editor. While studying History at the University of York, Kevin began covering UK club events as a freelance reporter for *Autosport* and *Motorsport News*. He joined the *Autosport* staff as Editorial Assistant on the magazine in 2006, winning what is now known as the Motorsport UK Young Journalist of the Year Award. He became National Editor in 2008 and over the next few seasons covered a range of international events, including the Le Mans 24 Hours, as well as the British Touring Car Championship and British GT. Kevin became Features Editor before switching to edit *Motorsport News* in 2014.

He returned to *Autosport* in 2016 to become editor of the magazine, a dream job that is still part of his role.

He became Chief Editor in 2020, helping to plan content for *Autosport*.com and *Autosport*'s podcast as well as seeing the magazine through the coronavirus pandemic. Kevin also led work on the special publication celebrating 70 years of *Autosport*, oversaw the magazine's switch from a weekly to a monthly in 2025, and has been a judge on the Silverstone *Autosport* BRDC Young Driver Award, formerly known as the McLaren *Autosport* BRDC Award, since 2008. He lives in Warboys with his wife and two children.

FORMULA 1
ALL THE RACES